Phinally!

Phinally!

The Phillies, the Royals and the 1980 Baseball Season That Almost Wasn't

J. DANIEL

McFarland & Company, Inc., Publishers
Jefferson, North Carolina

ISBN (print) 978-1-4766-7088-1 ♾
ISBN (ebook) 978-1-4766-3398-5

Library of Congress cataloguing data are available

British Library cataloguing data are available

Front cover: The Philadelphia Phillies celebrate their first ever world championship after winning the 1980 World Series (National Baseball Hall of Fame Library, Cooperstown, New York)

Printed in the United States of America

McFarland & Company, Inc., Publishers
Box 611, Jefferson, North Carolina 28640
www.mcfarlandpub.com

For Sue,
who believed in me when I didn't,
and Brady and Michael,
my two all-time favorite baseball players

Acknowledgments

No project like this is done in a vacuum, and there are a lot of people I need to thank. Each of them contributed in different ways but they all contributed. Were it not for them you may not be reading this. I wish I could list everyone but it would get boring, and I seriously might break down.

Chris Lamb gave this book legitimacy in its infancy, and for that I'm forever grateful. Sachin Waikar guided me down the road towards getting a publishing deal. His input and friendship has been invaluable. Dan Epstein and Doug Wilson were always available to answer writing questions and lend advice.

Gary Mitchem at McFarland took a shot on some dude from Indiana who had never written a book before and had no platform.

My parents, Patricia Harkin and Jim Sosnoski, instilled a love of reading and learning and multiple lifetimes' worth of support.

My sons, Brady and Michael, allowed me to see the game through their eyes both as fans and players, and I enjoyed watching them play more than they'll ever know.

Part of this project has been a companion blog and Facebook page, and the support I've received through those outlets, as well as many words of encouragement on Twitter, has truly been humbling. Speaking of websites, this book simply doesn't happen without Baseballreference.com.

Finally, my wife, Susan, put up with me during this project, allowed me to retreat into a room for hours on end to write when dishes and laundry needed to be done and the grass kept growing, and listened to me talk endlessly about all the small victories along the way. Somehow, she's been with me since 1991, and I couldn't have done this without her.

Table of Contents

Preface

The 1980 World Series was the culmination of an amazing season and the end of an era for the game and the country. On the field, the game was changing rapidly. Free-agency was here to stay, despite the protestations of the team owners. It was an issue which nearly ended the season prematurely and would permanently alter the game's finances. Nolan Ryan became the first player in history to earn $1 million per season when he signed a free-agent contract with the Houston Astros after a contentious breakup with his former team, the California Angels. By the end of the decade, the average player salary was nearly half a million dollars. The changing financial structure of the game would eventually force two owners to sell their teams before season's end, in large part because they felt that they could no longer afford to compete.

Two third basemen, Philadelphia's Mike Schmidt and Kansas City's George Brett, made the leap from good players to superstars. The two became professionals on the same day in 1971, when they were drafted back-to-back in the second round, and nine years later they went head-to-head in the World Series. Just reaching the World Series was a victory for both of them after coming so close in years past. In the 1980 season, they and their teams finally broke through, and they produced a World Series to remember.

In the 1970s, Major League Baseball was dominated by a select few teams. From 1972 through 1978, just three franchises—the Oakland A's, Cincinnati Reds and New York Yankees—won World Series titles. The Pittsburgh Pirates won championships in 1971 and 1979, while the Baltimore Orioles won in 1970 and lost two others.

But the dynasties were crumbling. The A's had been blown up shortly after winning their third straight championship in 1974, and the Reds had begun to disassemble their Big Red Machine piece by piece. A new decade of parity was about to begin.

The 1980s are a somewhat forgotten decade of Major League Baseball. They didn't even get a full inning in the Ken Burns series. But the 1980s were when the changes instituted in the 1970s began to alter the game seriously. Players could move freely from team to team, and general managers built teams suited to play on plastic grass in multi-purpose stadiums. Small-market teams still had a shot at the post-season, and disagreements between players were settled with fists, not tweets.

Sufficient time has passed that we can now look upon the 1980s as a different era, in the same vein that some view Twisted Sister as "Classic Rock." In baseball, technology and pop culture, the 1980s had a distinct personality, one that still has a hold on many people. Exciting new technologies emerged that changed forever the way we lived our lives. Cars couldn't fly, but by the end of the decade we could make a phone call from them. What follows is a look back at the first year of a transitional decade in the United States and in Major League Baseball. Between the white lines, speed and pitching were phased out and replaced by juiced-up sluggers, while Willie (Mays), Mickey (Mantle) and The Duke (Snider) were replaced by Willie (McGee), Mickey (Hatcher) and The Duke (John Wathan).

This is the tale of 1980, the personalities involved, and the stories behind the stories.

Introduction

Late fall in Pennsylvania's Delaware Valley is gorgeous. Entire vacations are planned around taking in the scenery. From fall foliage tours by car or train to music festivals and pumpkin patches, the region has something for everyone. But the mustachioed man wasn't there for the scenery and he didn't need a pumpkin, at least not yet. For him, this was a business trip. There were some people in the area who worshipped him and others who couldn't stand him. Very few didn't have an opinion.

Inside the safety of his luxury sedan, he was just another guy driving to work on an unseasonably warm October day. He wasn't a doctor or lawyer, and he didn't save lives; but he did alter them. His work was meaningless in the grand scheme of things, but seemingly life and death in the small world in which he operated. Once he reached his workplace and changed into his employer-issued uniform, the emotional fortunes of hundreds of thousands of people, not just in the Delaware Valley, but across the country, were in his hands.

The man behind the wheel was one of the most important figures in Philadelphia sports history. Although Wilt Chamberlain, Norm Van Brocklin and Bobby Clarke had each brought championships to the city in the previous 20 years, they weren't baseball players. Philadelphia is a baseball town and its citizens lived, and mostly died, with the fortunes of Phillies.

It was the early afternoon of October 21, 1980, and Mike Schmidt was heading south on Palmer's Mill Road to pick up a friend. His Phillies were one win away from securing the first World Series championship in franchise history. It was a history that went back to 1883, and it was littered with disappointment.

Being a Philadelphia Phillies fan has never been easy, and the misery extends to the very beginning of the franchise's history. Their predecessors, the Philadelphia Quakers, burst onto the scene in the summer of 1883 and immediately made a name for themselves as one of the worst teams in baseball, winning just 17 of 98 games in their inaugural season.

The team changed their name to the Phillies in 1890 but that didn't help matters. Four years later, all three of their starting outfielders hit over .400, yet they still finished fourth in the National League, 18 games behind the Baltimore Orioles. Year after year, the team played very bad baseball in an unsafe ballpark under lousy ownership.

Among the worst was Horace Fogel. A former newspaperman, Fogel obtained funding to purchase the team under suspicious circumstances and immediately upon assuming control in November of 1909 decided to put his stamp on the team by firing manager Billy Murray and changing the team's uniforms. He also wanted to change the team name. He didn't like the name "Phillies," and "Quakers" didn't fit the bill either. He was looking for something to get the fans excited and decided on the Philadelphia Live Wires.

Fortunately the name didn't catch on, but Fogel wasn't finished. He hosted three-ring circuses on the field and released pigeons in the city with tickets attached to their legs. But it was the volatile combination of alcohol and a big mouth that eventually did him in.

Toward the end of the 1912 season, Fogel began accusing the National League of fixing the season in favor of the New York Giants. The fact that his team finished 30½ games out of first place was seemingly irrelevant. Fogel was relentless in his accusations, but an investigation ensued which turned up absolutely nothing to substantiate his claims. The National League had had enough of him, and Horace Fogel became the first professional sports team owner to be banned from the game for life. A later Phillies owner, William Cox, was also kicked out of baseball when it was revealed that he had bet on Phillies games.

In between Fogel and Cox came William Baker, an owner so cheap that he brought in sheep to control the growth of the outfield grass rather than pay a groundskeeper. Even when the team did well, Baker found a way to hamstring his players in the interest of making money.

In 1915, the nucleus of pitcher Grover Cleveland Alexander and outfielder Gavvy Cravath helped the team set a franchise record by winning 90 games and the National League pennant, thus earning a spot in the World Series against the Boston Red Sox.

Philadelphia won Game One, 3–1, behind Alexander, but that proved to be the high point of the Series for them. The low point came in the decisive Game Five, when Baker decided he would make some extra cash by roping off an area in right field so he could sell more tickets. The move made the outfield smaller and Baker's gate receipts bigger. Financially it was brilliant, but it also may have cost his team a World Series title. The Red Sox hit three home runs into the shortened right field, including two by the left-handed-hitting Harry Hooper, who hit a total of two homers in 149 games during the regular season. Boston won the game, 5–4, and the Series, four games to one. It would be another 62 years before the Phillies would win a post-season game.

Fans had to endure bad baseball as well as the fact that attending a Phillies game could actually prove fatal. On two occasions, once in 1903 and again in 1927, the grandstands at the Phillies' home ballpark, the Baker Bowl, collapsed, killing 13 spectators and injuring hundreds more.

While the stands were falling down, the team was falling into the abyss. They hit bottom in 1942 by losing 109 games and finishing 62½ games behind the National League, and eventual World Series, champion St. Louis Cardinals.

The on-field product was terrible and it was dangerous to attend home games, but at least the players were safe. That is, until 1949 when first baseman Eddie Waitkus was shot by a crazed fan named Ruth Ann Steinhagen in a Chicago hotel room. The story became the basis for the 1952 Bernard Malamud novel, *The Natural*.

"We used to wait for them to come out of the clubhouse after the game, and all the time I was watching him, I was building in my mind the idea of killing him," Steinhagen wrote later in a court-ordered autobiographical sketch. "As time went on, I just became nuttier and nuttier about the guy. I knew I would never get to know him in a normal way, so I kept thinking, I will never get him, and if I can't have him, nobody else can."[1]

Waitkus miraculously recovered and was part of a team that made the summer of 1950 among the brightest in Philadelphia sports history. The Phillies battled the Brooklyn Dodgers down to the wire, and the two teams faced each other on the final day of the season. A Brooklyn win meant a three-game playoff, while a Philadelphia win would earn them a trip to their second World Series.

The game was scoreless through five innings before Philadelphia's Willie "Puddinhead" Jones singled to center field to score Dick Sisler and give the Phillies a 1–0 lead. But Brooklyn shortstop Pee Wee Reese's solo homer in the bottom of the inning tied the game at 1–1.

Phillies starting pitcher Robin Roberts was still on the mound in the bottom of the ninth inning, but the 302 innings he had logged to that point in the season were starting to catch up to him. Brooklyn's Cal Abrams led off the ninth inning with a walk, and Reese followed with a single to left field to bring up Duke Snider.

Snider was exactly the man the Dodgers and their fans wanted up in this situation, and one of the last people a weary Roberts wanted to face with the winning run on second base. Snider was a star and was one of three Dodgers to drive in 100 or more runs in 1950.

"The Duke" drilled Roberts' first pitch for a single. Phillies center fielder Richie Ashburn fielded the ball on a hop as Dodgers third-base coach Milt Stock waved Abrams home. Ashburn would become one of the most beloved players in Phillies history, and this game was a big reason why. As Abrams headed towards the plate, Ashburn threw a strike to catcher Stan Lopata.

Lopata was two inches taller than Abrams and outweighed him by 25 pounds. A collision at the plate might favor the Phillies catcher, but when he caught the ball and looked up, Abrams was about 25 feet up the third-base line. Instead of bracing for a collision, Lopata chased Abrams up the line and tagged him for an easy out. Stock's decision to send Abrams was not a good one and cost him his job. He was fired after the season. Roberts walked Jackie Robinson to load the bases, then got out of the inning to preserve the tie.

In the top of the tenth, Dick Sisler's three-run homer off Don Newcombe gave the Phillies a 4–1 win and the National League pennant. Unfortunately for Sisler and the rest of the Phillies, their luck ran out as they were swept in the World Series by Joe DiMaggio and the New York Yankees.

The amazing summer the "Whiz Kids" of 1950 gave the city was followed by another 13 years of ineptitude and a monumental collapse in 1964 known as "The Phold." Under manager Gene Mauch, the Phillies built a 6½ game lead in the National League pennant chase with just 12 games to play, but they couldn't hold it.

Philadelphia lost ten straight games and finished tied for second place, while the St. Louis Cardinals won the pennant and beat the Yankees in seven games to win the World Series.

As was the case after 1915 and 1950, a season of success was followed by a decade or more of misery. The Phillies floundered, averaging 87 losses per season from 1965 through 1974. But then young talent like Schmidt, Bob Boone, Larry Bowa and Greg Luzinski began to arrive.

Under manager Danny Ozark, the Phillies won the National League East flag three years in a row, from 1976 through 1978, but they still couldn't break through. A sweep at the hands of Cincinnati's Big Red Machine in 1976 was followed by playoff losses to the Los Angeles Dodgers in 1977 and 1978. The team failed to qualify for the post-season in 1979.

Such was the history Schmidt and his teammates were up against as they faced Game Six in the 1980 World Series. The Phillies led the Kansas City Royals three games to two in the best-of-seven Series, and if this team didn't win, they would likely be broken up.

"We're in the perfect spot," manager Dallas Green had told the media two days earlier. "One game to win and our ace is pitching on our home field."[2] The ace Green referred to was Steve Carlton, the 35-year-old who had two Cy Young Awards to his credit and was poised to win his third. "Lefty" had won 24 games in the regular season and another two in the post-season.

The Royals weren't so lucky. They were starting Rich Gale, who hadn't won a game since August 23. The crucial sixth game of the 1980 World Series, the culmination of a season which dawned when the teams reported to spring training in Florida some eight months earlier, would pit one of the game's top pitchers, at home, against a marginal pitcher riding a two-month winless streak, 249 career wins vs. 36 career wins. Eight-time All-Star vs. zero-time All-Star. The odds were certainly in favor of the Phillies.

But as Schmidt wound through the western Philadelphia suburb, he knew that while Carlton and Gale would play a large role in their team's fortunes, the outcome of the game would in all likelihood be decided by the man he was on his way to pick up.

Tug McGraw was a fan favorite and one of the best closers in baseball. He was also Schmidt's carpool buddy. For home games, Schmidt would often pick McGraw up and they would ride to the ballpark together. Some days, Schmidt would drive and McGraw would read him the sports page. Other days, Schmidt would nap while McGraw drove Schmidt's car.

On this day, Schmidt drove while McGraw read the newspaper accounts of Game Five, two days earlier in Kansas City. McGraw was being hailed as a hero for holding the Royals at bay to preserve the win. He had thrown the final three innings, striking out five, but he had also loaded the bases in the ninth inning before striking out former Phillie Jose Cardenal to seal the win.

Schmidt had had enough of the media's idolatry. He jokingly mocked McGraw, telling him he was tired of him getting all the good press for getting himself out of self-induced crises while Schmidt played Gold Glove defense, hit home runs, and was scorned for not doing more.

Schmidt predicted that the game would come down to McGraw striking someone out in a dramatic situation to win it. He told McGraw that after that happened, he should be ready because Schmidt was going to ruin his photo op by diving on top of him. The two men were both great players enjoying fantastic seasons, yet in many ways they were exact opposites.

McGraw was outgoing and great with the media and the fans. When asked what he planned to do with his 1973 World Series share, McGraw replied, "Ninety percent I'll spend on good times, women and Irish Whiskey. The other ten percent I'll probably waste."[3]

Schmidt was moody and had a difficult relationship with the media and the Veterans Stadium faithful. Phillies fans cheered him when he homered and booed him mercilessly if he seemingly did anything else. When asked about the local media, Schmidt famously said, "Philadelphia is the only city in the majors where you can experience the joy of victory one day and the agony of reading about it the next day."[4]

McGraw won five games in 1980, saved 20 more and was a major reason why the Phillies were in the World Series. After a slow start, he was practically unhittable in the second half of the season. In 52⅓ innings pitched over the last half of the season, McGraw had allowed just three earned runs while recording 42 strikeouts. While the Phillies battled the Pirates and the Expos for the National League East division title in September and October, McGraw surrendered just one earned run in 26⅓ innings of work. On the pitching staff, the reticent Carlton was the undisputed leader, but the boisterous McGraw was its beating heart.

Schmidt turned in his finest season in 1980, leading the National League in home runs with 48 and runs batted in with 121. His hot streak in May earned him Player of the Month honors and coincided with the Phillies' 17–9 record, which put them back in the race after a sluggish April. Like McGraw, Schmidt was at his best down the stretch. He hit .311

with 21 homers and 50 RBI over the last three months of the season and was a few weeks away from being named MVP for the first time in his career. But none of it would matter if his Phillies didn't win one of the next two games. They would be labeled chokers again. This was the closest the franchise had ever come to a championship, and they couldn't let it slip away.

"This year, we've found a way to win at an important time in the season," Schmidt told the *Associated Press*. "That's so important, more than great statistics. That's what every team wants to find—a way to win. That's what makes this team great."[5]

Great teams win the games they're supposed to win and sneak in some they're not supposed to win. Game Six of the 1980 World Series was a game the Phillies were supposed to win. If they didn't, it would be another example of how this group of players in particular, and the franchise in general, had failed the city.

1

Spring Training
Dollars, Dallas and Dissension

The would-be assassin prowled the hallway while the prey returned to his office. He had many enemies both in business and in his personal life. There was no shortage of people who would want him dead. Tonight someone was here to ensure it happened. Peering out his office window, the man heard a noise in the hallway.

"Who's there?"[1]

No response.

Tie loosened after a long day and wearing a grey suit vest over a white shirt, the handsome man went to investigate. As he stepped into the hall a shot rang out. Then another. J.R. Ewing slumped to the floor, near death.

"A House Divided" aired on March 21, 1980. It was the season finale of the wildly popular show, *Dallas*, and featured the first big cliffhanger in television history. The show was watched by nearly 50 million people in the U.S., second only to the Super Bowl, and the result was a worldwide pop culture phenomenon.

As the summer progressed, there was one question on the mind of nearly everyone in America. The question appeared on t-shirts, in magazines and on the lips of millions of TV viewers. It was a simple question, really, and despite the fact that everyone realized they wouldn't know the answer until the fall, the speculation was endless. In his book, *Hello Darlin*, actor Larry Hagman, who played J.R., summed it up: "Ronald Reagan was campaigning against Jimmy Carter, American hostages were being held in Iran, Polish shipyard workers were on strike and all anyone wanted to know was, 'Who shot J.R.?'"[2]

The burning question was finally answered when the episode titled "*Who Done It?*" aired on November 21. More than 83 million people in the U.S. finally learned that J.R.'s mistress, Kristen Shepard, played by Bing Crosby's daughter, Mary, was the culprit.

J.R. Ewing's near-death experience notwithstanding, the spring of 1980 was filled with excitement and optimism. The first spring training of a new decade offers the kind of hope rarely seen in professional sports. If your team has struggled, the decade can signal the beginning of the turnaround. If your team has dominated, there's reason to believe it will continue.

That was especially the case as spring training camps opened in March of 1980. The previous year's division winners, Baltimore, California, Cincinnati and Pittsburgh, were looking to stay on top. But challengers like Montreal and Houston had taken the division races down to the final weekend in the National League in 1979. Both teams were loaded with talent and ready to take the next step.

Chuck Tanner's Pittsburgh Pirates reported to Bradenton, Florida, to defend their title with a very strong offensive nucleus returning. Dave Parker was a bona-fide star, having hit .321 with 114 home runs and 490 RBI over the previous five seasons. Bill Madlock joined the Bucs midway through the 1979 season and hit .328, followed by a .375 batting average in the World Series. Omar Moreno provided speed, stealing 77 bases in 1979, while Tim Foli and Phil Garner provided solid defense up the middle. First baseman and Pittsburgh icon Willie Stargell was coming off a co–MVP season, an honor he shared with Cardinals first baseman Keith Hernandez, and was the unquestioned heart and soul of the team.

Their lineup was all but set. The team welcomed back eight different players who appeared in at least 100 games the previous season, while Madlock logged 85 after the mid-season trade. Rennie Stennett was gone via free agency, but Madlock's acquisition enabled Garner to move to second base, which helped the offense. There was no doubt that Pittsburgh would score runs, but pitching looked to be a concern, particularly in regards to health. Rick Rhoden and Don Robinson had medical issues heading into the spring, and 13-game winner Bruce Kison signed with the Angels in the off-season. To top it off, 14-game winner John Candelaria suffered back and facial injuries in a car accident driving home from a spring training workout midway through March. It was "The Candy Man's" second car accident in nine months.

The injuries forced Tanner and the front office to consider opening the season with unproven arms like Rick Jones, Gene Pentz and Rod

Scurry. Veteran swingman Jim Bibby, who had made 17 starts the year before, was a candidate for the rotation, along with 37-year-old Jim Rooker and free-agent signee Andy Hassler. For detractors of the relatively new world of free agency, Hassler could have been considered a poster boy for the harm the process had caused the game. He entered 1980 with a 32–60 career record, which included a string of 13 consecutive months without a win, and an ERA north of 4.00, yet he still signed a six-year contract with the Pirates worth more than half a million dollars. This was coming off a 1979 campaign in which he went 5–7 with the Mets and Red Sox. The deal also included a $50,000 incentive for winning the CY Young Award, which didn't seem likely. "It was the only thing I could bargain for," Hassler told *The Sporting News.*[3]

For the Philadelphia Phillies and their fans, 1980 represented a crossroads. The team had won division titles from 1976 through 1978, but 1979 was a disaster. That left fans, and some in the organization, wondering if 1979 was an aberration or the beginning of the end.

The 1980 Phillies were a very talented group. Their roster boasted a future Hall of Famer as a #1 starter, another at third base, and the future all-time hits leader. But they couldn't put it all together, and there was a perception that they were soft.

They didn't get along with each other, the press or the fans. The pitchers didn't like the hitters, and vice versa. Some of the newer players didn't like the laid-back attitude some of the veterans had. While the 1979 Pirates won with a tight-knit "We Are Family" theme, the Phillies more closely resembled the Ewing family on *Dallas* than the Pirates. About the only thing most of them could agree on was dislike for their manager.

Midway through the 1979 season, it became clear that Danny Ozark had lost the team and a change was needed. At one point during the season, Ozark confided in team president Bill Giles, "I can't control these guys. They're making ten times more money than me."[4]

On August 31, the popular Ozark was fired and replaced by Farm Director Dallas Green, whom Giles described as tall and blunt "with a voice like a foghorn."[5] Green took over with 30 games left in the season and used that time to evaluate what he had and what he needed. One of the biggest things he felt was lacking was attitude. When players groused about his style, he told them it was their fault that he was the manager because their play had gotten Ozark fired.

For a comfortable veteran, Green was a nightmare. He was on solid footing with the organization, had the full support of the front office, and didn't care if he lost his job as manager, in large part because he never really wanted it in the first place.

When the Phillies reported to the Carpenter Complex in Clearwater, Florida, for spring training, one of the first things they saw were signs that said, "We, not I," an indication of what Green felt was the major issue on the team. Too many players were playing for themselves rather than the team. If a player got a few hits but the team lost, he was okay with that. It was exactly the kind of attitude Green wanted to address. His theory was reinforced by the snickers the signs induced from many veterans.

"When do the pom-pom girls arrive?" asked shortstop Larry Bowa.[6]

Adding to the tension in spring training were rumors that all three of the Phillies' starting outfielders had been on the trading block over the winter. Left fielder Greg Luzinski was rumored to be headed to the Chicago Cubs in a deal involving Bruce Sutter and others. He was also supposedly headed to the San Diego Padres in a deal involving Dave Winfield, and to the Texas Rangers for Al Oliver. None of it mattered to Luzinski, who took the rumors in stride.

"The trade stuff hasn't bothered me," he told *The Sporting News*. "I've been in that situation before. I almost went to the Cubs two years ago for Manny Trillo and Rick Monday, and my first year here I was one player away from going to Baltimore. It's just part of the game."[7]

Trade rumors didn't affect Luzinski, but right fielder Bake McBride was not as forgiving. McBride had spent two and a half seasons in Philadelphia after coming over from St. Louis in a mid-season deal in 1977, but the constant trade talk affected him. "If they want to trade me then go ahead and trade me and get it over with," he said. "This whole winter, every time the phone would ring, I would think it was Owens calling to tell me I'd been traded. It got to the point where I wouldn't answer the phone."[8]

One deal involving McBride centered on the front office's desire to acquire bullpen help. The Phillies had long coveted former Cy Young Award winner Sparky Lyle and had a deal in place with the Rangers to acquire him, along with pitcher Adrian Devine and Johnny Grubb, in exchange for Tug McGraw, McBride, Larry Christenson and a minor leaguer.

The deal fell apart because Texas owner Brad Corbett had given Lyle a ten-year, $500,000 contract that allowed him to do radio work when he retired. Phillies General Manager Paul Owens wanted Lyle, but he didn't feel he could ask owner Ruly Carpenter to come up with an additional $500,000 in order to get him.

Owens' attempts to acquire new corner outfielders were further complicated by center fielder Garry Maddox's desire to get out of Philadelphia, feeling he was underpaid. Coming off a season in which he hit .281 with 13 homers and 26 stolen bases while playing his usual outstanding defense, Maddox was asking for Pete Rose–type money, but the Phillies weren't interested in giving it to him.

So the players disliked each other, were upset about their contracts, and hated their manager. In response, Green turned up the heat. "It's our job to push them and we plan to do that," Green said. "There are good players on this team who want to win. We won the division three years in a row and then the thing fell apart last season. Most of them have a sincere desire to win a championship, and it's got to start in spring training."[9]

The Phillies and Pirates won all but one of the NL East titles in the 1970s (the Mets won it in 1973), but the Montreal Expos were knocking on the door. Montreal had never finished higher than fourth in the division after entering as an expansion team in 1969, but General Manager John McHale was putting together a very talented roster. Led by manager Dick Williams, who had won back-to-back World Series titles with Oakland, and young stars like Gary Carter and Andre Dawson, Montreal finished just two games behind the Pirates in 1979. At the end of September, the Expos came to Pittsburgh for a crucial four-game series. The two teams were tied for the division lead with a week to go. After splitting a doubleheader on September 24, the Pirates outscored Montreal, 20–5, in the final two games and ultimately won the division. Dawson knew his team had a bright future, but he also witnessed first-hand what his team was missing. "The difference between their demeanor and ours was astounding," he said in his autobiography, *Hawk*. "They seemed to love the pressure. It increased their abilities. For us, it did the opposite. Though we were the more talented team, their very presence rattled us. They took advantage of our youth."[10]

The new decade represented a new start for the Expos, and they were ready to take the next step. "Going through the race we went through last year has to make us that much stronger," said Williams.[11]

Entering their fourth year at Olympic Stadium, the Expos were learning the nuances of their ballpark and decided to focus on speed. To that aim, they dealt lefty Dan Schatzeder to the Detroit Tigers in exchange for outfielder Ron LeFlore, who had led the American League in swipes in 1978 and finished second to Willie Wilson in 1979. Coupled with second baseman Rodney Scott, the addition of LeFlore gave Montreal a potent top of the lineup.

The middle of the order featured Dawson, Ellis Valentine, Larry Parrish and Gary Carter, all of whom were beginning to assert themselves as feared hitters. Parrish was coming off his finest season in the big leagues, hitting .307 with 30 home runs in 1979, while playing 153 games at third base. Parrish may have been eclipsed in notoriety at third base by bigger names like Mike Schmidt, George Brett, Graig Nettles and Ron Cey, but opponents knew and respected him. Pirates manager Chuck Tanner went so far as to single him out during a speech at a January banquet in Montreal. "Just look at that young man," Tanner said. "He deserved to be your MVP and he's not even gotten good yet. He came into Pittsburgh one time and we heard he had two bad wrists, but he had a big series against us. I don't want to have to face him when he's healthy."[12]

Any goodwill the remarks may have possibly garnered were offset by Tanner's assertion that the Pirates "won the World Series for our division. We won it for you fans in Montreal. It goes to show that your Expos are the second best team in the world."[13]

While Montreal was trying to break through in the NL East, the Houston Astros were looking to do the same in the West. The Astros showed they had serious talent in 1979 as they contended for the Western Division title throughout the season before finishing second to the Reds. It was the best season in their history, and they had a lot to look forward to in 1980.

Houston boasted one of the best pitching staffs in the National League in 1979. Joe Niekro won 21 games, Ken Forsch threw the major league's only no-hitter, and 6-foot-8 fireballer James Rodney Richard led the league in strikeouts. Those three were a big part of why the Astros posted a 3.20 team ERA, second only to Montreal. But new owner John McMullen wasn't satisfied, and in November he shook up the baseball world, and angered his fellow owners, by signing Nolan Ryan for the unheard-of price of $1 million per season.

Ryan had established himself as one of the top pitchers in the game in his eight seasons with the California Angels. He won 138 games and recorded nearly 2,500 strikeouts, leading the American League every year but 1975. But a rift developed between Ryan and Angels General Manager Buzzie Bavasi in 1979, and that rift grew to a chasm as the season progressed.

Ryan's contract was up at the end of the year and, after a 1978 season in which he went 10–13, Bavasi was in no hurry to sign him to a big-money, long-term contract. Both men drew a line in the sand. Bavasi indicated that he wouldn't negotiate until the season was over, while Ryan said he would become a free agent if he wasn't signed by Opening Day. Things got more contentious as the summer wore on. Ryan and his agent Dick Moss gave Bavasi permission to seek a trade to Texas or Houston, but a proposed swap involving Al Oliver was turned down by the Rangers, and Houston's offer of slugger Bob Watson and pitcher Joe Sambito was rejected by Bavasi.

Ryan finished 1979 with a 16–14 record and a league-leading 223 strikeouts, along with a 3.60 ERA, while helping the Angels win their first-ever division title. His 16 wins tied for the team lead, but Bavasi wasn't impressed, telling the media he could simply replace Ryan with two 8–7 pitchers. "Buzzie did not understand," said Don Baylor in his 1989 biography, *Nothing but the Truth: A Baseball Life.*[14] "They could replace the win total, but they could not replace the pitcher, the wear and tear he saved the bullpen, the fear he put in the opposition. He was the only pitcher in the majors capable of pitching a no-hitter any time he took the mound."[15]

The animosity extended to Ryan's agent, Dick Moss, who also took shots at Bavasi, saying, "Buzzie still thinks this is the mid–'50s and he is the general manager of the Dodgers and the name of the game is trying to sign a player for $15,000 when he's been authorized by Walter O'Malley to give him $16,000."[16]

"Those two young men [Ryan and Moss] deserve each other," countered Bavasi. "We've had no trouble with any other agents."[17]

Whether or not that was true, Ryan would definitely not be returning to the Angels and, as a free agent, had multiple suitors. George Steinbrenner and the Yankees offered $1 million per season, but after beginning his career with the Mets, Ryan had little interest in returning to New York. He told Moss that if the Astros matched the Yankees' offer, he would sign. His three-year, $3 million deal gave him the highest annual salary in team sports history. In his autobiography, *Miracle Man,* Ryan said the money was embarrassing, even for him, but he wasn't about to turn it down. The move gave Houston both defending strikeout champions in Ryan and Richard. They became even more devastating as bookends to the knuckleballing Niekro.

But McMullen wasn't finished signing future Hall of Famers. He was still looking for a veteran leader who could teach his team to win. Second baseman Joe Morgan was looking to prove he could still contribute as he entered his age 36 season. After winning back-to-back MVP Awards and two World Series with the Reds in 1975 and 1976, Morgan's offensive numbers had fallen sharply. He hit just .236 in 1978 and .250 in 1979, while his home run total slipped from a high of 27 in 1976 to just nine in 1979. He also wanted out of Cincinnati. In his 1993 autobiography, *Joe Morgan: A Life in Baseball*, he cited the Reds firing Sparky Anderson after 1978 as a tipping point for him. "With Tony, Pete and now Sparky gone, the heart of the Big Red Machine had all but ceased. It was ... before the 1979 season was even under way that I decided to play out my contract and move on."[18]

Morgan entered the free-agent draft and was selected by the Dodgers, his preferred destination. His signing with Cincinnati's long-time rival was predicated on incumbent second baseman Davey Lopes agreeing to move to center field. But Lopes balked, and Morgan didn't want to be the reason for a fracture on a pennant-contending club, so he announced that he wouldn't be signing with anyone and went back into the secondary phase of the draft.

This time he was selected by the Yankees and the Astros. As was the case with Ryan, George Steinbrenner's Yankees lost out to Houston. On January 31, Joe Morgan agreed to a deal to return to the city where he began his career in 1963. "The Astros are a contender, that's why I'm here," Morgan said at his introductory news conference. "This team has a lot of talent. I like the way they played last year. They hustled and played the game the right way.[19] ... With a pitching staff of J.R. Richard, Joe Niekro, Ken Forsch and Nolan Ryan that is the best in the National League. And if pitching is 80 percent of the game like so many people say, then we are in pretty good shape."[20]

Adding Ryan and Morgan was a boost to any team, but the Astros' biggest weakness was a lack of run production, particularly from the right side. As a team, Houston hit just 49 home runs in 1979, one more than Dave Kingman hit by himself for the Cubs. They led the NL with 190 stolen bases but finished last in runs scored, and General Manager Tal

Smith knew a big bat could be the thing to put them into the post-season for the first time in their history.

Smith nearly pulled off a trade at the winter meetings with the Pirates that would have sent pitcher Joaquin Andujar to Pittsburgh for Bill Robinson and another player, but when the Astros wouldn't renegotiate his contract, Robinson nixed the deal. His decision was all the more frustrating for Houston because he could play first base, which was a position of need for the Astros.

Without Robinson, manager Bill Virdon was forced again to consider having Gold Glove center fielder Cesar Cedeno open the season at first base. But the additions of Ryan and Morgan and a talented young outfield of Jose Cruz, Jeffrey Leonard, and Terry Puhl had Virdon feeling good about the upcoming season.

"We made great strides during the 1979 season and the pennant race provided some experience for our players," said Virdon. "That should make us a better club in 1980. If we can get good overall offensive production, the pitching we're capable of and consistency, I feel we'll be legitimate contenders this year and will have as good a chance as any club in our division of winning the division crown and more."[21]

The Astros were legitimate contenders, but to win the division they would have to knock off both the defending champion Cincinnati Reds and the Los Angeles Dodgers. The Reds won six NL West titles in the 1970s, including 1979, despite injuries to many key players. Manager John McNamara returned all but one of his starters from the previous season and liked his team's chances heading into the new decade. The only question heading into spring training was who would take over for Morgan. "I'm just hoping Junior Kennedy or the kid, Ron Oester, can do the job at second that Knight did last year at 3rd as a replacement for Pete Rose."[22]

Kennedy was 29 and had spent parts of three seasons in the big leagues with mixed results. Oester was a Cincinnati native, and the Reds liked what they had seen of him in the minor leagues.

"No matter who wins the job, I have to think we'll be stronger at the position this season,"[23] said McNamara in a not-so-thinly veiled shot at the departed Morgan. Oester was the first product turned out by a Reds youth movement that had the team excited and was a big reason why they chose not to venture into the free-agent market. Also on the horizon were catcher Dave Van Gorder, outfielders Paul Householder and Eddie Milner, and pitchers Bruce Berenyi and Charlie Liebrandt. Most of that talent was at Double-A Nashville, but team President Dick Wagner didn't want to spend big money on stop-gap guys when he felt that his farm system was loaded.

The other reason Wagner didn't aggressively bid for free agents was that, like many teams, the Reds were led kicking and screaming into the free-agent era. Horrified Reds fans watched star after star leave Cincinnati either in trades or via free agency in the late 1970s. Despite drawing 2,000,000 fans per season for seven consecutive years, the Reds were determined not to pay top dollar for players. *Sporting News* columnist Bill Conlin wrote that Wagner was clinging tenaciously to the old way of doing business and that unhappy Reds quickly become former Reds. Morgan was the latest to depart Cincinnati, following Rose, Tony Perez, Fred Norman, Pedro Borbon, and Rawly Eastwick.

Be it confidence or arrogance, the Reds felt they were poised to repeat in 1980. Injuries to Ken Griffey, George Foster, first baseman Dan Driessen and staff ace Tom Seaver had cost them in 1979, and they still won the division. A healthy lineup was key, as was good pitching, which started with Seaver. Back problems limited "Tom Terrific" early in 1979, but after recovering, he returned to his old ways, reeling off 11 straight wins. Behind Seaver were Frank Pastore, who had pitched well after making his major league debut in 1979, Mike LaCoss, Liebrandt and veteran Bill Bonham.

While the Reds were looking for pitching, the Dodgers had an embarrassment of pitching riches. Entering spring training, LA had seven pitchers who could lay a legitimate claim to one of the five spots in the Dodgers' rotation. Don Sutton and Burt Hooton were both coming off seasons of ten or more wins, while Rick Sutcliffe's 17-win season had earned him Rookie of the Year honors in 1979. Then there were Bob Welch, Jerry Reuss, and knuckleballer Charlie Hough, all in contention for spots in the rotation.

As if that weren't enough pitching, LA signed former Twins starter Dave Goltz, who won 20 games in 1977, to a free-agent contract in the off-season. Goltz grew up in Minnesota and loved playing for the Twins, but when the Dodgers offered him a six-year deal worth $3 million, he left the Twin Cities for Tinseltown. The fact that Minnesota's final offer was $250,000 a year made leaving home a bit less difficult from a financial standpoint, but not an emotional one. "I'm nervous here," Goltz told the *Minneapolis Star-Tribune*. "I have to show I can pitch."[24]

"Dave is a class young man," said Dodgers manager Tommy Lasorda.

"He comes with credentials. He's won 20 games. He's a workhorse. He's a competitor."[25]

Terry Forster was expected to return to help a bullpen that had been a weakness the year before, and 24-year-old Bobby Castillo was back after earning seven saves and striking out 25 batters in 24 late-season innings. Non-roster invitees to camp included 1979 first-round draft pick Steve Howe and an intriguing lefty out of Mexico named Fernando Valenzuela.

The Dodgers won the National League pennant in 1977 and 1978 but slipped to third place in the NL West in 1979 with the pitching staff taking much of the blame. Dodgers pitchers led the NL in earned run average in 1977 and 1978, but slipped to seventh in 1979.

The offense was certainly not to blame as Steve Garvey, Ron Cey, Davey Lopes, Joe Ferguson, and Dusty Baker each hit 20 or more homers en route to leading the NL with 183. This was despite Reggie Smith missing more than half the season with an ankle injury. The loss of Smith didn't keep the Dodgers from outscoring their opponents or outdrawing every other team in Major League Baseball. Nearly 2.9 million people filed into Dodger Stadium to see the stars both on and off the field.

Unfortunately, the laid-back atmosphere of Los Angeles wasn't translating well to the Dodgers clubhouse. Pitcher Don Sutton was late to spring training because a bookkeeping error resulted in $100,000 coming up missing at his company, Suttcor International. Sutton held most of the franchise pitching records, including starts, strikeouts and shutouts, but distractions such as this didn't endear him to his teammates. He wanted out of Los Angeles, and everyone knew it. "He's an excellent pitcher, but he wants to be traded," said General Manager Al Campanis. "We are in a position where we can possibly do something. But we're not going to give him away. He can be a valuable asset for a club."[26]

Sutton was still a valuable asset, but some in the organization were ready to pack his bags for him. At the head of the line was catcher Joe Ferguson, who told the media he was "sick and tired of Sutton's act."[27] That act included supposedly planting trade rumors that had him heading all over the league, including a straight-up swap for Seaver which ultimately didn't pan out.

Sutton had also famously gotten into a fight with Steve Garvey in the visitors' clubhouse in Shea Stadium a few years earlier. Garvey took exception to Sutton's comments in the press about Reggie Smith being the "real MVP" of the team. The two rolled around on the floor for a while before being separated, but not before someone yelled, "Stop the fight! They'll kill each other!" to which Ferguson replied, "Good."[28]

But the Sutton feuds were nothing compared to the pugilistic actions of Dodgers manager Tommy Lasorda, whose off-season included a fight with former coach Jim Lefebvre. The two got into it at the studios of KNBC in Burbank after shooting separate interviews. Bad blood had existed between the two since Lasorda fired Lefebvre as hitting and first base coach after the 1979 season. Lefebvre won Rookie of the Year honors for the Dodgers in 1965 and parlayed his time in LA into some acting gigs, including playing one of The Riddler's henchmen on the "Batman" TV series. The henchman experience proved handy when the two squared off in Burbank. Both men claimed that the other started the fight, but there was little doubt who finished it. LA sportscaster Steve Sommers reported that "Lasorda left with blood on his face and Lefebvre left with a smile on his."[29]

In the American League, the Baltimore Orioles began the new decade with hopes of continuing as one of the junior circuit's top teams. The Birds won three pennants and one World Series in the 1970s, knocking off the beta version of the Big Red Machine in 1970.

At the helm was feisty, 49-year-old Earl Weaver. In 11 full seasons as Baltimore's skipper, Weaver had never finished below .500 and had topped 100 wins four times, based on a simple philosophy of baseball being a game of pitching, defense and three-run homers.

That philosophy had guided the Orioles to a major league-leading 102 wins in 1979, including a stretch of 50 wins in 66 games. They easily topped Milwaukee in the AL East and then beat the Angels three games to one in the American League Championship Series. Weaver's squad held a commanding three games to one lead over the Pirates in the World Series and then collapsed. Baltimore had outscored the Pirates, 24–16, through the first four games of the Series. They had Mike Flanagan, the eventual Cy Young Award winner, on the mound for Game Five and champagne on ice. The Pirates' Game One starter, Bruce Kison, was injured, so Chuck Tanner had to go with Jim Rooker, who had won all of four games in 17 starts.

Trailing late in the game, the Pirates scored seven runs in their final three at-bats to take Game Five, 7–1, then shut out Baltimore, 4–0, in Game Six behind Candelaria. They took Game Seven, 4–1, thanks to Willie Stargell's 4-for-5 night at the plate and strong relief pitching by Grant

Jackson and Kent Tekulve. After scoring 24 runs in the first four games of the Series, the Orioles managed just two in the remaining three games, all Pittsburgh victories.

But despite the collapse, the Orioles felt good about the new decade. The 1979 team had nine position players appear in at least 120 games, and they all returned for 1980. Al Bumbry set the table at the top of the order, while Eddie Murray, Ken Singleton, Lee May and Gary Roenicke combined to hit more than 100 home runs. For all the potent bats in the lineup, the Orioles' strength throughout the 1970s was pitching, and that didn't change with the new decade. Baltimore had one of the top pitching staffs in the game, comprised of Flanagan, Scott McGregor, Dennis Martinez, Steve Stone, and three-time Cy Young Award winner Jim Palmer.

Back problems limited Palmer to just 22 starts and a 10–6 record in 1979. Those back problems weren't helped when he aggravated the injury in a tug-of-war competition against the Los Angeles Rams in the made-for-TV *Superteams* event right before spring training. *Superteams* was a small part of a busy off-season for Palmer. There were the ubiquitous Jockey underwear ads, which earned him support in a poll of Playboy Bunnies for athletes they'd most like to see appear in a magazine. He was also talking to people about hosting a new TV series called *That's Incredible*, which ultimately starred former Minnesota Vikings quarterback Fran Tarkenton. But the big news heading into camp was Palmer's seemingly annual contract squabble.

Palmer was 34 years old and coming off one of the worst years of his career, but that didn't stop him from asking for a six-year contract worth $3.5 million. He led the major leagues in wins in the 1970s with 186, but Baltimore was understandably hesitant to offer him a long-term deal worth big money. The Orioles countered with a three-year extension of his current contract that bumped his salary from $260,000 per season to $325,000, along with a $250,000 signing bonus and $100,000 in deferred payments for each of the last three years. Palmer's response was that the Orioles weren't being realistic, and he threatened to sit out the year or ask for a trade.

Those demands didn't sit well with the Orioles or Palmer's agent, Ed Keating, who said, "I think Jim should cool it ... the negotiations are getting serious and there's no question [the Orioles] don't appreciate some of the things Jim says to the press. But you know Jim; when he wants to make a point, he wants to make a point."[30]

Billy Martin revitalized a moribund Oakland franchise with his aggressive style that came to be known as "Billy Ball." The A's returned to the playoffs in 1981 after a six-year absence (National Baseball Hall of Fame Library, Cooperstown, New York).

1. Spring Training

Baltimore's 1979 division title broke a string of three consecutive division championships for the New York Yankees. Broadway is the home of drama in America, and the Bronx remained the home of drama in major league baseball. Act I took place at the end of October 1979, when manager Billy Martin was fired once again by team owner George Steinbrenner after an altercation in Minneapolis with marshmallow salesman Joseph Cooper. According to Cooper, Martin challenged him to a fight and then sucker-punched him on the way outside. Cooper, whom the *Associated Press* described as "a family man with two sons and a productive sales job,"[31] received 15 stitches in his lip and a place in baseball lore.

Cooper didn't come forward initially because he didn't want Martin to lose his job as a result of the incident. But once Steinbrenner fired Martin, Cooper decided to tell his side of the story. Martin's side of the story was that Cooper tripped and fell, at which point Martin returned to his room. But Steinbrenner wasn't buying that version, and he fired Martin for the second time in 15 months, naming Dick Howser the new Yankees skipper.

Howser's 1980 Yankees team had a very different look from Martin's 1979 club. Thurman Munson's tragic death in a plane crash in August was devastating to the entire organization. Reggie Jackson considered himself "the straw that stirred the drink,"[32] but Munson was the most respected member of the team, especially in the clubhouse. The emotional and leadership void would be difficult to fill, but from a strictly baseball standpoint, the Yankees needed a catcher.

General Manager Gene Michael addressed that need by dealing first baseman Chris Chambliss to Toronto in a six-player deal that brought Rick Cerone to New York. One week later, Michael signed free agent Bob Watson to play first base and help balance a lineup that was heavy on left-handed bats. The last piece was acquiring center fielder Ruppert Jones from Seattle to replace Mickey Rivers, who was dealt to Texas the year before. Paired with second baseman Willie Randolph at the top of the order, Jones represented a major upgrade coming off a season in which he hit 21 home runs and stole 33 bases. The combination of speed and power from the left side was a perfect fit for Yankee Stadium and its short right field dimensions.

Left-handed pitchers Ron Guidry and Tommy John combined to win 39 games and were 1–2 in the American League in ERA in 1979. But the Yankees' team ERA of 3.83 was still more than a half-run off the pace set by Baltimore, who led the league. To address the lack of depth, Michael added Tom Underwood from Toronto in the Chambliss deal. Underwood won only nine games the previous year, but had a respectable 3.69 E.R.A. and was expected to win more with a better team surrounding him. The Yankees also added veteran Rudy May to the bullpen; he won ten games while posting an ERA of 2.31 for Montreal.

Change was the theme in Fort Lauderdale, but one thing stayed the same: Reggie Jackson was late to camp. The 33-year-old Jackson was in his 14th season, had five World Series rings and an MVP Award, and was closing in on 400 career home runs. The Yankees were supposed to report on March 1, but Reggie was on his own schedule. He showed up a few days late, met with the Yankees brass and was fined, with the money eventually going to the New York Public School Athletic Association. For Jackson, it was a financial transaction he was more than happy to make. "I don't consider it punitive," Reggie said. "I had business commitments and loose ends I needed to tie up. They did what they had to do. There's no bitterness."[33]

In the AL West, the Kansas City Royals were looking to get the train back on the tracks in 1980. KC had won the division three years in a row before the California Angels edged them out in 1979. The fallout cost Royals manager Whitey Herzog his job. Despite amassing a 410–304 record over four-plus seasons, Herzog was fired two days after the 1979 season ended. Almost immediately, fans began cancelling their season tickets and threatened to boycott.

In his place, the Royals hired former Baltimore first base coach Jim Frey. "Sure, I'm gonna be on the spot, like 25 other managers,"[34] Frey told reporters at his introductory news conference. "I came in here fully aware of the fact Whitey Herzog is a very popular man here. I can accept the fact that people will not openly welcome any man who comes in after him."[35]

Welcome to Kansas City!

Once the team reported for camp in Fort Myers, Florida, Frey was able to focus on his roster rather than his predecessor. As with every other team, health was an issue. But while sore muscles and hamstring pulls are fairly routine, starting pitchers nearly severing their fingers in boating accidents are not.

Dennis Leonard had done just that on Christmas Eve of 1979. Fortunately for him, the injury was on his left (non-pitching) hand. The righty won 14 games in 1979, and Frey needed him healthy if his new team was to regain their rightful spot atop the division. The rest of the rotation seemed fairly set with Larry Gura, Paul Splittorff and Rich Gale. None of them had pitched all that well in 1979, but they were veterans and could be counted on to deliver once the season began. The back of the bullpen was another question. Closer Al "The Mad Hungarian" Hrabosky had signed with the Braves as a free agent, and the issue of who would finish games was in doubt. Submariner Dan Quisenberry, who had come up at the end of 1979 and pitched well, figured to take over the job, but there were other candidates as well, including righty Renie Martin.

There was change at other positions, too. Phenom Clint Hurdle was penciled in to take over the outfield spot vacated when Al Cowens was traded to the Angels. In return for Cowens, the Royals got slugging first baseman Willie Aikens, who was coming off knee surgery. Despite playing only 116 games in 1979, Aikens hit 21 homers and drove in 81 runs. His season was cut short after he suffered a knee injury sliding into second base in Kansas City on September 18, but Frey was counting on the kind of production he'd shown before the injury to add to an already potent offense. "I think that with the acquisition of Willie Aikens and if Clint Hurdle would fulfill his potential as our right fielder, you've got a great combination of power and speed," Frey told reporters. "We've got four or five guys who can hit 20 home runs or more."[36]

The batting order was one area that didn't concern the rookie manager. Hal McRae, Amos Otis, Frank White and George Brett, who had blossomed into one of the best hitters in the game, provided a solid foundation. At the top of the order, Willie Wilson had hit .315 in 1979, and his 83 stolen bases led the majors. He was one of seven Royals who hit double-digits in swipes, which helped KC lead all of baseball with 207 stolen bases.

The Royals were in good shape heading into the season, but camp was not without drama. The team was negotiating a new contract with George Brett, and the numbers being thrown around were grabbing attention. Once White, who was in year two of a six-year deal, heard the news, he wasn't happy. He was making about $150,000, while Brett was close to a deal worth $800–900,000 per year. White wasn't asking for that kind of money but thought he should be paid among the top five second basemen in the American League. "I just want to be paid what I'm worth," he said. "But when a guy is making $600 or $700,000 more than you are, you get a funny feeling. Are they going to take care of one guy, or everybody who helped build this team?"[37]

"Everybody is trying to be fair, but free agency has changed things," said McRae. "Guys are wondering if they can't get more unless they threaten to play out their contracts. If the club wants to be fair, it should try to resolve the situation."[38]

McRae had hit the nail on the head. Free agency was still new, and the definition of fair was constantly changing. It was also different depending on whether you asked a player or an owner or a GM. All the talk put Brett in a difficult position. "When you see everybody upset at what they're making and they're throwing your name around, it's a funny feeling," he said.[39] "I haven't signed anything yet. I don't think the guys are mad at me, they're just trying to get the Royals attention and using me as an example. I don't think they resent me. I haven't signed a contract. I haven't asked to renegotiate."[40]

So the Royals' three-year string of first-place finishes in the AL West snapped, and they fired a popular manager. One of their best pitchers had nearly cut off his hand, and a handful of others were griping about their contracts. Then things got bad.

Former major league pitcher Don Newcombe came to Royals camp to address the players about the dangers of addiction. Newcombe's career was cut short due to an alcohol problem, and he was making the rounds to counsel players. His speech hit home with one player in particular.

Darrell Porter had had a career year in 1979. He hit .299 with 20 home runs and 112 RBI while drawing a league-leading 121 walks. His season had earned him an All-Star Game selection and a ninth-place finish in the American League MVP voting. But off the field he was out of control. Drugs and alcohol had taken over, and he had finally reached a breaking point. While many players relaxed in the off-season and then prepared for spring training, Porter's off-season was a bit different.

"Get up about noon, drink coffee, do a Quaalude, sniff cocaine and drink beer," he detailed in his autobiography, *Snap Me Perfect!* "Mixing it with tomato juice, I could guzzle an entire case [of beer] in a couple of hours while doing cocaine."[41]

After Newcombe's speech, the team was out on the field stretching when Porter told teammate Pete LaCock that he had a drug problem. LaCock tried to ease his mind, saying it was no big deal. But Porter knew it was and that he needed help right away. Sensing the severity of the situation, LaCock headed into the clubhouse and told Newcombe what was going on. A few minutes later, Porter laid everything on the table, telling Frey and Newcombe about his eight-year battle with substance abuse. Porter was expecting Newcombe to understand his plight and lend a sympathetic ear. He did anything but.

"Porter, you're a jerk," Newcomb said in an expletive-laden tirade. "You're a real idiot! You ought to cry. You're a disgrace to baseball and that uniform you're wearing."[42]

After more choice words from both sides, Newcombe told Porter he had to come clean with General Manager Joe Burke. Burke was supportive, but after speaking to Newcombe on the phone he told Porter it was a lot more serious than he had thought, and the Royals were sending him to rehab. They told him he couldn't come back until he had a clean bill of health.

As spring training wound down, one issue loomed above all others: The threat of a players' strike. Ever since Peter Seitz's ruling in December of 1975, which struck down the reserve clause, MLB owners had been trying to turn back time. The collective bargaining agreement was set to expire, and the owners' proposal of free-agent compensation was the major sticking point. Owners wanted a system in which a team signing a free agent would be able to protect up to 15 players, and the team losing the free agent could select any unprotected player as compensation for the loss.

Player's Association head Marvin Miller advised the players not to accept the proposal, feeling it would keep teams from aggressively bidding on free agents, which it certainly would have done. On April 1, the players voted to walk out of the final week of spring training and to go on strike on May 22 if an agreement was not reached. The final vote was 967–1 in favor of a strike. The single no vote came from Royals infielder Jerry Terrell, who objected on religious grounds. Terrell didn't admit to casting the lone dissenting vote, but there was little doubt as to where he stood.

"The players know my views and there is mutual respect,"[43] he said. Terrell was the Royals' player representative, but surprisingly, none of his teammates had a problem with his stance, despite the fact that he reportedly told a teammate that he would cross the picket line and play if he had to. They understood that it came from a religious standpoint and not because he thought the owners were in the right. Regardless of Terrell's vote, the battle lines had clearly been drawn, and neither side showed signs of backing down. The mini-strike cost the owners revenue from 92 spring training games and put the regular season in doubt.

The players had an unlikely ally in Orioles manager Earl Weaver, who felt that free agency was a good thing and was against the system of teams receiving active major league players as compensation for losing a free agent. He recognized the compensation system for exactly what it was: a deterrent. Weaver felt free agency would help to level the playing field and keep teams from dominating like the Yankees did in the 1950s and early 1960s.

He even went so far as to propose an alternate system where all teams could protect 35 of the players on their 40-man roster, with the team losing a free agent selecting one of the remaining five. Baseball owners were in favor of teams only being able to protect 15 players off their 25-man roster. Potentially losing your fourth starter or a key member of the bullpen would make teams think twice about pursuing free agents. Weaver saw that and was decidedly against it.

Angels owner Gene Autry, a union member during his days as an entertainer, suddenly had a change of heart and took a hardline stance. "If I had my say and the other owners agreed with me, I'd close down for the season," he said. "What's the sense in going out again? It's a waste of time … and I would just as soon forget about the season."[44]

He also had some words of advice for the players about their chief negotiator, Marvin Miller. "One of these days, the players are going to have to take a deep look at what their leader has gotten them into,"[45] he said. What Miller had gotten them into was a new system in which they were free to move from team to team and make more money doing it. The average player salary had more than doubled since 1976, and the highest salary in the game had gone from Henry Aaron's $240,000 in 1976 to Nolan Ryan's $1 million per year.

Miller had also educated the players about labor practices and how the owners had been manipulating them for decades with cries of poverty. He noted that the owners had built up a strike fund of more than $20 million and also had taken out an insurance policy to further protect themselves. The intent was clear: The owners *wanted* the players to go on strike, and they were financially prepared to wait them out.

"Their intent has been to provoke a strike," Miller said. "They see this as a time to take the players on, to dismantle the association. I'd say 95 to 98 percent of the time has been spent talking about what they want, not what we want."[46]

Delaying a potential strike until mid–May served multiple purposes. The first was that players would receive three paychecks before walking off the job, which could help ease their financial burden. Secondly, May 22 was the Thursday before Memorial Day, so a strike could inflict more financial damage on the owners due to traditionally high-attendance games being cancelled.

Owners said they would leave camps open for players who wanted to work out, but they wouldn't pay expenses such as hotels and meal allowances. As the week progressed, teams began to hold workouts and intra-squad scrimmages. Some on their own, some with coaches present. The workouts were not mandatory, and some players took the opportunity to head home for a few days before the season started.

In Clearwater, Florida, every member of the Phillies stayed in town and attended workouts run by Dallas Green and the coaching staff before going their separate ways in the afternoons. Mike Schmidt, Steve Carlton and Tug McGraw chartered a fishing boat and lived on it during the week. The three got a great deal on the boat and, since the team wasn't paying for their hotel rooms anymore, they decided to live it up.

The situation was odd for the scores of baseball writers as well. Instead of reporting on final roster battles or writing Cardinals/Phillies game stories, they got a crash course in labor relations and wrote game stories about coach-led Team Krol vs. Team Ricketts in Cardinals camp.

The most bizarre incident took place in the Orlando airport when Enos Cabell decided to head home after the strike vote. Joe Morgan and J.R. Richard wanted Cabell to stay in camp and continue to work out with the team. Their desire for team unity was so great that the two of them, 5-foot-8 Morgan and 6-foot-8 Richard, were seen sprinting through the airport in full uniform trying to track down Cabell before he boarded his 12:40 p.m. flight to California.

"We didn't know which airline," said Morgan. "So we had to run around the airport looking for a flight that left at that time for Los Angeles."[47] "It tripped me out," said Cabell. "When I saw Joe and J—man, I couldn't believe it. Neither could anyone at the airport. They said we're a team and they wanted me with them. This just shows you how close we are on this team."[48]

That closeness would be tested in what was a turbulent but rewarding season for Houston.

2

April
Richard, RBIs and Rockin' Robin

Keen Babbage had been walking for two weeks. Four states, two pairs of shoes and more than 400 miles later, his trip was almost over. As he prepared to cross the Ohio River into Cincinnati, he wanted to keep going. The walk was part of an effort to raise money for the March of Dimes, but for Babbage it meant a lot more than that. "I loved it all," he said. "The walk rebuilt my faith in the fundamental strengths of this country. The energy, the strength of the people. Everybody welcomed me."[1]

During the trip, he had acquired blisters, new friends and great memories. But any thoughts of continuing were put on hold because he had a job to do. On the other side of the river, five-year-old Jason Edwards leaned on his walker and peered across the bridge. His face brightened as Babbage came into view. Edwards was the March of Dimes poster child, and he too had a job to do today. But Jason couldn't fulfill his obligation until Babbage completed his.

"We made it, Jason, we made it," Babbage said as the two met for the first time. "Here's the ball for you. I brought it 430 miles just for you."[2]

The baseball Babbage handed off was the one he had picked up at the Rawlings factory in St. Louis two weeks earlier. Now it was up to Jason. His job was simple but no less important. Throw a strike to Johnny Bench to begin the 1980 baseball season.

A few hours later, Jason stood on top of the Reds dugout and threw the first pitch of the new season to the best catcher in the game. The 1980 baseball season was underway.

Bench and his teammates hosted the lowly Atlanta Braves, a franchise that was looking to put a horrible showing in the 1970s behind them. The Braves won the inaugural NL West title in 1969 before being swept in the

NLCS, 3–0, by the "Miracle Mets." Since then things had been horrible. Eight different men managed the team during the 1970s, including owner Ted Turner's notorious one-game stint in 1977. But none of them could get the Braves higher than third place, including current skipper Bobby Cox.

The Braves' big off-season move was a five-player deal with the Toronto Blue Jays that netted first baseman Chris Chambliss, who brought a Gold Glove, post-season experience and a left-handed power bat. The addition of Chambliss also allowed the Braves to move their former catcher of the future, Dale Murphy, to the outfield, a position he hadn't played since high school.

Just 23 years old, Murphy had already had two knee surgeries, and the Atlanta front office was taking no chances with a player they deemed a future star. A move to first base in 1979 may have saved his knees, but his 15 errors in just 76 games at the position didn't help the team. Murphy needed a new defensive home, and the departures of Barry Bonnell and Rowland Office opened space in the outfield. "Murph is an athlete and an athlete can play left field," Cox told *The Sporting News*. "Greg Luzinski plays left, Dave Kingman plays left.... Dale Murphy can play left or just about anywhere."[3]

Just about anywhere no longer included first base or catcher. The addition of Chambliss and the fact that Murphy threw out just 16 percent of the runners who ran on him in 1979 meant that his days behind the plate were over. "It's going to be another adjustment," said Murphy. "But if that's what they want me to do, that's what we'll do. I feel like I have a good arm, but there is more to it than just letting it fly."[4]

His arm would be tested early on Opening Day as the Reds got to Atlanta starter Phil Niekro right away. After a Dave Collins groundout, Ken Griffey and Dave Concepcion singled, before George Foster doubled to Murphy in left to give Cincinnati a 2–0 lead. Two batters later, Bench also doubled to left as part of a four-run first inning for the Reds. Two more runs in the second inning chased Niekro and gave the Reds a 6–0 lead. For Niekro, it was the shortest of his seven Opening Day starts in an Atlanta uniform and continued a string of bad luck/bad pitching in season openers. He was tabbed with the loss as the Reds rolled, 9–0. The defeat brought his Opening Day mark to an ugly 0–6 with an ERA of 6.88. Clearly, the knuckleball is a warm-weather pitch.

Niekro's struggles on Opening Day were nothing new, but one thing was. At the beginning of 1980, Major League Baseball implemented Rule 1004-a, which established a new batting statistic called Game Winning RBI. A batter would receive credit for a GWRBI if he recorded "the r.b.i. that gives a club the lead it never relinquishes."[5]

Introduced during the spring by the Elias Sports Bureau, the intent of the statistic was to quantify something that many people weren't convinced even existed: the idea of "clutch hitting." Throughout baseball history, certain players seemingly always delivered when their team needed it most. Of course, the definition of "clutch" varied depending on who was doing the talking. Those who believed in clutch hitting would often conveniently forget the many times a certain player failed to deliver in those situations, but highlight the far fewer times that he did.

But baseball is a game driven by numbers, both good and bad, and on the surface the GWRBI was a nice idea. If a player drives in a run in the eighth inning of a tie game and his team wins, there should be a way to track that and reward those who accomplish this feat more than others.

Unfortunately for proponents of the rule, its flaws were exposed the very first time the stat was used. George Foster earned the first Game Winning RBI in the history of Major League Baseball. His first-inning double off Niekro drove in the first two runs for his team in a 9–0 shutout. Not exactly clutch hitting on his part.

Niekro's performance aside, it's often the case in the early going that pitchers are ahead of hitters. That was certainly true in Houston when the Astros hosted the Dodgers. Despite giving Nolan Ryan the largest contract in the history of team sports, he was a spectator as they opened their season. What he saw was his new teammate, J.R. Richard, making major league hitters look foolish.

"It was coming out of a cannon,"[6] said Los Angeles outfielder Rudy Law, who was making his first Opening Day start. "I've never faced anybody who can throw the ball like that, it was unbelievable. He's one of the greatest pitchers in the major leagues. I don't look forward to facing too many more like him."[7]

Richard was perfect through six and one-third innings before Law broke it up with a single in the seventh. Richard went eight innings and struck out 13 before giving way to Joe Sambito, who earned his first save in a 3–2 Houston win.

"Hitters don't like coming to the Astrodome anyway," said Sambito.

"With pitchers like that waiting for them, they like it even less."[8] The combination of Richard, Ryan, Joe Niekro and Ken Forsch gave Houston perhaps the best starting rotation in the game. But it was Richard's performance that had people buzzing. He had always had a big fastball, but there were often times when neither he nor his catcher had any idea where it would end up. What made his Opening Day start different was that in addition to the 98mph fastball and the 13 strikeouts, he issued zero walks, something he was able to do just three times in 1979. To begin the season that way was a big boost for him. "I think that's about the fastest I've ever been clocked," said Richard. "Being overpowering is a great asset—that and getting the ball over the plate."[9]

New Houston second baseman Joe Morgan had seen some overpowering pitchers in his career, and he felt Richard was among the best, saying, "You have to go back to Koufax, who was the best I've ever seen. And even he wasn't better than J.R. was for seven innings."[10]

Knowing they were facing Richard on the road was enough to put the Dodgers in a bad mood, but that paled in comparison to the feeling some had for manager Tommy Lasorda, who seemed to have a communication problem with certain members of the team. Tops among them were catcher Joe Ferguson and outfielder Rick Monday, who both felt that Lasorda wasn't truthful with them.

According to Monday, Lasorda told him that Law would start in his place because Monday was dealing with an Achilles tendon injury. Lasorda went on a radio show and said that Law had won the center field job outright. Making matters worse was the fact that Monday's wife was the one who delivered the news after hearing it on the radio. "Lasorda told me one thing and the radio station another," said Monday. "I have to assume he's lying to somebody."[11]

Ferguson was upset because published reports had him as the clear #2 catcher behind Steve Yeager after the two split time in 1979. Again, Lasorda sad nothing to Ferguson about the situation, which angered the veteran. "I have to be very cautious here," said Lasorda. "It's a very delicate situation. Whichever one doesn't play is going to be angry."[12]

That was certainly the case, but by saying nothing to the parties involved, Lasorda succeeded only in making everyone angry. Hard feelings aside, pre-season prognosticators assumed that the NL West would come down to either the Dodgers, Houston or Cincinnati. In the East, getting the answer to a few key questions would likely determine the champion.

Were the Phillies finished or could they return to their former glory? Were the Expos ready to break through? Could the Pirates repeat?

Pittsburgh opened the season against the Cardinals in St. Louis and carried the looseness of a defending champion. In the visitors' clubhouse, Jim Rooker donned Mike Easler's black and gold robe emblazoned with the nickname, "Hitman," and danced around imitating boxer Sugar Ray Leonard. In another part of the room, Willie Stargell gave center fielder Omar Moreno grief, saying Cardinals starter Pete Vuckovich was certain to pick him off first base. That was if Moreno was lucky enough to even get there.

Vuckovich had found a home in St. Louis after spending time with the White Sox and the Blue Jays. The 6-foot-one righty racked up 27 wins in two seasons as a Cardinal and did not allow a run during spring training. His success carried over into the regular season. In the bottom of the second inning, St. Louis right fielder George Hendrick's double to left field off Pirates starter Bert Blyleven scored Bobby Bonds, and the Cardinals had a 1–0 lead.

After that, the two starters were dominant. Blyleven retired ten of the next 12 batters he faced, surrendering just a fourth-inning walk to catcher Ted Simmons and a fifth-inning single to Ken Reitz. Meanwhile, the Pirates could get nothing going against Vuckovich, who did not allow a hit through the first five innings. With one out in the top of the sixth, Pittsburgh second baseman Phil Garner's single broke up the no-hit bid and brought up Blyleven's spot in the order. Seeing a chance to tie the game, Tanner lifted Blyleven and sent Easler up to hit. The move backfired as Easler hit into an inning-ending double play.

The Buccos had one more chance in the ninth inning after Lee Lacy and Moreno both reached to put two on with nobody out. Despite Stargell's dire prediction, Vuckovich didn't pick Moreno off, but instead bore down on shortstop Tim Foli, one of the best contact hitters in the game. Foli struck out just 14 times in 1979 and figured to put the ball in play. A well-placed ground ball seemed certain to score Lacy and tie the game. Instead, Vuckovich struck him out as well as Dave Parker and Stargell to end the game.

"These Pirates keep coming at you," Vuckovich said. "Growing up in Johnstown, Pennsylvania, I got to know the Pirates. After all I've been rooting for them my whole life. They play the game with such intensity. They just don't give up."[13] Vuckovich displayed his own intensity during the game. But afterwards he was anything but, telling reporters, "Look, I'm just a pitcher. I go out there and throw. Some days it's good, some days it's not so good.... Now, will you pass me another beer? I drink six-packs when I win and 12-packs when I lose."[14]

In Philadelphia, the new decade began with the triumphant return of "Kiteman" for his third attempt at flying in the ceremonial first pitch. The original Kiteman was Richard Johnson from Cypress Gardens, Florida, and it was his job to pilot his hang glider from the upper deck of Veterans Stadium to the pitcher's mound with a baseball. His first attempt, in 1972, ended with him crashing into a railing thanks to a crosswind before he ever got out of the upper deck. He tried again in 1973 with greater success, making it all the way to the outfield before crashing. The empathetic crowd booed lustily as catcher Bob Boone jogged out to retrieve the ball.

But in 1980, things were different, including Kiteman himself. Johnson was replaced by T.J. Beatty, who also brought a new "kite," complete with running lights and smoke bombs attached to tips of the wings. The launch position had also changed. The upper deck was abandoned in favor of a platform between the 500 and 600 level of The Vet. The plan was that Beatty could glide smoothly off the platform and straight to the pitcher's mound.

As he left the platform, Beatty hit the switches to ignite the smoke bombs, which promptly caught fire. Like a fighter pilot nursing a wounded plane, he valiantly maneuvered toward his target and actually overshot the mound, landing just short of home plate. Members of the grounds crew, as well as the Phillie Phanatic, came to his rescue before his craft, and the artificial turf, were engulfed in flames. Beatty handed the ball to Philadelphia mayor Bill Green, who then threw out the first pitch.

Once the game started, the Phillies wasted little time in showing they were back after a dismal 1979 campaign. Greg Luzinski's three-run homer in the bottom of the first inning off Expos starter Steve Rogers gave the Phillies a lead they never relinquished, and Steve Carlton went the distance in a 6–3 win. As his blast cleared the left field fence, Luzinski shot his huge fist in the air and charged toward third base coach Lee Elia. Luzinski was a head taller and 75 pounds heavier than his third base coach, but he showed no mercy in delivering a crushing high-five. "He hit my hand so hard that I thought he knocked my arm off at the shoulder,"[15] said Elia.

The Opening Day home run was exactly what Luzinski needed after a horrible 1979. At 6-foot-1 and 250 pounds, he earned the nickname "The Bull" by smacking more than 30 home runs in 1975, 1976 and 1978. But his power numbers fell off dramatically in 1979 with just 18 homers, and the Philadelphia fans let him know they weren't happy with his lack of production, especially at home, where he hit just .187.

"Last year I went through more or less hell out there and I just wanted to get off to a good start and break the bubble,"[16] Luzinski said. After the game, Dallas Green reminded reporters of his prediction that Luzinski would bounce back in 1980. "I told you I'd bet my house that Bull would have a helluva year," he said. "The first payment's down and I couldn't be happier for him."[17]

"There's no question that he's in my corner," Luzinski said of his manager. "It's great to have him on your side and know he's behind you."[18] Unfortunately, the Opening Day love between the two of them wouldn't last.

In Kansas City, Jim Frey had to keep pinching himself to make sure he wasn't dreaming. After 16 years as a player and manager in the minor leagues and another 15 as a coach under Earl Weaver in Baltimore, he was finally a major league manager. By contrast, the manager in the other dugout, Sparky Anderson, had amassed more than 900 wins as a major league skipper, along with four pennants and two World Series championships. Managerial credentials aside, oddsmakers liked Frey and the Royals in the season opener. Jimmy the Greek established the Tigers as 7-to-5 underdogs for the first game of the new decade, and Sparky Anderson was having none of it. "I'd take that bet," he said. "You damn right I would. I can't take it—make sure the commissioner hears that—but if I could I would."[19]

All bets aside, what looked like a managerial mismatch became irrelevant as Frey's Royals were dominated by a young pitcher who was just beginning to make a name for himself. Despite beginning the 1979 season in the minor leagues, Jack Morris still led the Tigers in wins with 17, which was enough to earn his first Opening Day start the following year. At the age of 25, he was the second-oldest member of the Detroit starting rotation, behind Milt Wilcox, but was undoubtedly the most talented pitcher on the staff. Anderson, who was never shy when it came to platitudes, called Morris the best right-handed pitcher in the American League, and he looked the part on Opening Day in a 5–1 win. "I think that's the first complete game I've ever had as a manager in a season opener," said Anderson, who earned the nickname "Captain Hook" in Cincinnati for his proclivity to go to the bullpen at the first sign of trouble. "He reminds me a lot of the real good ones."[20]

Buried in the American League East, the Tigers had slowly been building around a talented young core consisting of Morris, catcher Lance Parrish and middle infielders Lou Whitaker and Alan Trammell. Kirk Gibson was the latest to join that group. A star wide receiver at Michigan State, Gibson made his debut in Single-A Lakeland in 1978 and jumped to Triple-A Evansville in 1979. He had tremendous power, but the question was whether or not he could consistently hit major league pitching. After a pre-game pep talk from Tigers great Al Kaline, Gibson looked very comfortable against Royals starter Dennis Leonard, going 2-for-4 with a triple and a home run. "I had a feeling like I had when I was playing football," Gibson said after the game. "I was standing there near home plate and the guy was playing the anthem right in front of me and jingles went through my body, you know what I mean?"[21]

While Gibson and Morris were taking care of the Royals, lefties Jon Matlack of the Rangers and Ron Guidry of the Yankees dueled each other through nine scoreless innings in Arlington, Texas. It was still tied at 0–0 into the bottom of the 12th when former Yankee Mickey Rivers led off with a single off Tom Underwood and advanced to second on Graig Nettles' throwing error. Bump Wills' sacrifice bunt moved Rivers to third, which brought up Al Oliver, who had hit .323 the year before. Yankees manager Dick Howser ordered Underwood to walk Oliver and Buddy Bell intentionally to load the bases. He then went to the bullpen to summon one of the game's most-feared relievers.

Six-foot-3 Richard "Goose" Gossage had led the American League in saves twice in large part by simply throwing the ball past people. His fastball, paired with his size and Fu Manchu mustache, cut an intimidating figure on the mound. He was used to the pressure of being on the mound with the game on the line, but the situation he found himself in this time had a more familiar feeling to it.

Two years earlier, on Opening Day against Texas, Guidry and Matlack had faced each other and been masterful. The game was tied in the bottom of the ninth inning when Gossage gave up a game-winning home run to Richie Zisk to lead off the inning.

Now, with the bases loaded, Gossage was set to face Zisk again. He peered in for the sign from catcher Rick Cerone and unleashed his fastball.

The ball was low and away, got past Cerone and went to the screen. Rivers scored easily and the Yankees were 0–1 in Howser's debut as manager.

As the month progressed, things didn't improve for the lowly Braves. Atlanta lost nine of their first ten games and found themselves 8½ games out of first place by April 20. It was time for a change, and one of the casualties was third baseman Bob Horner. After beginning the season 2-for-34, the Braves sent the 1978 Rookie of the Year Award winner to AAA Richmond, much to his dismay. The 22-year-old Horner hit .314 with 33 homers and 98 RBI in 1979, but President and General Manager Ted Turner, calling on his four years of baseball experience, felt it best to send Horner down to the minor leagues to regain his stroke. "This is incredible," said Horner. "It's beyond incredible. It's something words can't describe, really."[22]

But Horner wasn't the only one who felt Turner's wrath. Left fielder Gary Matthews, coming off a season in which he hit .307 with 27 homers and 90 RBI, found himself on the bench. It's not often that a team dumps its Opening Day three and four hitters after just ten games, but Turner did just that. After recovering from the shock of being sent down just six months after a 33-homer season, Horner refused to report to the minor leagues and went on the offensive. "If I felt that there was any justification for being sent down to the minors, I would go," Horner said. "But when everyone calls me—fans, friends, teammates, high-level people in the front office—and tells me that it's just Ted going a little whacko again, it confirms what I already know. Ted Turner is a jerk, an absolute jerk."[23]

"I don't want to punish him. That's ridiculous," said Turner. "I've even been thinking of offering to go with him to the minors. If I was vindictive, why did I give him a three-year, $1-million contract? I didn't have to do that. It's me and the Atlanta Braves who are being punished for Mr. Horner's terrible play."[24]

While the Braves were battling internal strife and poor play, the Reds looked every bit the defending divisional champion, winning their first eight games of the season, including three shutouts in their first four games. Interestingly enough, none of the three shutouts came from Tom Seaver, but instead were thanks to Frank Pastore, Mike LaCoss and Charlie Liebrandt. pitchers who had 28 combined career wins entering the season.

Offensively, slugger George Foster, with his menacing muttonchop sideburns and even more menacing black bat, paced the team, while Ray

Knight and Junior Kennedy also got off to hot starts. On April 23, Dave Concepcion's 12th-inning single off Joaquin Andujar scored Harry Spilman to give the Reds a 3–2 win over Houston and a 12–2 record to open the season. The Astros also began the season on a high note behind the strong pitching of Richard, Joe Niekro, and Ken Forsch. Even better news for Houston was the fact that they were actually scoring runs. Bill Virdon's club finished last in the National League in runs scored in 1979, but scored nearly five runs per game in early 1980. The renewed offense was coupled with a pitching staff that allowed the fewest runs in the major leagues in April, and Richard was the undisputed leader.

On April 19, more than 50,000 fans packed the Astrodome to watch Richard outduel Bob Welch in a 2–0 Houston win. Joe Morgan's fourth-inning sacrifice fly was followed by a Jose Cruz RBI single to score Cesar Cedeno. That was more than enough for Richard, who went the distance and struck out 12 while allowing just one hit. Two starts later, Richard beat Seaver, 5–1, in Cincinnati to run his record to a perfect 4–0. But the undefeated record didn't pay justice to how dominant he was. In 37⅔ innings, the big right hander surrendered just 13 hits while striking out 48 and recording a 1.67 ERA. Perhaps most impressive was the league batting average against him, a paltry .104.

Not to be outdone, Niekro posted a 2–1 record and a 1.52 ERA and Forsch went 3–0, 2.12. The weak link in April appeared to be Ryan, who went 1–0 with an ERA of 3.33, somewhat pedestrian compared to the numbers put up by his fellow starters. Houston's April record of 13–5 was good for a half-game lead over Cincinnati, who finished month at 13–6.

Not far behind were the Dodgers, who began the season losing five of their first six but soon ran off ten straight wins, nine against the Giants and Padres. As with their NL West counterparts Houston and Cincinnati, pitching was the key. Tommy Lasorda's club never scored more than six runs during the streak, but the pitching staff allowed just 17, including three shutouts against San Francisco.

Jerry Reuss went 3–0 with a 0.66 ERA out of the bullpen, and starters Don Sutton, Bob Welch, Dave Goltz and Burt Hooton combined for a 7–4 mark. At the plate, Reggie Smith hit .387 with four homers and 17 RBI to pace the offense.

Opening Day is a time for optimism and hope, unless you happened to be a member of the Chicago Cubs in 1980. "There is a negative feeling around this club," said pitcher Mike Krukow. "It was that way all spring too."[25] Many Cubs players felt their season was over before it began, and the feeling came from the top. General Manager Bob Kennedy allegedly told Bruce Sutter, whose 37 saves for the club in 1979 had earned him the Cy Young Award, that if the team got off to a slow start, he would likely be traded. Once Rick Reuschel, who led the team with 18 wins the year before, heard that, he said he wanted out too. In fairness to Kennedy, it was clear to all involved that he wasn't looking to deal Sutter on a whim. The order had come from the Wrigley family to trim payroll, and Sutter's $700,000 contract was first up.

New manager Preston Gomez was brutally honest in assessing his team's chances in the NL East. "We aren't going to win it. Not unless EVERYTHING falls into place."[26] The headline for Bob Verdi's *Chicago Tribune* column after an Opening Day 5–2 loss to the Mets summed up the feelings in the Cubs clubhouse. "With 161 games left, Cubs already are playing dead."[27]

But as April hit the midway point, a bizarre thing began to happen in Chicago. The Cubs started playing winning baseball. On April 19, the Cubbies found themselves down, 9–5, in the bottom of the eighth inning to the New York Mets at Wrigley Field. Mets skipper Joe Torre called on closer Neil Allen, who surrendered seven runs in a 12–9 Cubs win. Chicago's 2–3–4 hitters, Ivan DeJesus, Bill Buckner and Dave Kingman, went a combined 9-for-14 with 9 RBI. The big blow was Kingman's grand slam in the eighth, one of two long balls he hit on the day. "The man's phenomenal," said starting pitcher Mike Krukow, who lasted just four innings. "He's our money man. All I had to do was hold 'em close, right?"[28]

Despite possessing amazing power, the enigmatic Kingman was already with his sixth major league team in ten years. He held the distinction of homering for teams in each of the four divisions in the same year in 1977 and led the NL with 48 homers in 1979. But his surly mood with both teammates and the press often caused him to wear out his welcome. He stopped talking to the media in 1980 and dumped a bucket of ice water on a reporter's head in spring training. Former Mets teammates bristled at the fact that he would enter the clubhouse, get dressed and head to the field without uttering a word. They noticed he didn't tip the clubhouse attendants. They also didn't care for his seeming lack of interest or concentration during games.

"He'll never really get what he wants in baseball—to be left alone," said Torre, who had managed him with the Mets in 1977. "He's too big, he gets paid too much money, he does too many sensational things—whether it's hitting a ball 600 feet or striking out. He's a story."[29]

In many ways, Kingman was similar to Bobby Bonds, with whom he had played in California and San Francisco. Two immensely talented players who produced year after year and were subsequently let go by whichever team they were on. Bonds was the Opening Day left fielder for the Cardinals in 1980, his eighth team in the last seven seasons.

Just three days after Kingman's slam proved the margin of victory, it was a lesser-known teammate providing the late-inning heroics. On April 22, the Cubs and Cardinals were tied 12–12 in the bottom of the ninth inning when Barry Foote stepped to the plate with the bases loaded and a 22mph wind at his back. Foote's eighth-inning home run off Roy Thomas had tied the game, 12–12, after the Cardinals jumped out to a 12–6 lead. Cardinals reliever Mark Littell hung a slider and Foote hit it into the basket in right-center field for a game-winning grand slam, one of three homers on the day for the suddenly surging Cubs.

Things were going well on the South Side too as the White Sox finished April on top of the American League West with a 12–6 record. The Sox were supposed to be a pitching-heavy team with a suspect offense and shaky bullpen. Instead, they averaged nearly five runs per game while their starting pitching stumbled, and Ed Farmer provided solid relief work in the back of the bullpen.

After losing the season opener to Baltimore, the Sox won four in a row, including a 14-inning thriller that ended with Chet Lemon's bases-loaded single off Yankees reliever Jim Kaat. Eleven days later, Chicago scored another extra inning win over the Yankees in New York. Tony LaRussa started an all right-handed lineup against lefty Ron Guidry, and once again the Sox offense proved formidable, scoring four runs off Guidry in seven innings. Unfortunately for LaRussa, his starter, Ken Kravec, was worse, lasting just 5⅓ innings and running his early-season E.R.A. to a robust 8.50.

The game was tied after nine innings and again after ten, when each team added a run. Thad Bosley led off 12th inning with a walk off Tom Underwood, stole second and moved to third on Bob Molinaro's single. LaRussa called for a suicide squeeze, and Mike Squires laid it down perfectly to score Bosley and win the game. "It looks like they're going to be pesky," said Yankees manager Dick Howser. "They have natural speed and they're hitting well right now. They're hot."[30]

The White Sox bats were, indeed, hot. Molinaro, whose pinch-hit, two-run homer off Goose Gossage in the eighth inning gave the Sox a brief lead, was having a fantastic April. A second-round pick of the Tigers in 1968, Molinaro had been waived by Detroit in 1977, waived by the White Sox in 1978 and waived again by Baltimore in 1979, when he was reclaimed by the White Sox. In his second stint in Chicago, the 29-year-old hit .375 in the season's first month. On the mound, starter Rich Dotson went 3–1, while rookie Britt Burns added a 2–1 record and an ERA of just 0.42. Burns made two starts as a 19-year-old in 1978 and six relief appearances in 1979, but he came out of the chute in 1980 allowing just one run in his first three starts. Ed Farmer anchored the supposedly shaky bullpen with six saves in April.

At the beginning of 1980, the Minnesota Twins were riding a streak of losing baseball that had lasted nearly a decade. Led by Tony Oliva, Harmon Killebrew, Rod Carew and a pitching staff anchored by Jim Perry, Jim Kaat and a 19-year-old Bert Blyleven, the Twins won back-to-back American League West titles in 1969 and 1970, but had never placed higher than third in the ensuing nine seasons.

Calvin Griffith inherited ownership of the ball club in 1955 after his uncle, Clark Griffith, passed away. The junior Griffith had served many roles in the organization, including bat boy, minor league player and manager, but he would make his mark early as the team's owner.

Clark Griffith was a Hall of Fame pitcher and manager who took over the Washington Senators in 1912. Seven years later, he purchased controlling interest in the team, along with William Richardson. As owner of the Senators, Griffith played a part in keeping baseball going during the war years by lobbying Woodrow Wilson and later Franklin D. Roosevelt about the importance of the game for the morale of the country.

Upon his death, his nephew Calvin took control of the team and, mindful of the famous saying coined by sportswriter Charles Dryden, "Washington—first in war, first in peace, last in the American League,"[31] moved the team to greener pastures in Minnesota in 1961 after a long courtship. Speaking to civic leaders in 1978, Griffith attributed the move in part to the fact that "you only had 15,000 blacks here."[32]

"Black people don't go to ball games," Griffith told the stunned gathering at the Waseca Lions Club. "But they'll fill up a rassling ring and put up such a chant it'll scare you to death. It's unbelievable. We came here because you've got good, hardworking, white people here."[33]

Those comments didn't endear him to black stars such as Carew, whom Griffith also singled out in his speech for being foolish enough to play for the low salary Griffith paid him. A few months later, Carew was dealt to the California Angels in exchange for four players, including outfielder Ken Landreaux. When Landreaux returned to California for the first time as a member of the Twins, he told reporters he thought enough of his abilities to suggest that it should have been an even swap: him for Carew. "I know Carew is a seven time batting champion. But I feel, if I continue to work hard, someday I can produce just as much as Carew did for this club,"[34] said the 24-year-old Landreaux, who had all of 77 big league hits to his name at the time of the deal.

In 1979, Landreaux had shown a lot of promise, hitting .305 with 15 homers and 83 RBI while playing 151 games in the outfield, somewhat easing Twins fans' angst over losing Carew. Twins skipper Gene Mauch told *The Sporting News*, "If we leave him in left, he could become one of the best in the game."[35]

The Twins opened the 1980 season with a 12-game road trip and thus didn't have their home opener until April 22, when they beat the Angels, 8–1. The next day, in front of just 4,772 fans at Metropolitan Stadium, things didn't go so well as California righty Bruce Kison held Minnesota hitless into the ninth inning. If that wasn't bad enough, the Angels also held a 17–0 lead as Landreaux stepped to the plate with one out. He doubled to left field, breaking up Kison's no-hit bid. For Landreaux, the double proved the beginning of what would become a 31-game hitting streak, the longest of the year and the longest in the American League since Dom DiMaggio's 34 in 1949.

However, Landreaux's hot bat didn't help the Twins' fortunes as they went 12–20 during the streak. He drew a walk as a pinch-hitter in a May 7 loss to the Orioles, accounting for the extra game. During late April and most of May, Landreaux was seemingly the only Twin who was hitting, as he scored just 13 runs. The streak finally came to an end against Baltimore and lefty Scott McGregor on May 31, but Landreaux felt it was first of many in his career. "I don't feel sad; it's all right," he said. "It just wasn't meant for 32. The best thing for me is to start over. I'll just keep doing what I've been doing. There's no sense in changing anything now."[36]

Gene Mauch had been involved in professional baseball since 1943 as a player or a manager. He'd seen a lot of good hitters, and he put Landreaux right up with the best. "The remarkable thing about this," Mauch said, "was that he hit so many lefthanders. I only know two left-handed hitters consistently as good as Landreaux against left-handed pitchers. One is Stan Musial. The other is Ted Williams."[37]

The end of the streak was a bummer, but a decision by Bowie Kuhn ended up costing Landreaux a lot of money. After Pete Rose's 44-game hitting streak in 1978, Aqua Velva offered a bonus of $1,000 per game to the person who recorded the longest hitting streak each season. Rose himself took the prize home in 1979, but Kuhn stepped in in 1980, saying the bonus put too much pressure on official scorers. Kuhn and Aqua Velva eventually reached an agreement which allowed Landreaux to donate the money to the Little League and Pop Warner programs in his home town of Compton, California.

Landreaux missing out on a $31,000 bonus paled in comparison to the money problems experienced by Ozzie Smith. The Padres shortstop was in debt and needed an influx of cash sooner rather than later. So he did what anyone would do in that situation. He put an ad in the *San Diego Union* looking for a second job. "Padre baseball player wants part-time employment to supplement income," the ad read. "College education, willing to work, prefer PR-type employment. Need hours tailored to baseball schedule, but would quit baseball for the right opportunity. Call Mr. Gottleib, 714-571-8800."[38]

Mr. Gottleib was Smith's agent, Ed, one of many people to whom Smith was in debt. Once the ad ran, the offers poured in. Ozzie was offered positions as a pizza delivery guy, an exotic dancer and office jobs at brokerage houses. He was also offered a part-time gardening gig on the estate of Padres team owner Ray Kroc by his wife, Joan. Mrs. Kroc had gone so far as to clear bringing Ozzie on board with the head gardener, Luis, who she explained was a big Ozzie Smith fan.

There were even rumors that Smith was mulling over an offer to ride in the Tour de France, a side job which might have been difficult to fit in with Padres games, played at the same time on a different continent. In the end, Smith was able to secure work with an unnamed company from Los Angeles that paid him $500 per week plus commission and also allowed him to stay in the U.S. so he could keep his day job.

As April came to a close, things began to shift for the Pittsburgh Pirates. The team that danced on the Three Rivers Stadium turf in Pittsburgh with Sister Sledge at their home opener at the beginning of the month now found themselves facing dissension on the pitching staff. During spring training, Pirates manager Chuck Tanner indicated that he wanted to see more complete games out of his starting pitchers. If the Pirates were to repeat, Tanner needed a fresh bullpen, and getting complete games from his starters definitely fit the bill.

Tanner's Opening Day starter, Bert Blyleven, supported his plan 100 percent. From 1971 through 1978, Blyleven had completed nearly half of the games he started. In 1979, that number slipped to just four in 37 starts, and he was not happy about it, feeling it robbed him of the chance for more wins which, more importantly, equated to a larger contract.

Through his first four starts of the season, Blyleven was excellent but had nothing to show for it. His record was 0–2, but he had an ERA of 2.42 and was allowing less than one baserunner per inning while posting 26 strikeouts in 26 innings. The problem was offense. The Pirates bats had produced just eight runs in his four starts. But for Blyleven, the other issue was again not being permitted to finish what he started, and he wasn't alone. Despite Tanner's pre-season proclamation, through their first 14 games, Pirate pitchers had completed just three starts. Jim Bibby had one and John Candelaria had two. Blyleven had none.

Game number 16 of the season, on April 29, was at Three Rivers Stadium against the Montreal Expos with Blyleven on the mound. Through five innings, the Pirates led, 4–2. But a sixth-inning Montreal rally tied the game at 4–4 and brought Tanner out of the Pittsburgh dugout once again to remove Blyleven after 5⅔ innings. The Pirates eventually won the game, 5–4, in ten innings, but Blyleven was livid, so much so that he requested a trade and left the team the following day. "I felt I had to speak up. If I didn't, maybe 20 years from now, I'd be wishing that I had spoken up. Maybe 20 years from now I'll wish I hadn't spoken up. I've been thinking about it for more than a year. Sometimes, last year, I took my frustrations home with me. I don't want to do that."[39]

Needless to say, Blyleven going AWOL after five starts was not met with approval within the organization. Executive Vice President Pete Peterson told the press that he considered Blyleven semi-retired and would make an attempt to trade him. Teammate Dave Parker said, "I hope Bert comes to his senses and rejoins the greatest club in baseball."[40]

3

May
Fear, Fights and Fergie

"What a piece of...," thought Betsy Palmer after she read the script. "Nobody is ever going to see this. It will come and it will go."[1]

But she needed a new car and the job paid $1,000 a day for ten days of shooting, which happened to be the exact amount she needed for the new VW Scirocco she'd had her eye on. It seemed a small price to pay. Work for a few days on an obscure movie and get a new car. She wasn't a fan of horror films, but a new car is a new car. She said yes.

Kevin Bacon had a bit role in *Animal House* and had recently completed a film called *Starting Over*. In the credits he was listed as "Husband—Young Couple." He was back in New York waiting tables when his offer came. He needed rent money. He said yes, too.

Sean Cunningham had recently finished two G-rated movies about youth sports and was looking for a new project when he saw the 1978 film, *Halloween*. He called his friend Victor Miller and asked if he was interested in making a horror movie. He was, and together they banged out a script. "A filmmaker must be part magician, part gypsy and part huckster,"[2] Cunningham told the *Toronto Globe and Mail*. Critics were nearly unanimous in their assertion that he bypassed parts one and two and went straight to hucksterism in *Friday the 13th*.

The *Boston Globe* called it "nauseating,"[3] while a headline in the *Globe and Mail* suggested it was a "clunker"[4] and added that it was difficult to assess individual performances in the film because no actor was on screen long enough before suffering a grizzly death. In spite of, or perhaps because of, the horrible reviews, the film scored big at the box office. Made on a budget of less than $600,000, *Friday the 13th* grossed $31 million in its first six weeks in theaters. Advantage, Jason.

A few weeks later, another controversial horror film hit theaters. The promotional poster billed Stanley Kubrick's *The Shining* as "A Masterpiece of Modern Horror" when it debuted on May 23 in New York and Los Angeles. This time it was a different Gene who went on the offensive. The "Today Show"'s Gene Shalit panned the film, saying, "After a year of buildup, it is a letdown. *The Shining* is a horror picture. It cost $18 million. That's part of the horror. The rest is the wasting of excellent performances by Jack Nicholson and Shelly Duvall, and the gall of calling it a Masterpiece in the advance ads."[5]

Life on the set was nearly as terrifying as the film itself. Kubrick, who was notoriously difficult to work with, rewrote the script almost daily, and Duvall spent so much of her screen time crying that she became dehydrated. Critical reviews were a bit more favorable than for *Friday the 13th*. The *New York Times* called it "Meticulously detailed and never less than fascinating,"[6] while another headline suggested that the film might become "the ultimate horror film."[7]

In a limited release of just ten theaters, *The Shining* grossed more than $600,000 in its first weekend and contained a baseball-related Easter egg for sharp-eyed viewers. At one point, Shelly Duvall whacked Nicholson with a Carl Yastrzemski model Louisville Slugger.

But *Friday the 13th* and *The Shining* were no match at the box office for the summer's most anticipated release. Late in June, *The Empire Strikes Back* opened in 126 theaters and grossed nearly $9 million in its first week. By the end of the year, it would rake in $209,398,025, more than twice as much as its nearest competitor, the campy office comedy *9 to 5*, starring Dolly Parton, Jane Fonda and Lily Tomlin.

As May began, the defending champion Pirates held a 1½-game lead in the NL East over the Chicago Cubs, but all was not well. Bert Blyleven's trade demands proved an unwanted distraction to a team trying to repeat. General Manager Pete Peterson sent a message to the other 25 teams announcing Blyleven's availability via trade and requesting a pitcher in return. Rumors flew that he was headed to the Yankees in exchange for Ed Figueroa, or the Red Sox with Pittsburgh receiving Mike Torrez, but he eventually returned to the Pirates a few weeks later and was inserted back into the rotation against the San Francisco Giants. He went the distance in a 5–0 loss. "I can understand a lot of things about ballplayers," said Bill Madlock. "But going home.... I don't know why he did that."[8]

Soon the tables were turned on Madlock as his teammates could rightly question his actions as well. On May 1, the Pirates were wrapping up a three-game series with the Montreal Expos at Pittsburgh's Three Rivers Stadium. The game was tied, 1–1, in the bottom of the fifth inning when Madlock faced the Expos' David Palmer with two outs and runners on second and third. Palmer delivered a 3–2 pitch, Madlock checked his swing, and home plate umpire Jerry Crawford called strike three to end the inning.

Madlock went back to the dugout to retrieve his glove and headed to his position at third base. Pirates shortstop Tim Foli asked Crawford if Madlock had swung at the pitch, and Crawford said he had. When Madlock heard that, he snapped. "Mad Dog" headed towards Crawford and began berating the umpire while jabbing his glove in the air. Chuck Tanner raced out of the dugout to get between his player and Crawford, but not before Madlock's glove made contact with Crawford's face. Crawford immediately ejected Madlock, and a suspension seemed certain.

But National League President Chub Feeney didn't rule immediately on the situation, saying he needed to look at films of the incident. Umpire-in-chief John Kibler felt that films weren't necessary, especially considering that newspapers across the country carried a photo of Madlock jamming his glove into Crawford's nose. "Films? What does he need films for?" Kibler asked. "What about us? What about the safety of the umpires? Suppose Madlock gets angry again and comes at one of us with a bat?"[9]

When the Pirates faced Atlanta in their next series, Kibler and his crew, which included Dick Stello, Bruce Froemming and Terry Tata, threatened to boycott the game if Madlock was in the lineup. Fortunately Tanner was able to talk them out of it, but it was clear that the situation wasn't going away.

After an 0-for-5 day against the White Sox on April 26, Reggie Jackson's batting average stood at an anemic .177. But then he caught fire, going 8-for-18, including five hits in nine at-bats with a home run in the first two games of a four-game set against the Twins in Bloomington.

In the third game of the series, on May 4, Reggie led off the second inning against Jerry Koosman, who quickly got ahead in the count, 0–2. Koosman's next pitch sealed his fate in the game, and potentially Jackson's fate in the Yankees clubhouse. Koosman delivered his 0–2 offering directly at Jackson's head, causing him to hit the deck at the last second and come up extremely unhappy. Not satisfied, Koosman brushed Jackson back again, prompting him to tell Twins catcher Butch Wynegar, "If the next one comes in close, I'm going to get you."[10]

With the count now 2–2, Koosman couldn't afford to deck Jackson for a third time, and his next pitch caught a bit more of the plate. Jackson unloaded, sending it more than 400 feet to straightaway center field for a home run. Reggie Jackson had hit a lot of home runs in pinstripes. He made history in Game Six of the 1977 World Series with three off three different Dodgers pitchers en route to leading the Yankees to their first championship since 1962. But his cockiness rubbed a lot of people the wrong way, and there were high-profile run-ins with former manager Billy Martin and catcher Thurman Munson that caused many people, both in and out of the Yankees clubhouse, to dislike him.

Reggie Jackson hit .300 for the only time in his career, tied for the AL lead in home runs and was almost shot twice. It was an eventful summer (National Baseball Hall of Fame Library, Cooperstown, New York).

Jackson's blast gave the Yankees a 1–0 lead in the game but more importantly, it may have been the tipping point in his relationship with his teammates. As he rounded the bases and headed back to the dugout, Jackson saw a number of Yankees waiting for him. "I was thrilled to see my teammates standing there," he said. "Half of them told me they would have gone out there to defend me."[11]

This was in stark contrast to his first year in New York when, stung by public criticism from his teammates, Jackson snubbed those looking to congratulate him after hitting a home run. All seemed to be forgiven now, and the Yankees were rolling. Spurred by Reggie Jackson's heroics, New York knocked Koosman out of the game after just 3⅓ innings and cruised to a 10–1 win. Tom Underwood exacted some revenge by drilling Wynegar in the back later in the game, prompting home plate umpire Vic Voltaggio to warn both benches.

The show of support from his teammates was a big moment for Jackson and the Yankees. It also added to his reputation as a guy who could deliver in the big moment. "The good ones, Frank Robinson, Al Kaline, Mickey Mantle, they're better hitters when they get knocked down," said Howser. "Reggie's like that. We need Reggie. He has to have a good year for us to win."[12]

No one, with the possible exception of owner Bill Veeck, thought the White Sox's hot start would continue, but that didn't mean they wouldn't be entertaining or innovative. A 12–6 start begat a three-game losing streak heading into their May 4 game against Milwaukee, and then things got really ugly. The Sox jumped out to a 1–0 lead in the bottom of the first when Mike Squires scored on a Bob Molinaro groundout, but then the Brewers took over, scoring 11 unanswered runs, including six in the top of the eighth inning. An inning later, Chicago skipper Tony LaRussa did something no manager had done since 1958.

On September 21 of that year, the Chicago Cubs trailed Sandy Koufax and the Dodgers, 2–1, in the bottom of the eighth inning when they loaded the bases with no one out. Koufax was lifted for Roger Craig, who induced a double play, and LA eventually escaped the inning. In the top of the ninth, Cubs manager Bob Scheffing needed a catcher, having pinch-hit for starter Cal Neeman in the previous frame, and moved first baseman Dale Long from first base to catcher. It was the second time that season that Long had caught, which was significant because Dale Long threw left-handed. Since then, no lefty had caught an inning in the major leagues. That streak came to an end on May 4, 1980, when LaRussa sent Mike Squires from first base to catcher in the top of the ninth against Milwaukee. To keen observers, there was little doubt as to where the move originated.

"You might say I had something to do with it," admitted Veeck. "[Squires is] such a good athlete that I might even try him at shortstop or third base just to prove a point."[13] When asked what point he would be trying to prove, Veeck had an answer at the ready.

"The point that the entire world is designed to the needs of right-handers," the left-handed owner said. "Did you ever try to wind your watch in a phone booth?"[14] "Well, it's impossible."[15]

The following day, things got even more interesting at Comiskey Park. Milwaukee held a 7–6 lead in the fourth inning with Ben Oglivie facing Chicago relief pitcher Mike Proly. "Gentle Ben" had spent the previous three games of the series pounding White Sox pitching, going 8-for-14 with a home run. Doing what pitchers do to set up hitters, Proly came inside with a slider to set up another one on the outer half. But his next pitch hit Oglivie on the shin, prompting him to charge the mound and deliver a right cross to the White Sox pitcher before the benches emptied.

"I saw him throw down his bat and his helmet and take five or six steps towards the mound," said Proly, who was suddenly dubbed "Sugar Ray" by his teammates. "If I'm going to hit him I'm not going to hit him on the foot with a slider. If that's grounds for charging the mound then he's an idiot."[16]

Oglivie wasn't available to give his side of the story when reporters entered the visitors' clubhouse. After he was ejected, he enjoyed a beer shower courtesy of the White Sox faithful and then drove back to Milwaukee on his own. For Proly, it was the second time in just over two weeks that one of his pitches had touched off a bench-clearing brawl. On April 20, Baltimore third baseman Doug DeCinces had taken exception to Proly pitching him inside.

"I've hit three guys in two years and two of them charged the mound," Proly said. "I have to pitch inside to be effective. These guys, if they think I won't pitch in because they come out, well, they're wrong."[17] Proly must have been effective because Chicago was 2–0 in games in which he sparked bench-clearing brawls, but his personal mark wasn't quite as good. He fared well in the DeCinces bout, but not so much against Oglivie. "I'm 1–1 in fights," he said while sporting a bruised check courtesy of an Oglivie right cross. "I won that one [DeCinces], but I lost this fight."[18]

Another loser was LaRussa, who suffered a dislocated shoulder in the pile-up. After getting his shoulder popped back into place, LaRussa returned to the bench just in time to see Lamar Johnson's sixth-inning homer, which proved to be the game-winner for the Sox.

The physical punishment the Brewers doled out paled in comparison to the damage their hitters did on opposing pitchers. Led by Oglivie, who earned Player of the Month honors by hitting .337 with eight home runs and 23 RBI, the Brewers scored a major-league high 170 runs in May.

Milwaukee began the month with an 8–0 win over the White Sox and finished May with a 19–8 win over the Red Sox. In between, they had four other games in which they scored ten or more runs. Their main offensive weapons—Oglivie, first baseman Cecil Cooper, second baseman Paul Molitor and shortstop Robin Yount—combined to hit .348 with 19 homers and an amazing 79 runs batted in. Center fielder "Stormin'" Gorman Thomas added five homers and 18 RBI to an extremely potent lineup. But the biggest letdown for the Brewers and the city of Milwaukee was that their manager wasn't there to see any of it.

George Bamberger took over as the Brewers manager prior to the 1978 season after serving as a pitching coach under Earl Weaver in Baltimore from 1968 through 1977. Under his tutelage, Orioles pitchers won at least 20 games 18 times along with four Cy Young Awards. His managerial career began well as the Brewers won 93 games in 1978, which earned him *Sporting News* Manager of the Year honors. In 1979, he guided Milwaukee to a second-place finish in the AL East. After nine years of struggle before Bamberger's arrival, the late–1970s success had many in Milwaukee thinking a breakthrough was imminent. But Bamberger suffered a heart attack during spring training and was forced to sit out the beginning of the season to recuperate, making Buck Rodgers the interim manager. "Bambi" recovered at his home in Florida, following the team through the newspaper and television.

By May 5, National League President Chub Feeney had finally watched enough video to render a decision on the Bill Madlock incident. The verdict: a 15-day suspension and a $5,000 fine. When lost pay was added into the equation, Madlock stood to lose more than $20,000, and he wasn't happy. "There's no reason for it," he said. "There was no intent on my part. If I wanted to hit the man, I would have hit him. I pushed the glove near his face. There was no intent to hurt him."[19]

Madlock appealed the ruling and, along with Players Association head Marvin Miller, also took issue with Kibler's assertion that he and his fellow umpires felt threatened by Madlock even being on the field. The comments angered Madlock to the point where he considered legal action against Kibler. "There is some question that quotes attributable to other umpires may be actionable," said Madlock's attorney, Steve Greenberg. "We'll have to wait and see. Meanwhile, Bill will be playing third base for the Pirates. If the umpires don't want to work those games that is up to them."[20]

At 8:32 a.m. Pacific Time on May 18, the ground in southwestern Washington state began to shake. A 5.1 magnitude earthquake caused the entire north face of Mt. St. Helens to collapse and precipitated a volcanic eruption equal in magnitude to that of Mt. Vesuvius. The resulting eruption column rose nearly 80,000 feet in the atmosphere and caused the largest landslide ever recorded. More than 500 million tons of volcanic ash were released into the atmosphere and deposited over an 11-state area, reaching as far as eastern Oklahoma. The blast flattened everything within a 15-mile radius and resulted in more than 50 deaths. Additional eruptions went on throughout the summer, and the damage estimates would reach more than $1 billion.

A few hundred miles south of Mt. St. Helens, another seismic shift was taking place. After dominating the early part of the 1970s, the Oakland A's hit bottom in 1979 both on and off the field. The 1979 A's lost 108 games, which was bad enough, but they also did so while drawing only 306,763 fans the entire season, dead last in the major leagues. An April 17 game against Seattle drew an announced attendance of 653, though the actual number of fans in the building was reportedly closer to 250.

The city of Oakland sued Charlie Finley for breach of contract, claiming he had failed to put a respectable team on the field. They sought $1.5 million for lost revenues from parking and concessions and an additional $10 million in punitive damages.

The A's were for sale, and the asking price was $12 million. Among those interested were future San Francisco 49ers owner Edward DeBartolo, Sr., who planned to buy the team and move it to New Orleans, and billionaire oil man Marvin Davis, who planned to move the team to Denver. Finley and Davis had even struck a deal earlier in the 1970s, which had fans in Denver preparing for their own team. That was when the Oakland-Alameda County Coliseum pointed out that the A's lease ran through 1987, and if they moved to Denver someone would have to compensate the Coliseum for the lost revenue.

One scenario to rectify that issue included each AL team contributing $77,000, Finley kicking in $1 million and the San Francisco Giants contributing another million in order to get the Bay Area to themselves. The money would be enough to buy out the A's lease, and the Coliseum could then use the money for capital improvements which could keep the NFL's Raiders from moving to Los Angeles. But when Raiders owner Al Davis announced that he was moving regardless of improvements to the Coliseum, Finley was stuck. After years of neglecting his franchise, he needed to find a local buyer, and to do that, he needed to make the team less horrible.

A few weeks before spring training began, Finley made his first move by firing manager Jim Marshall and hiring Billy Martin as his replacement. Martin inherited a young team coming off a terrible season, but there was some talent there, especially offensively. Speedy outfielder Rickey Henderson made his debut in June of 1979 and hit .274 with 33 stolen bases in 44 attempts. Playing alongside Henderson in the outfield were Dwayne Murphy and Tony Armas, who showed promise, and Mitchell Page, who hit 38 home runs in his first two seasons in Oakland before slipping to just nine in 1979.

One thing Oakland fans could count on was a new style of baseball. With Martin at the helm, that style meant running, and it didn't matter if you weren't a base stealer. Guys like Henderson, who did have speed, were set loose, while guys like Wayne Gross, who had a total of nine stolen bases in his career when Martin took over, were pressed into service. By the end of May, Gross had stolen home twice.

Things got bad for one catcher in particular. Oakland's fun began on May 19, a 6–5 Royals win in Kansas City. Dwayne Murphy, Rickey Henderson and Mitchell Page each stole bases against Royals backstop John Wathan. The next night, the same Oakland trio combined for five stolen bases in five attempts. Billy Martin was onto something. On May 21, Henderson got two more in two attempts. In the four-game set, Oakland stole ten bases in 12 attempts.

The two teams got together again a week later in Oakland, with the A's stealing three bases in the first two games. But in the series finale, Oakland really did some damage. In the bottom of the first inning, singles by Murphy and Page put runners on the corners with one out. With Gross at the plate, Page took off for second while Murphy broke for home seconds later. Wathan's throw went into center field, allowing Murphy to score and sending Page to third base. With Gross still at the plate, a Rich Gale pitch got past Wathan, scoring Page.

Later in the inning, with Gross on third and Jeff Newman on first, Martin reached into his bag of tricks. Newman took a big lead off first and then "fell down," drawing a throw from Wathan. This gave Gross the opportunity to steal home, while Newman got up and ran to second for the fourth stolen base of the inning. The play was one Martin cooked up in the off-season and unveiled in spring training of 1972 against Ted Williams and the Texas Rangers.

"I've heard of that play but I never saw it," said Wathan.[21]

"That play is designed for guys like me and Wayne who aren't considered fast runners," said Newman. "They're not expecting us to steal, so when I fell down, they thought they'd caught me napping."[22]

Wathan exacted some revenge by gunning down Henderson trying to steal second in the next inning, but Billy Martin and the A's weren't through with him yet. They would steal three more bases in the game, running their total to an amazing 20 in 24 attempts against Wathan, who also committed a throwing error and a passed ball. The 20 stolen bases against a single catcher were just the beginning for Billy Martin and the A's as they ran wild against their opponents, stealing 42 bases in 51 attempts. Henderson alone stole 16 bases while being thrown out only twice.

Martin also showed that he hadn't given up his feisty ways despite their costing him his job with the Yankees. In a late April series against the Twins in Bloomington, Martin exchanged words, and nearly blows, with a fan who was throwing marshmallows at him. Security intervened before things got physical, and the fan was ejected, but Martin pulled no punches in his post-game press conference. "I can tolerate a lot of things, but I can't tolerate throwing stuff on the field," he said. "There are good fans here in Minnesota and we don't need a jerk like that here. He could have put somebody's eye out."[23] He added, "It was a young kid with a French queer's hat on. When I went up there I didn't know whether to kiss him or punch him. I thought he would have caressed me. He was a big, fat fag."[24]

While Billy Martin was dodging marshmallows and hurling homophobic slurs, Major League Baseball had a bigger problem. Division leaders, records and left-handed catchers were fun, but there was serious concern that the season would end prematurely. A strike date of May 23 was in place, and negotiations were not going well. At the heart of the matter was the issue of free-agent compensation. The owners wanted it and the players didn't, and neither side was willing to budge. Ever since free agency came into being, the owners had been trying to turn back the clock to an era when they held absolute power over the players. Those days were over but, like a toddler with a favorite toy, the owners stubbornly tried to hold onto the way things used to be. It was arrogance, and they clearly underestimated the power and solidarity of the Players Association and its chief, Marvin Miller.

Talks went on throughout May with little progress, despite the efforts of federal mediator Ken Moffitt, who was brought in to referee the proceedings. On May 22, the last day before the players were set to walk out, Moffitt, Miller and Ray Grebey, the owners' lead negotiator, and their teams met in a New York hotel in an attempt to salvage the season. A strike seemed certain, and moods were sour after a morning meeting that lasted less than 90 minutes.

American League President Lee MacPhail told the media things didn't look good, but Miller was more to the point. When asked what it would take to avoid a strike, he said it would take a miracle. Negotiations continued throughout the day and into the night, and just before dawn on May 23 the two sides finally struck a deal on a new four-year collective bargaining agreement.

Minimum player salaries would gradually increase from $21,000 in 1980 to $35,000 in 1983, and the owners also agreed to increase their contribution to the players' pension fund. Players would be eligible for salary arbitration after two years instead of three and gained other benefits such as life insurance and major medical coverage. But there was one glaring omission from the agreement, and everyone knew it. The issue of free-agent compensation was not resolved. Instead, the two sides agreed to form a four-man committee, two from each side, to further study the issue and issue a report by January 1, 1981. That report would be followed by a 30-day bargaining session, and if no agreement was reached, the owners had the right to implement their proposal, while the players had the right to go on strike. It was a win as far as the continuation of the 1980 season, but few saw it as a solution.

"It is possible that a baseball strike was postponed rather than avoided when the Major League [Baseball] Players Association and owners reached an agreement Friday in New York,"[25] wrote Mike Kiley in the *Chicago Tribune*. He wasn't the only one who saw it that way.

"I hate to open up a can of worms," said Dodgers pitcher Jerry Reuss. "But by appointing a one-year study committee on the compensation issue, what we might be doing is just delaying the fight. There is a remote possibility that we could be right back in this situation in another year if nothing is resolved."[26]

"What's important is that there will be baseball," said Cubs first baseman Bill Buckner. "I don't think there would have been much sympathy from the fans for either side. They wouldn't have cared much for the players or owners if there were no games."[27]

With the issue of a work stoppage avoided, at least for the remainder of 1980, Texas Rangers pitcher Fergie Jenkins could get back to etching his name in baseball's record books. Jenkins made his major league debut with the Phillies in 1965, but the Phillies, in one of many short-sighted

Ray Grebey (left) and Marvin Miller (right) shake hands after reaching an agreement to avoid a player strike. The deal saved the 1980 season, but the lack of an agreement on free-agent compensation led to a strike the following year (National Baseball Hall of Fame Library, Cooperstown, New York).

moves, dealt him to the Cubs in April of 1966. In Chicago, Jenkins won at least 20 games in six consecutive seasons from 1967 through 1972. After a 14–16 season in 1973, he was dealt to the Rangers for Bill Madlock and promptly regained his winning form in 1974, tying Catfish Hunter for the major league lead with 25 wins.

A native of Chatham, Ontario, Jenkins celebrated his 25-win season by going home to do what Canadians do—play in an industrial hockey league. All was going well until someone decided to test Jenkins' mettle. "A guy speared me," Jenkins told the *New York Times*. "I hit him in the head about 25 times and broke a bone in my [pitching] hand. I didn't tell anyone about it until I was having trouble during the [1975] season. That's why I only won 17 games."[28]

Jenkins was traded to Boston after 1975, then came back to Texas two years later. By 1980, his career was on the down slope but he was still an effective pitcher. "He's like a surgeon," said Yankees catcher Rick Cerone. "When he's ahead of you and working the corners, he's tough. When you get to him is when he's behind."[29]

He wasn't behind often. Entering the 1980 season, Jenkins averaged nearly seven strikeouts per nine innings against fewer than two walks. He made his living on the corners of the plate at a time when guys like J.R. Richard, Rich Gossage and other were blowing the ball by people. Jenkins had a good fastball, but considered himself a craftsman rather than a brute. "I enjoy the art of pitching," he said. "Some say it's a lost art. The league doesn't have many pitchers now. It's a lot of throwers."[30]

On May 3 in Arlington, Texas, Jenkins was in full artist mode as he beat the Baltimore Orioles, 3–2, giving him 100 wins in both the AL and NL, joining Cy Young, Jim Bunning and his teammate Gaylord Perry as the only pitchers to accomplish the feat. Twenty days later, he made history again, beating Martin and the A's, 3–1, on a two-hitter. The win was the 250th of his career and pulled the Rangers to within two games of the division-leading Royals and a half-game ahead of Oakland.

The defending AL West champion California Angels were just 3½ games behind the Rangers but they were reeling. Slugging catcher Brian Downing was out with a broken ankle, Dan Ford was in and out of the lineup with knee problems, and other regulars were battling mild injuries. They had lost nine straight home games and 12 of 16 overall when they faced the Rangers at "The Big A" on May 26, and the frustration was due to boil over.

Texas was up, 2–0, in the top of the sixth inning when Angels pitcher Bruce Kison knocked Buddy Bell off the plate with an inside pitch before retiring him on a fly ball to end the inning. But instead of heading to the dugout to get his glove, Bell headed to the mound to get Kison, sparking a bench-clearing brawl. Bell was ejected, but Kison wasn't.

In the bottom of the seventh, Rangers reliever Jim Kern played policeman by throwing a pitch behind Angels third baseman Carney Lansford's head. Unfortunately for Kern, Lansford then hit a two-run homer to give the Angels a 5–2 lead. A Rod Carew double chased Kern, who was replaced by Bill Babcock, whose first pitch was behind the head of Dan Ford, sending him to the showers.

This didn't sit well with Kison, who returned to the mound in the next inning and plunked Johnny Grubb in the ankle with a pitch, which caused the benches to empty again. Kison was new to the American League, but he had established a reputation in the National League as someone who wasn't afraid to pitch inside. "I read an article this spring where Don Baylor said it was nice to have a pitcher like Kison on his side," said Rangers catcher Jim Sundberg. "A pitcher who protects his hitters."[31]

"He has that reputation," said Angels manager Jim Fregosi. "He even had me on his list. He once hit me in the ribs."[32] When asked if he charged the mound, Fregosi responded, "Any guy who hit me with a pitch was doing me a favor."[33]

There were fisticuffs on the East Coast as well when the Phillies and Pirates began a four-game series on May 26. Led by eventual NL "Offensive Player of the Month" Mike Schmidt and eventual NL "Pitcher of the Month" Steve Carlton, Philadelphia had won four straight games to cut Pittsburgh's lead in the division to just a half-game. The series was a chance for the Phillies to reassert themselves as the class of the NL East. The Pirates were in a foul mood after losing six of their last eight, including dropping a 5–2 game on "Bat Day" in Pittsburgh on May 25. The loss so incensed the Pirates faithful that a few of them took their new bats and smashed the back window of Willie Stargell's Rolls Royce.

Pittsburgh sent Blyleven to the mound, while the Phillies countered with rookie Bob Walk, who was making his major league debut after going 5–1 in Triple-A Oklahoma City. For Walk, it would be his first time atop a major league pitching mound, but not his first time throwing objects at big leaguers. As a teenager, he was once arrested at Dodger Stadium for throwing a tennis ball at Astros outfielder Cesar Cedeno from the bleachers.

Pittsburgh took a 2–0 lead on Willie Stargell's first-inning home run. In the bottom of the third inning, with the Pirates lead standing at 3–1, Blyleven threw inside to Mike Schmidt and Schmidt took exception, heading to the mound to confront the Pirates' hurler, and the benches quickly emptied. Home plate umpire Doug Harvey, who carried the nickname "God" for the clout he earned among players and other umpires, was able to intercept Schmidt before he reached the mound, and order was restored.

Walk lived up to his name in his debut, issuing free passes to five Pirates hitters in 2⅔ innings before being replaced by Lerrin LaGrow. When Kevin Saucier took over for the Phillies in the fifth inning, he had revenge on his mind. After getting Dave Parker to ground out, Saucier plunked Willie Stargell, causing the Pirates dugout to take notice. In the sixth, Saucier finally got a chance to get even with Blyleven and did so by drilling the Pirates' starter with a pitch. None too pleased, Blyleven picked the ball up and prepared to throw it back at Saucier. Harvey was able to stop Blyleven, but he wasn't able to prevent the swarm of Phillies and Pirates from rushing the field. Someone tackled Saucier, and a nearly five-minute brawl ensued. Things were seemingly under control until Pirates outfielder Lee Lacy began hurling insults towards the Phillies.

"I told Lacy to stop trying to instigate things," Harvey said. "He was cursing and I threw him out of the game. The next thing I knew, [Phillies pitching coach] Herm Starrette was shouting at someone and I told him to stop instigating. He kept yelling and I threw him out of the game."[34] But Starrette wasn't the only Phillies coach causing problems. Bullpen coach Mike Ryan began jawing with several Pittsburgh players, and a second brawl broke out, this one bigger than the first. For the Pirates, there was no doubt who was to blame. "It was Ryan's fault," said Lacy. "He ran into a pile of players and started kicking everyone, even his teammates."[35]

"I didn't kick anyone," Ryan said. "As a coach, I was trying to be a peacemaker. Some of the Pirates, two or three of them, started pointing at me. I said, okay, if you want a piece of me, try me."[36]

After the teams finally returned to their dugouts, the Pirates carried a 6–5 lead into the ninth inning with their closer, Kent Tekulve, on the mound. Tekulve faced five batters in the bottom of the ninth and retired none of them. Larry Bowa's single to right field scored Bob Boone, and the Phillies had a win and sole possession of first place in the NL East.

"Dammit, we're a baseball team that's going to stick together," said Dallas Green. "They've got 'The Family,' or whatever and that's great. Well, we've got our own family here. I think today we showed we're not going to back off. We're not going to be intimidated. We're going to come after anybody that's coming after us. And that's not a challenge. That's not a threat. That's just us."[37]

Harvey, in his 18th season, had seen it all, and he felt tensions were a bit high for this time of year. "It's only May," he said. "A little early for this kind of thing."[38]

North of the border, the Montreal Expos were doing their best to keep pace despite a banged-up roster. Andre Dawson was nursing an arm injury and missed a week of action, and third baseman Larry Parrish was hit by an Ed Whitson pitch on May 3 against San Francisco. Parrish returned to the lineup on May 9, but the wrist was still bothering him, and it showed as his batting average steadily fell.

Montreal limped from April into May with a 1–5 road trip in Atlanta and Pittsburgh that left them six games back in the division after just 17 contests. But beginning with the second game of a doubleheader against the Giants on May 4, the Expos won 13 of 17 games to pull to within 1½ games of the lead.

On May 5, fans at Stade Olympique barely had time to get situated before the Expos put up four runs against J.R. Richard and the Astros in the bottom of the first inning before rain delayed the game for nearly three hours. Montreal starter David Palmer ignored the delay and went 6⅔ innings while allowing just one run as the Expos won, 10–1. It was part of a nice month for Palmer, who went 3–1 with a 1.96 ERA. Rotation mates Scott Sanderson (4–1, 2.36) and Steve Rogers (3–3 2.96) helped the Expos turn things around.

Offensively, Gary Carter hit his 100th career homer as part of a .310 month with seven longballs, while Ron LeFlore stole 16 bases. But no one was hotter than Ellis Valentine, who hit .345 and drove in 18 runs. Valentine played in 23 games in May and got at least one hit in 19 of them. But in the sixth inning of a May 30 game against the Cardinals, St. Louis pitcher Roy Thomas threw a pitch that slammed into Valentine's face and broke his cheek in six places. The injury required surgery to insert a pin into Valentine's face to hold the bones in place while they healed. Valentine was hitting .297 at the time of the injury, but he wouldn't return until after the All-Star break, leaving a big hole in the Montreal lineup.

In the NL West, the Big Red Machine was leaking oil. Cincinnati led the division at the end of April, but their pitching seemingly fell off a cliff in May, surrendering an NL-high 140 runs as part of a 13–14 month. Frank Pastore posted a respectable 3–1 record with a 3.27 ERA but five other Cincinnati starters, including Tom Seaver, combined to go 7–7 with an ERA of 5.99.

In Houston, the Astros had the opposite problem. Nolan Ryan and J.R. Richard were superb, starting 12 of the team's 26 games and posting a combined 2.30 ERA, and they weren't alone. Houston pitchers surrendered just 91 runs the entire month. Unfortunately for them and manager Bill Virdon, they posted an anemic .232 team batting average during the month.

The offense was so bad that 36-year-old Joe Morgan, he of the .256

April batting average and one home run, spent much of the month in the cleanup slot as the Astros managed to score a mere 79 runs while being shut out four times and enduring a 24-inning scoreless streak mid-month.

The struggles of the Astros and the Reds gave the Los Angeles Dodgers a chance to take early control of the NL West. The Dodgers won ten of 11 games mid-month, including an 8–1 homestand against the Cubs, Pirates and Cardinals.

First baseman Steve Garvey paced the offense, batting .289 with seven homers and 21 RBI, while Bob Welch went 4–0 with a 2.21 ERA in five starts to lead the pitching staff. Those numbers were even more impressive considering Welch's bumpy start in May. He began by surrendering six runs in five innings of work against the Pirates in Pittsburgh. A Dodgers comeback meant that he escaped without a loss, but he was ready to atone for his poor outing when the two teams met in LA twelve days later. Welch did more than that as he delivered 8⅔ scoreless innings before being pulled, much to the chagrin of the Dodger Stadium crowd, in favor of rookie reliever Steve Howe.

With two outs in the ninth inning and the Dodgers holding a 2–0 lead, Dave Parker singled to bring up Willie Stargell. Dodgers manager Tommy Lasorda emerged from the dugout and signaled to the bullpen for the lefty, Howe, while a chorus of boos filled Chavez Ravine. "Howzer, you better get this guy out because they're gonna run me out of town for pulling Bobby,"[39] Howe recalled in his biography, *Between the Lines*.

The decision may have been unpopular, but it also worked as Howe's first offering was up and in. As Stargell backed away, the ball hit his bat and bounced harmlessly in front of the plate, where catcher Steve Yeager picked it up and tagged him for the final out. Two starts later, on May 29, Welch was even better, facing the minimum of 27 batters against the Atlanta Braves. He allowed just a single to Atlanta outfielder Larvell Blanks but got the next hitter, Chris Chambliss, to hit into a double play. "It's the best he's ever thrown," said catcher Joe Ferguson. "I've never caught anyone who had that great command on one pitch."[40]

That one pitch was his fastball. In fact, the only hit Welch surrendered was when he hung a curveball to Blanks. Welch was on a roll, having allowed one run in his last 30⅔ innings. More importantly, the 3–0 win gave L.A. a two-game lead over Houston and Cincinnati in the division. There was a lot of season left, but the races were beginning to take shape, and baseball fans were in for a great ride.

4

June

Richard, Reggie and Reuss

On most evenings, residents of Parthenia Street in Northridge, California, could look out their windows and not see a man on fire running down the street. But June 9 wasn't an ordinary evening.

Richard Pryor had been free-basing cocaine for about seven months, and his habit was out of control. On the evening of June 9, in the middle of a free-base binge, Pryor poured a bottle of 151 rum over his head, pulled out a lighter and lit himself on fire. Fortunately for Pryor, his cousin entered the house just as this was taking place. In the confusion, his aunt yelled at his cousin to smother him with a nearby comforter. But Pryor thought the command meant to kill him, so he jumped out a window and ran down Parthenia Street. When he finally made it to the hospital, doctors determined that he had suffered third-degree burns over more than half his body.

The rumor mill kicked into full gear surrounding the circumstances of the incident and Pryor's chances of survival. Friends and family lied about what actually happened, and Pryor lied to verify their stories. Once he finally recovered, Pryor set the record straight in his 1982 concert, *Live at the Sunset Strip*. "I dipped my cookie in the milk, and the shit blew up."[1]

The Pryor story provided material for a fledgling cable network that launched at the beginning of the month. At 6 p.m. EST on June 1, CNN, the brainchild of Atlanta Braves owner Ted Turner, officially went on the air and changed television news forever.

Since arriving in New York in 1977, Reggie Jackson had been on a quest to etch his name in Yankees lore. His World Series heroics made him a legend on the field and made him a star off the field as well, particularly when it came to the city's night life. In the early-morning hours of June 1, that night life proved dangerous.

After smacking a game-winning home run against the Toronto Blue Jays on May 31, Jackson was headed to dinner at one of his favorite restaurants when a car blocked his path. He honked his horn, and 25-year-old Angel Viera, who was in the passenger's seat, began shouting obscenities. Jackson went on and looked for another place to park until Viera began yelling racial insults. That's when Jackson had had enough and began chasing Viera down East 83rd Street. After a short chase, Viera turned around, pulled a gun and fired three shots before fleeing the scene. Jackson escaped unharmed, then went to dinner, where he was questioned by police, who eventually caught Viera and charged him with attempted murder, among other things.

The Yankees were playing good baseball. The Mets were not. By the first week of June, the Mets were already a non-factor in the NL East. They were five games under .500, seven games off the pace, and had a manager, Joe Torre, in whom the team didn't even have enough confidence to give a full-season contract. When new general manager Frank Cashen took over just before spring training, he told Torre that his performance would be evaluated at the All-Star break, and a decision about his future would be made at that time. Cashen and the Mets had a month to decide on Torre's future, but they had a big decision about the future of the entire franchise.

The team owned the overall number one selection in the June draft for the third time in history, and they had missed badly the previous two times. They couldn't afford to miss again. In 1966, the Mets chose a high school catcher named Steve Chilcott with the top pick, passing on an outfielder from Arizona State named Reggie Jackson, who was snapped up by Kansas City at #2. Two years later, the Mets selected infielder Tim Foli with the first pick. The cross-town Yankees held the fourth selection and took a catcher from Kent State named Thurman Munson.

The kid everyone had their eye on this year was 18 years old, stood 6'4", and weighed just 180 pounds. His name was Darryl Strawberry, and he had already signed a letter of intent to play baseball at Oklahoma State. It was a commitment his mother wanted him to keep, but the prospect of big league baseball, and big league money, would be tough to turn down.

Strawberry attended Crenshaw High School in Los Angeles, which was familiar territory for baseball scouts. The year before, they flocked to

Crenshaw to see Chris Brown, a second-round selection who would later become an All-Star with the San Francisco Giants. Brown and Strawberry led Crenshaw to the 1979 City Championship game at Dodger Stadium, where they faced another powerhouse team from Granada Hills. Strawberry pitched well in the game but was outdueled by Granada Hills star John Elway who, despite hitting .491 and posting an ERA of just over 1.00 as a senior, decided to eschew baseball in favor of a football career.

On June 3, the Mets made Strawberry their choice and assigned him to their Appalachian League farm club in Kingsport, Tennessee, a world away from Crenshaw. Playing alongside future big league managers Lloyd McClendon and John Gibbons, Strawberry enjoyed some success, batting .268 with five homers, but he made a bigger splash as a marketing tool. The Yankees' Appalachian League affiliate in Paintsville, Kentucky, pulled out all the stops for Strawberry's first appearance. A helicopter dropped a load of strawberries on home plate, much to the delight of all the fans who gained free admission, provided they showed up with a strawberry. The team served strawberry shortcake and strawberry sundaes, free of charge, in between innings, sold only strawberry soda in the concession stands, and planted a strawberry patch beyond the wall in right field. Darryl Strawberry even got a kiss from a local beauty queen who also gave him a gift of ... a pint of strawberries.

Just below the Mets in the NL East standings in early June were the St. Louis Cardinals. Under manager, and former Cardinals player, Ken Boyer, the Birds endured a horrific stretch in May during which they lost 16 of 18 games and earned the worst record in the major leagues. The issue was pitching. As May turned to June, Cardinals pitchers had given up 25 more runs than any other National League staff. On June 3, the team embarked on a ten-game road trip to face the Mets, Expos and Braves. It wouldn't go well.

Two straight wins were followed by three straight losses, and by June 8, Cardinals management had seen enough. General Manager John Claiborne flew to Montreal to relieve Boyer of his responsibilities as Cardinals manager. But bad weather in Chicago delayed Claiborne's departure, and he didn't arrive in Montreal until the following day, placing him in the awkward position of firing Boyer on the road in between games of a doubleheader. Making matters worse, Boyer was in the middle of filling out his lineup card for the second game when Claiborne appeared in the visiting manager's office.

Jack Krol piloted the Cardinals in the second game of the doubleheader in Montreal, which they lost, and later that day Cardinals owner Augie Busch introduced Whitey Herzog as his new manager at a news conference at his suburban St. Louis home. "[I was] so impressed with Whitey, I felt we had to make [a change] right now," Busch said. "Something had to be done in my opinion."[2]

The change didn't sit well in the Cardinals clubhouse, and the players voiced their displeasure, saying Boyer's hands were tied because of the roster he was handed. "It doesn't matter who's managing if you don't hit, pitch or field,"[3] said Bob Forsch. Keith Hernandez agreed. "The worst team I've been on in the major leagues," he said. "We are bad. The manager is only as good as his horses and [we] don't have the horses."[4]

Herzog flew to Atlanta to join his new team while the Expos stayed in Montreal to prepare for the San Diego Padres. Montreal was slowly climbing back into the NL East race after dropping seven games off the pace in early May. But by the time the sweep of the Cardinals was complete, the Expos led the division by one game. Even more impressive was that the climb came despite injuries to some key players.

Larry Parrish and Ellis Valentine were both out with broken bones thanks to being hit by pitches. Chris Speier dislocated a finger playing a game of pre-game pepper, and Andre Dawson was also in and out of the lineup with a wrist problem. Dawson's injury wasn't severe enough to warrant a trip to the disabled list, but it did sap a lot of his power. "The Hawk" recorded just six extra-base hits in 21 May games. Still, the Expos kept right on rolling. Their winning streak hit ten straight on June 13 with a 4–3 win over the Dodgers. In the seventh inning, with a runner on and the game tied, 3–3, Dodgers manager Tommy Lasorda went with the percentages and walked catcher Gary Carter intentionally to go lefty on lefty with Steve Howe against Warren Cromartie. Cromartie's single up the middle scored Rodney Scott to give Montreal the lead and eventually the win.

"Lefty/Lefty is the biggest misconception in baseball," Cromartie told the *LA Times*. "Every time I hit in that situation I try to put a dent in 'the book' to show how dumb it is."[5]

The Montreal run would have been bolstered by the presence of Bill Lee, but the "Spaceman" fell victim to a horrific late-night injury. After beating St. Louis on June 6, Lee claimed he was out for a late-night/early-morning run when he was startled by a cat and fell, thus suffering a very painful hip injury. It quickly became another chapter in the legend of Bill Lee.

Lee ran a 10K race through Central Park in 1979 while the Expos were playing a weekend series against the Mets. He emerged from that unscathed, but running in Montreal seemed to be hazardous to his health. In one incident the previous year, Lee was out jogging when he was struck by a cab, and now he was being attacked by cats at all hours of the night. "Let's make the streets safer for Spaceman,"[6] said a headline in the *Ottawa Journal* on June 10.

In his book, *No More Mr. Nice Guy*, Expos manager Dick Williams claimed the real story was that Lee injured himself while engaging in a different sort of exercise. According to Williams, Lee was having a rendezvous with a woman when her husband came home. Lee's only means of exit was to climb out a second-story balcony onto a trellis, which subsequently broke. According to Williams, the hip injury occurred when Lee fell onto an iron fence.

While the Expos were surging, the Phillies were treading water thanks to injuries and inconsistent play. Pete Rose's 4-for-5 night on June 13 against the Padres kick-started a six-game winning streak that moved the Phillies into a first-place tie. The hits also moved Rose ahead of Honus Wagner into fifth place on the all-time list and, while he was happy to pass a legendary name, he also wasn't satisfied. "I'm just happy to get the base hits," Rose told the *Philadelphia Inquirer*. "When you have in your mind you can be No. one, you don't get excited at being fifth."[7]

The Phillies began the game with seven straight hits off Randy Jones and John D'Acquisto and were up 6–0 before they made an out. But Dick Ruthven hurt his shoulder in the seventh inning when he caught his spikes in the turf and fell while fielding a Tim Flannery grounder. The injury forced Ruthven to miss two weeks and put Dallas Green in quite a bind. With Ruthven out, the Phillies' pitching rotation was essentially Steve Carlton and any warm body they could find. Nino Espinosa won 14 games in 1979, but hadn't pitched at all in 1980 due to a shoulder injury. Green was also missing Larry Christenson, who was out with bone spurs in his elbow.

The six-game winning streak was followed by a dismal string of eight losses in ten games, including losing two of three to the Expos at Veterans Stadium. The first game of the series was especially tough. Tied 6–6 in the top of the tenth inning, Dallas Green, apparently not a student of recent history, walked Gary Carter intentionally to set up a lefty/lefty matchup with Tug McGraw facing Warren Cromartie. As was the case against the Dodgers earlier in the month, Cromartie delivered the game-winning hit. When asked about his proclivity for delivering game-winning hits, Cromartie responded, "I don't count them. Maybe Pete Rose does. I don't keep tabs on that stuff. I just go out and play baseball."[8]

Tom Cushman's column in the following day's *Philadelphia Daily News* carried the headline "Expos Are No Joke."[9] Indeed they weren't. It appeared that the NL East would be a three-team battle right to the end.

The race in the AL West was quickly becoming a joke thanks to the hot start of the Kansas City Royals. By early June, KC was in the midst of an eight-game winning streak to bump their lead to 5½ games. But the June 10 win against the Indians proved costly. Up 3–1 in the top of the third inning, George Brett drew a walk from Cleveland starter Len Barker. Royals manager Jim Frey flashed the steal sign, and Brett took off for second. Moments later, Brett's teammates reported hearing a pop before seeing their star third baseman writhing in pain near second base.

Brett was one of, if not the, hottest hitter in baseball at the time of the injury. Over the previous 18 games, he had hit .447 with 24 RBI and six homers, including a first-inning shot off Barker. Now he was leaving the field on a stretcher. "I had bad thoughts when I saw him rolling over in the dirt," Frey said after the game. "He's an excellent, aggressive, alert baserunner. I just hope he'll be out only a week or so. In the meantime, I'll be using Dave Chalk, Jerry Terrell and also maybe Jamie Quirk at 3rd base."[10]

That was not an exchange that any Royals fan was eager to make. The situation became even worse when it was revealed that Brett had torn a ligament in his right ankle, and he was placed on the disabled list a week later. But even Brett's absence couldn't slow down the Royals, who actually increased their divisional lead while missing their best player. Willie Aikens did his part to pick up the slack by hitting .308 for the month with seven homers. Aikens had had a chip on his shoulder ever since the season began after he felt slighted by Tigers manager Sparky Anderson.

In the season-opening series, Anderson ordered pitcher Dave Rozema to walk Hal McRae intentionally to pitch to Aikens with the bases loaded in a one-run game. Aikens delivered a single to center to drive in two runs and ultimately give the Royals the win. When asked after the game about the move, Anderson, who had managed McRae in Cincinnati, said he'd do it again. "I will walk McRae and pitch to Aikens a thousand times," he said. "Who do you think is a better hitter? I think McRae is a better hitter."[11]

Those words, especially coming from a manager of Anderson's stature, hurt Aikens, and he began to put pressure on himself to produce, which only made things worse. But in the two weeks after Brett went down, Aikens hit .364 with six homers while driving in 13 runs in 16 games. Willie Wilson continued to set the table at the top of the lineup, and veteran Amos Otis also contributed six homers in June. The Royals were rolling and were showing the rest of the American League that even without Brett, they were still very dangerous.

The summer movie releases kicked off with a bang as "Saturday Night Live" alums John Belushi and Dan Aykroyd starred in the action/musical, *The Blues Brothers.* Set in Chicago, the film portrayed Jake (Belushi) and Elwood (Aykroyd) Blues as two brothers on a mission to raise $5,000 to save the Catholic orphanage they grew up in. Like *The Shining, The Blues Brothers* came with a big price tag and many sub-par reviews.

The *LA Times* called it "A $30-million dollar wreck, minus laughs,"[12] and said, "It destroys more real property than any other event since the bombing of Dresden and all by itself it solves Detroit's inventory problem by totaling enough automobiles to transport four Army divisions and the cast of 'Ben-Hur.'"[13]

The *Times* had a point. One of the signature scenes of the film took place in the recently closed Dixie Square Mall in Harvey, Illinois The mall opened in the mid–1960s but closed in 1979 as increased crime in the area kept shoppers away. For director John Landis, it represented the perfect opportunity to film a car chase the likes of which had never been seen.

"Will there be anything else?"[14] asked the smiling Toys 'R' Us clerk.

"Yes," said the customer, holding up a stuffed Grover doll from Sesame Street. "Do you have a Miss Piggy?"[15]

Just then, Jake and Elwood crashed "the Bluesmobile" through the back of the store, closely followed by two of Illinois' finest in what became a nearly three-minute orgy of destruction. Shot after shot of cars driving through plate glass windows filled with store displays and extras playing mall shoppers diving out of harm's way were punctuated with one-liners from Belushi and Aykroyd. When the scene was finished, Landis and his crew left without bothering to clean up. The ensuing lawsuit was eventually thrown out of court, and the mall sat vacant until it was finally torn down in 2012. While not fine art, *The Blues Brothers* was big fun and earned nearly $5 million at the box office in its opening weekend.

There was plenty of entertainment in ballparks on June 20 as well, and it began at Fenway Park in Boston. By the time the Angels made it to Boston on the evening of Friday, June 20, they were off to the worst start in franchise history, stood 17 games behind the Royals in the division, and were riding a nine-game losing streak. California skipper Jim Fregosi sent Frank Tanana to the mound, sporting a 2–7 record and an ERA of 6.79, against a potent Boston lineup that included Fred Lynn, Jim Rice, Tony Perez and Dwight Evans. Don Zimmer countered with Steve Renko, and the Boston faithful settled in for what looked to be an easy victory. They were wrong.

In the top of the second inning, Freddie "The Flea" Patek, all 5'5" of him, doubled to left field as part of a seven-run inning that chased Renko from the game. The next inning, Patek stepped to the plate with teammates Bobby Grich and Larry Harlow aboard against relief pitcher Dick Drago and hit a three-run shot to give the Angels a 10–0 lead. Two innings later, Patek homered again, the first of two California would hit in the frame to chase Drago. Sensing history, the Boston fans gave Patek a standing ovation.

"Some people get married more often than Patek hits homers,"[16] wrote Mike Littwin the next day in the *Los Angeles Times*.

Now he had hit homers in consecutive at-bats, but Patek wasn't finished. After grounding into a double play in his fourth at-bat, he came to the plate in the eighth inning, again with Harlow on base, and homered again, this time off Jack Billingham, to give the Angels a 17–0 lead. This time the Fenway faithful not only gave him another standing ovation, they wouldn't settle down until Patek gave *them* a curtain call.

He had a chance to become just the 11th player in major league history to hit four home runs in a game when he came up in the ninth inning, but struck out against Boston reliever Bill Campbell. Still, it wasn't a bad night. He went 4-for-6 with three homers and seven RBI in a 20–2 Angels win. "He was really pumped that last time," said Don Baylor, whose stint on the disabled list, along with that of Brian Downing, was a big reason why the Angels were struggling so badly. "Every swing, Freddie was looking at me."[17]

The three home runs accounted for 60 percent of Patek's season total of five. In his career, he totaled 41 round-tippers, but June 20, 1980, was the only multi-homer game of his career.

On the same night that Patek was putting on a power display at Fenway, Detroit outfielder Al Cowens put on a display of an entirely different sort. Cowens and the Tigers were in Chicago to take on the White Sox. The game was tied in the top of the 11th inning when Cowens stepped in against Chicago relief pitcher Ed Farmer. Farmer was looking to keep the Tigers off the board in hopes of picking up a win. Cowens was looking for revenge.

On May 8, 1979, the two had faced off when Cowens was with Kansas City and Farmer was with Texas. Farmer, making his first start since 1974, hit Royals second baseman Frank White with the second pitch of the game, breaking his hand. Then with one out in the top of the fifth, Farmer's first pitch to Cowens sailed inside and shattered Cowens' jaw.

Farmer denied that he threw at Cowens on purpose, saying he was nervous and Texas manager Pat Corrales cited a line drive off the bat of Patek that hit Farmer as another potential reason for his wildness. Farmer and Buddy Bell visited Cowens in the hospital the next afternoon to apologize, bringing a copy of Sparky Lyle's book, *The Bronx Zoo*, as an olive branch of sorts, but Cowens was in no mood for the visit. "He's going to get his some kind of way," said Cowens. "It's all right brushing back a player but don't throw at his head. He could have killed somebody."[18]

In their first matchup since the incident, Farmer brushed Cowens back on the third pitch of the at-bat and eventually coaxed him to ground out to shortstop Todd Cruz on a 3–1 pitch. But as the ball bounced to Cruz, instead of heading to first base, Cowens charged the mound and went after Farmer, causing a bench-clearing brawl. Farmer, whose back was turned when Cowens charged the mound, escaped with a few scratches and a bloody nose, while Cowens was ejected from the game. Never one to shy away from controversy, Sox broadcaster Harry Caray called it "the worst sneak attack since Pearl Harbor."[19]

No sooner had Cowens sat down in the visitors' clubhouse at Comiskey Park to try and cool down than he was approached by two Chicago police officers, who told him to get dressed so they could place him under arrest. Fortunately for Cowens, he wasn't alone in the clubhouse. Infielder Tom Brookens had been ejected from the game earlier for arguing balls and strikes, and when he realized what was going on, he ran back to the Tigers dugout to summon Sparky Anderson to come to the aid of his outfielder. "I told 'em to get their ass out of here," said Anderson, "and I told 'em they aren't taking anybody out of here. They have no business in here."[20]

The fact that Anderson managed to convince Chicago police to buzz off should have instantly earned him the American League Manager of the Year award, but there was still a game to finish. Detroit scored two runs in the inning to win the game, 5–3, but that quickly became secondary as emotions were still running high in both clubhouses.

White Sox skipper Tony LaRussa called Cowens' actions "about the most gutless thing I've ever seen."[21] Bill Veeck was beside himself. "It was an attack on an unprotected man," he said. "Cowens should be barred from baseball for the rest of the year."[22]

"I don't have anything to say about it,"[23] was all the media would get from the suddenly reticent Cowens.

American League President Lee MacPhail acted swiftly, suspending Cowens for seven games and fining him an undisclosed amount. But that wasn't the only legal trouble he faced. Farmer filed charges against Cowens in Cook County Circuit Court, and a judge issued a warrant for Cowens' arrest on an assault-and-battery charge. It was clear that this was not a run-of-the-mill baseball fight.

While Farmer and Cowens exchanged blows in Chicago, there was an even bigger fight taking place in Canada. The World Boxing Council welterweight championship was on the line at "The Brawl in Montreal," featuring Sugar Ray Leonard defending his title against Roberto Duran, the number one contender.

With the Expos on a West Coast swing, the bout took place at Olympic Stadium, and many of the Expos weighed in on their favorite. Leonard was a 3–2 favorite in Vegas, and the Expos clubhouse favored the defending champ, but it wasn't unanimous. "I've got to go with Duran," said first base coach Felipe Alou. "I'm Latin and it's difficult to betray your ancestry. Duran's been good for the Latins."[24]

Unbeknownst to Alou, Duran was also in Leonard's head and had been for quite some time. As Leonard climbed through the ropes at the beginning of the fight, he said he felt a sense of impending doom, and the early rounds fed that feeling. Duran took control early and, though Leonard battled back and took the fight the full 15 rounds, he lost for the first time as a professional.

Farmer/Cowens and Leonard/Duran garnered most of the headlines, but one other fight took place in the early morning hours of June 20 in Cincinnati. This bout took place just after the St. Louis Cardinals had finished a two-game series against the Astros in which they scored zero runs, courtesy of Joe Niekro and Nolan Ryan.

"I wasn't feeling well at all," Ryan told reporters after the final game of the series, a 2–0 Houston win. "I felt like I might be coming down with the flu before the game."[25] St. Louis pitcher Bob Sykes, whom Ryan defeated, was less than sympathetic. "Send my condolences, please," he said. "That takes some nerve to throw a one-hitter and say he's been sick."[26]

It was an unhappy bunch that pulled up to the Stouffer's Cincinnati Towers the next morning. Tension was still running high after the dismissal of Ken Boyer, and there were warring factions within the team. Some veterans were unhappy with recently added minor league players, and there was also friction between the pitchers and the position players. Making matters worse, some members of the team had to stand on the ride from the airport to the hotel because the team bus didn't have enough seating. During the ride, Keith Hernandez began needling pitcher John Fulgham about his recent inability to pitch because of a sore shoulder.

As the two stepped off the bus, things came to a head and a shoving match broke out. As many as ten players may have been involved, but order was quickly restored thanks to Ted Simmons and Ken Reitz, who separated the combatants. No punches were thrown, and the only casualty was Fulgham's shirt, which was torn in the melee. New manager Whitey Herzog didn't seem bothered by the incident. "Nothing wrong with it," he told the *St. Louis Post Dispatch*. "Just a few beers. I kind of like it, myself. It's not going to hurt anybody."[27]

Fists were flying out west, too, but in San Francisco it wasn't between teammates; it was in the manager's office. On June 18, John "The Count" Montefusco faced the Mets for the second time in five days. In the first start, Giants manager Dave Bristol pulled Montefusco in the eighth inning with a 6–1 lead, and the bullpen couldn't hold the lead, costing "The Count" a win.

Four days later, Montefusco took an 8–2 lead into the ninth inning when the Mets loaded the bases with no one out. Once again, Bristol emerged from the dugout and signaled to the bullpen. The two argued on the mound, and Montefusco stormed off. His mood didn't improve when Al Holland gave up a two-run double to the second batter he faced. Greg Minton came in to put out the fire, but Montefusco was livid and stormed into Bristol's office to let him know. Shortly thereafter, the sounds of a scuffle were heard, and by the time players and coaches intervened, Montefusco had Bristol in a headlock.

"Bristol provoked it," Montefusco said. "He didn't like what I was saying and he told me to get out of his office. I was backing up and he kept pushing and pushing. I told him, 'You better stop it or I'll deck you.' He kept pushing me—at least 10 times—before he sucker punched me."[28]

Bristol denied hitting his pitcher and said he simply did what had to be done. "I told him to keep quiet, and he kept going on and on. It had to be done sooner or later. You can't get in a situation where a player is dictating to a manager."[29]

When asked to name a winner in the bout, Giants coach Jim Lefebvre rendered his decision without hesitation. "It was Dave Bristol, easily," he said. "Count picked on the wrong guy. [Bristol's] one tough son-of-a-gun."[30]

The battling Giants posted a 15–13 record in June, their first winning month of the season, but it wasn't enough to keep up with the Dodgers or the Houston Astros, thanks in large part to some outstanding pitching. For the month of June, Houston pitchers threw five shutouts and allowed just 87 runs while posting a team ERA of 2.85. "It's as good and deep as any I've ever seen," said Bill Virdon of his pitching staff. "We have no complaints about our pitching. It keeps us in every game."[31]

J.R. Richard continued to dominate hitters like never before. He began the month with back-to-back shutouts against the Giants and Cubs, capping a seven-start run in which he posted a 4–2 record and an amazing 0.78 ERA. Nolan Ryan was nearly as good in June though his record didn't show it. He went 2–1 with a 2.90 ERA, but the Astros went 5–1 in his starts. The continuing problem was a lack of offense. Houston batters hit only 11 homers in June, just one more than the National League Player of the Month Dusty Baker, and the Astros offense could muster only 102 runs.

As the June 15 trade deadline approached, there were rumors that the Astros and Phillies were talking about a swap of Joaquin Andujar for Keith Moreland and Lonnie Smith. Andujar made 23 starts in 1979, but was bumped from the rotation after Houston signed Nolan Ryan and had made just one start by mid–June. The Phillies were desperate for pitching, but the deal fell through for multiple reasons. Houston wanted established players, which Moreland and Smith weren't, and Dallas Green wasn't eager to part with two players who possessed so much potential.

The non-trade turned out to be fortuitous because just two days after the deadline, Richard left his start against the Cubs early, complaining of arm troubles. "I felt tired early," Richard told the *Chicago Tribune*. "I like to finish what I start, but this is the first time I've pitched this many innings this early in the season. There's no need to go out and hurt myself."[32]

Richard missed his next scheduled start, but came back to face the Reds on June 28. Pitching on 11 days' rest against a struggling Reds team at home figured to be a good matchup for Richard. It wasn't. In 3⅓ innings, the Reds scored more runs off Richard than he had allowed in his previous five starts. He left with forearm soreness but it was obvious that something wasn't right with the Astros pitcher. Many in the media suspected that the problem was more than physical or perhaps not physical at all, but rather mental. Yet despite Richard's sudden woes, Houston's pitching enabled them to pick up nearly five games in the standings. The 'Stros began the month two games out of first place, but entered July with a 2½ game lead over the Dodgers.

Like the Astros, the Dodgers got by on pitching in June. LA pitchers posted a 3.06 team ERA on the strength of seven shutouts in 28 games. Leading the way was a guy who started the year in the bullpen.

The 1980 Los Angeles Dodgers opened the season with an all right-handed starting rotation. Burt Hooton started on Opening Day against the Astros, followed by 1979 Rookie of the Year Rick Sutcliffe, future Hall of Famer Don Sutton, Dave Goltz and Bob Welch. Lefty Jerry Reuss opened the season as a long reliever.

Reuss won 108 games through his first ten years in the major leagues with St. Louis, Houston and Pittsburgh. He hit double digits in wins six times, including an 18–11 mark with the Pirates in 1975. But by 1978 he was relegated to the bullpen, and he wasn't happy about it. After five straight seasons of 200+ innings, he logged just 82⅓ in 1978, including enduring two strings of 19 days between appearances. He asked the Pirates to trade him, and they complied, swapping him to the Dodgers for Rick Rhoden in a rare one-for-one pitcher swap. "We are quite pleased with our acquisition of Reuss," Dodgers GM Al Campanis told *The Sporting News*. "We feel he has several fine years ahead of him ... and he gives us another left-hander."[33]

"Ever since my high school days, I wanted to play for the Dodgers." said Reuss. "Now it's a dream come true. I've always wanted to be a Dodger."[34]

As the 1980 season dawned, Reuss was lobbying for a spot in the rotation. Dodgers manager Tommy Lasorda said he would prefer to start Reuss, but he had seven starters for five rotation spots and something had to give, so the lefty opened the season in the bullpen as a long reliever. His first appearance of the season came on Opening Day, when starter Burt Hooton lasted only two innings. Reuss pitched well, allowing just one hit over five innings, but did not earn a decision. He pitched in relief for the first month and a half, picking up three wins and three saves.

Reuss made his first start of the season on May 16 against Pittsburgh at Dodger Stadium, facing John Candelaria. He gave up four runs in the first two innings, but the Dodgers scored six runs in the seventh inning en route to an 8–6 win to earn him his fourth win of the season. In a role reversal, Sutcliffe picked up the save, inducing Bill Robinson to pop out to first with a runner on to end the game.

Reuss went 4–1 over his next seven starts, including a June 16 game against Philadelphia where both he and Phillies starter Randy Lerch pitched ten innings. On June 27, he took the hill against the Giants at Candlestick Park in what turned out to be a special night.

The Dodgers took an early lead when Rudy Law's infield single scored Davey Lopes in the top of the first inning. In the bottom of the first, Giants right fielder Jack Clark hit a two-out ground ball to shortstop Bill Russell. Russell fielded the ball cleanly, but his throw was in the dirt and Steve Garvey couldn't dig it out. Russell was charged with an error. As it turned out, Clark would be the only baserunner of the game for the Giants.

Reuss had seen success in earlier starts with his sinking fastball and used it with great success on this night. The Giants managed to get only six balls out of the infield. The only real challenge came in the eighth inning, when Larry Herndon hit a ball to the left of third baseman Ron Cey, who dove to his left to make the stop and threw Herndon out at first.

In the ninth, catcher Mike Sadek grounded out to Cey and pinch-hitter Rennie Stennett grounded out to Russell, to bring Bill North up. Reuss' first pitch was a ball, but he then induced North to hit a comebacker to the mound, which he fielded and threw to Garvey for the final out.

"I just threw a no-hitter!" Reuss said after the game. "What could be a bigger thrill? I haven't pitched in the World Series yet."[35]

"He's been a godsend," said Lasorda. "In all the years I've been managing, I've never had a pitcher pitch a no-hit no-run game. It was really a thrill for me to sit there and watch him. He was awesome."[36]

Reuss' mound opponent was lefty Vida Blue, who threw a no-hitter for Oakland in 1975. "As a pitcher I can appreciate what he did. Personally, I'm glad for him. But as far as the San Francisco Giants go, I hate his guts."[37] The fact that Reuss would have had a perfect game but for his throwing error was not lost on Russell, who told reporters, "I threw it away. It was as simple as that."[38]

Old baseball superstitions abound when it comes to no-hitters. Lasorda sat in the same spot on the bench once he realized what was happening, going so far as to chase away players who had taken his seat. Giants fans did their best to put the hex on Reuss as well. One fan leaned into the dugout in the sixth inning and told him he was throwing a no-hitter and to keep up the good work. The no-no, along with a 3–0 record with a 0.82 ERA, helped earn Reuss National League "Pitcher of the Month" honors for June. Not too shabby for a guy who didn't have a spot in the rotation when the season began.

While the Astros and Dodgers were making gains behind their pitching staffs, the defending division champion Reds were losing ground thanks to theirs. Cincinnati hitters led the National League with 129 runs scored in June, but their pitchers gave up 144 runs, nearly 20 more than any other team in the league.

Reds pitching was so bad it even jump-started the Astros' offense. When the Reds got to Houston for a three-game series at the end of the month, the Astros had scored only 76 runs in 23 games. Once Cincinnati pitchers took the mound at the Astrodome, Houston put up 22 runs in three games. "We've struggled," Reds manager John McNamara told the *Indianapolis Star*. "We just haven't put things together."[39]

That was quite an understatement. After posting a team ERA of 2.80 in the season's first month, the numbers were heading steadily up. The team ERA jumped to 4.56 in May and 5.22 in June.

The starting rotation was not effective, but the bullpen was an absolute disaster, pitching to an ERA of 6.25 in June. "[The bullpen] has definitely been a problem," said Tom Hume. "Everybody was getting in a bad groove. The pitching hasn't been good for the last three or four weeks. We've been taking things for granted and not going after hitters."[40]

Not one to panic, Johnny Bench told writers not to count the Reds out just yet. "Consistency is the key word. Putting the pitching and hitting together. A lot of people picked us third behind Houston and Los Angeles. We're third. But we haven't put everything together."[41]

They would need to do just that if they wanted to stay in the race.

5

July
Stretch, Strikeouts and a Stroke

Zero Hour! hit theaters in November of 1957. The film featured a retired World War II pilot haunted by a decision he made that resulted in some of his men being killed. After the war, the pilot is on an airplane when passengers and crew are stricken with food poisoning. There's only one man who can safely land the plane. Can he pull it off?

Late one night in the 1970s, Jim Abrahams and his friends David and Jerry Zucker saw *Zero Hour!* and loved it. They bought the rights, and *Airplane!* was born. Shot in just over a month with a budget of about $3.5 million, *Airplane!* opened on July 2 and enjoyed immediate success. The *New York Times* called it "clever, confident and furiously energetic,"[1] while the *Los Angeles Times* said it "sends up a comic boom."[2]

The secret to the film's success was taking the unintentionally funny parts of *Zero Hour!* and making them intentionally funny. In many cases, *Airplane!* lifts parts of *Zero Hour!* shot for shot and line for line. The 1957 version also showcased the "talents" of Elroy "Crazylegs" Hirsch, a future pro football Hall of Famer, in the role of the co-pilot. Hirsch's performance was lacking to say the least, but it gave Abrahams and the Zuckers the idea to cast a professional athlete in their film, preferably one with no acting experience whatsoever. The original script called for Pete Rose to be the co-pilot, but production began in August of 1979 and Rose wasn't available, so the producers turned to Kareem Abdul-Jabbar.

Robert Hays played the part of the former pilot, Ted Striker, but among those who read for the part was a former weatherman named David Letterman. By year's end, *Airplane!* was the fourth highest-grossing film of the year, earning more than $84 million. The brothers Zucker and Abrahams appeared on Letterman's show in 1982, where they aired his awkward screen test. "Maybe if I had gotten the part that film would have made some money,"[3] Letterman said.

On the evening *Airplane!* was released, things weren't so funny at Comiskey Park in Chicago. Prior to the White Sox July 2 home game against the Angels, broadcaster Jimmy Piersall sought out *Arlington Heights Daily Herald* writer Bob Gallas to "discuss" Gallas' story about Piersall's dismissal as an unofficial outfield coach.

As a player, Piersall had a much-publicized mental breakdown that became the basis for the 1957 film, *Fear Strikes Out*. A two-time All-Star selection, Piersall's mercurial behavior made him tough to deal with for both teammates and management. As the 1980 season progressed, Tony LaRussa and the Sox felt it was a conflict of interest for Piersall to coach players and then go to the booth and criticize their play. After polling the players, he relieved Piersall of his coaching duties.

Adding to the intrigue was the fact that Sox owner Bill Veeck had been trying to get rid of Piersall as a broadcaster because he felt he was too critical of the players. Piersall responded that he could say whatever he wanted, which included taking shots at Veeck's wife, Mary Frances, on a local radio show, calling her "a colossal bore"[4] and suggesting that she should stay in the kitchen.

When Gallas' article made it public knowledge that Piersall was no longer coaching, Piersall confronted him in the clubhouse, and the two exchanged words. What happened next depends on whom you ask. In his book, *The Truth Hurts*, Piersall said that he and Gallas got into "a little scuffle"[5] before being separated. Newspaper accounts painted a much different picture, however.

"Jimmy jumped him; I saw it because it was right by the trainer's room," said Sox trainer Herm Schneider. "Gallas started turning blue in the face."[6]

Piersall's troubles didn't end there. Once Veeck was informed of the incident, he sent his son, Mike, to the broadcast booth to confront Piersall. "I gave him a dedicated introductory statement as to my intentions," said the younger Veeck. "I didn't want it to look like Cowens' sneak attack on Farmer. I said I wanted him to look at someone his own size."[7]

No sooner had Mike Veeck entered the booth to "announce his intentions" than he and Piersall were involved in a scuffle that took Piersall's broadcast partner, Rich King, and two writers to break up. In addition to potential embarrassment to his father's baseball team, Mike Veeck's intensity was most certainly ratcheted up by Piersall's comments about his mother. After meeting with Veeck in his office, Piersall left the stadium and spent the night in a local hospital with what Sox officials termed "exhaustion."[8]

Piersall wasn't the only one who began July by wanting to punch someone's lights out. Two days later, the Mets and Expos celebrated the nation's 204th birthday with a bench-clearing brawl at Shea Stadium. Just a day before, Lee Mazzilli's three-run homer gave the Mets a 7–2 win in the first game of the series. For Joe Torre's Mets, it was the ninth win in their last 12 games. Montreal held a slim one-half game lead over the Phillies at the All-Star break, while the Pirates were just one half-game behind Philadelphia.

Adding to their foul mood was the fact that catcher Gary Carter was the sole All-Star representative on a team that won 95 games the previous season and was in first place when the teams were announced. "We certainly should have had more than one player,"[9] said Dick Williams. Andre Dawson was hitting .290 with ten home runs, Warren Cromartie, who wasn't even listed on the All-Star ballot, was in the top ten in hitting, and Ron LeFlore lead all of baseball with 49 stolen bases.

On the mound, Steve Rogers was 10–6 with a 2.94 ERA but couldn't crack All-Star manager Chuck Tanner's staff. "I didn't anticipate being named anyway," said Rogers. "Chuck Tanner had it in his power to bestow an honor, and he's not very appreciative of me and I'm not very appreciative of him. It's a crying shame a team like ours rates just one guy."[10]

Such was the Expos' mood as they took the field for an Independence Day doubleheader at Shea Stadium. Their disposition worsened when they made five errors and lost the first game, 9–5, despite pounding out 14 hits. In the second game, the Mets came on strong again. Down 2–0 in the bottom of the first inning, Claudell Washington's triple scored Frank Tavares, and Joel Youngblood hit a two-run homer off Montreal starter Bill Gullickson, which brought first baseman Mike Jorgensen to the plate.

Gullickson buzzed Jorgensen with a pitch that sent him sprawling. No hitter enjoys being knocked down, but Jorgensen was a bit more sensitive than most, having been hit in the head with a pitch by Andy Hassler in 1979 that caused a blood clot and nearly killed him.

Jorgensen had some words for Gullickson and began walking towards the mound, bat in hand. Montreal catcher John Tamargo moved to get between Jorgensen and his pitcher, but he couldn't stop Mets catcher John Stearns from charging out of the New York dugout and straight for the mound. Unfortunately for Gullickson, Stearns reached the mound before anyone could stop him, and he had the rookie pitcher by the neck before help arrived in the form of the entire Montreal bench and bullpen. Once things settled down, Gullickson lasted two more batters before Williams pulled him from the game after just one-third of an inning. Montreal came back to win the game and regain first place, but Gullickson was making no excuses in just his sixth major league start. "I did what I had to do," he said. "I'm new to the league and I'm not going to be intimidated."[11]

"I wasn't going out there to fight," Jorgensen said after the game. "I just didn't appreciate what he did."[12]

Not surprisingly, both managers defended their players. Torre felt that Stearns was in the right in protecting his teammate, while Williams said Stearns escalated a situation that had begun to calm down.

The following day, Stearns came to the plate for the first time since the incident with one out and the bases empty thanks to a Steve Henderson homer that gave the Mets a 2–1 lead. Montreal pitcher Scott Sanderson's first pitch knocked Stearns down, but he simply dusted himself off and singled to left field. The fun continued in the series finale as Steve Rogers brushed back Henderson and Mazzilli, and Woodie Fryman came close to hitting Jorgensen again. Mets pitcher Craig Swan had seen enough and vowed revenge. "Our guys keep going in the dirt and we do nothing about it," he said. "That's got to stop.[13] ... If this continues, I won't ask anybody—the manager or the coaches—what to do. I'll take it upon myself to do something."[14]

Adding to the Mets frustration was the fact that Expos manager Dick Williams went to the mound to talk to Gullickson a few pitches before he knocked down Jorgensen. The implication was that the rookie had been on strict orders from a World Series-winning manager to knock down the next hitter. It's a charge Williams denied, but Swan wasn't buying it. "Williams is an old-style manager," Swan said. "His style has been obsolete for four or five years now. You let him know I'm going to get him. I can always throw one in the dugout. If I don't get him, then I'll get one of his hitters."[15]

On the same day the Mets and Expos went toe-to-toe, Nolan Ryan was making history in Cincinnati. Ryan entered his July 4 start against the Reds just three strikeouts shy of 3,000 for his career, a mark obtained by only three other pitchers: Walter Johnson, Bob Gibson and Gaylord Perry.

Ryan fanned Ken Griffey and Dan Driessen to end the first inning, and in the bottom of the second, he struck out Cesar Geronimo to reach 3,000. For Geronimo, the moment was a bit of ignominious history as he was also Gibson's 3,000th victim six years earlier. On the bright side for Geronimo and the Reds, Ryan was outdueled by rookie Charlie Liebrandt, who threw a complete-game four-hitter and matched Ryan's six strikeouts. Despite making history, Ryan lost the game and saw his record fall to a disappointing 5–6. Not exactly what he or the Astros were hoping for when they gave him the biggest contract in the history of the game.

"I need to start pitching better if I'm going to start helping this club," Ryan said. "I don't think I've kept them in the ball game the way I should have the last three games I pitched. I really don't know what the reason is."[16] The loss also put a damper on his joining an exclusive club. "I don't put that much emphasis on it. It's just another number. I think the main thing it shows is I'm durable and have good stuff over my career. To be able to strike out that many people sums it up."[17]

Ryan's troubles were part of a bigger problem for the Astros. After building a three-game lead in the NL West, Houston had lost six of their last nine games, and the lead had shriveled to just a half-game over the LA Dodgers. Fortunately for Houston, they would be facing Bruce Berenyi, a rookie making his first big-league appearance in the first game of a July 5 doubleheader. Berenyi's uncle, Ned Garver, won 129 games in the major leagues and had some advice for his young nephew. "Tell him to be aggressive," Garver told the *Cincinnati Enquirer*. "If you look and act confident, that's going to have an effect on the hitter. If the hitter looks out and sees you stammering around, he'll think you're afraid. Just get the ball from the catcher, look right back for the sign and go get 'em."[18]

The advice was solid. Unfortunately, Berenyi was unable to execute it. The Astros scored six runs in the top of the first inning to knock Berenyi out of the game after only one-third of an inning. He was relieved by Mario Soto, who threw 8⅔ shutout innings. That, combined with some timely Cincinnati hitting and five Houston errors, gave the Reds an improbable comeback win. Mike LaCoss beat Juaquin Andujar in the second game, and the Reds had themselves a sweep. Three straight wins against the division leader was exactly what the Reds needed. Cincinnati had dropped 12 of their last 18 games. They also lost their best pitcher.

Tom Seaver had been a workhorse since he came into the league in 1967. In the days before pitch counts and ramping up the inning totals of top prospects, Seaver averaged 35 starts per year from 1967 through 1979. He threw 251 innings as a rookie and had never thrown fewer than 215 innings in a season. But that streak was in jeopardy and so, potentially, was his career.

Seaver left his June 30 start against the Giants after giving up five runs and seven hits in just four innings. The loss dropped his record to 3–5 with an un–Seaverlike 4.76 ERA, thanks in part to allowing 16 home runs in his 14 starts. The problem was his shoulder, and he was scared. "My shoulder ached most of last year, but I pitched well," he said. "This year it's a sharp pain instead of an ache. [When I release the ball] the pain tightens my shoulder, pulling my elbow down. As a result, the ball stays up. By the time it gets to the strike zone, it's just floating up there."[19]

He was 35 years old, no longer in his prime, but still a very effective pitcher when he was healthy. For the first time in his career, he wasn't. "I can't keep pitching this way," he said. "It's not getting any better and it's not going to get any better as long as I keep pitching. It's not frustrating. It's depressing. I love what I do."[20]

While Seaver was worrying that his career might be over, another legend had already decided to hang it up. Willie Lee McCovey signed with the New York Giants at age 17 and made his major league debut four years later after batting .372 with 29 homers in 95 games for the 1959 Phoenix Giants of the AAA Pacific Coast League.

While many rookies are eased into the lineup, Giants skipper Bill Rigney threw McCovey right into the fire, batting him third in the order in his first game, right between Willie Mays and Orlando Cepeda. Unfazed, he went 4-for-4 with two triples against future Hall of Fame pitcher Robin Roberts and the Philadelphia Phillies. "He sure can swing a bat," said Phillies manager Eddie Sawyer. "But we didn't know how to pitch to him. After he's been around the circuit once, the pitchers will have a better line on what to use."[21]

Pitchers never did figure him out in 1959. Despite not making his debut until July 30, McCovey earned National League Rookie of the Year honors by hitting .354 with 13 homers. No position player has ever won the award while playing in fewer games. McCovey became one of the most-feared hitters in the National League in the 1960s. He hit exactly 300 homers in the decade and won the MVP Award in 1969. Age and knee problems began to catch up to him, though, and in October of 1973 the Giants traded him to the Padres, where he became a mentor for a young slugger named Dave Winfield.

In one game with Winfield on deck, McCovey came to bat and noticed the infield playing back, as they often did. He took a huge cut to keep the infielders where they were, then laid down a bunt to get on base. Winfield came up and knocked him in. After the game, McCovey told his protégé he bunted because he knew he could get on and was confident Winfield could bring him around. "[I] learned as much about strategy in that moment as I had in the 21 years preceding it,"[22] Winfield wrote in his 1988 autobiography, *Winfield—A Player's Life*.

After a disappointing 1976, McCovey returned to the Giants in 1977 and earned "Comeback Player of the Year" honors by hitting .280 with 28 homers in his age-39 season. By 1980, he was in the twilight of his Hall of Fame career. He was 42, but still felt he could contribute. The Giants disagreed. They hadn't finished higher than third place in the National League West since 1971, and it didn't appear they would be in contention in McCovey's baseball lifetime, so he was relegated to the bench. On May 4, he hit his 521st, and final, home run against the Expos in Montreal, and he used the platform to say he wanted more playing time. "Sure I'm 42. But I've got a couple of big years left," he said. "Not so-so years. McCovey years. Sometimes I get the feeling they're trying to force me into retirement."[23]

Willie McCovey wrapped up an amazing career when he retired in the middle of the 1980 season. He was inducted into the Hall of Fame in 1986 (National Baseball Hall of Fame Library, Cooperstown, New York).

By the end of June, McCovey had had enough. He announced that he would retire at mid-season, and on July 6 he pinch-hit for Rennie Stennett in the eighth inning against the Dodgers and drove in a run with a sacrifice fly in his final appearance. He was battling the flu and thus didn't start his final game. After his sacrifice fly drove in a run, he emerged from the visitors' dugout, acknowledged the crowd, and was gone. He didn't stick around to talk to the media.

"He's been through a lot this week," said manager Dave Bristol. "There's a lot of emotion in retiring."[24]

On the same day McCovey ended his historic career, the Cubs made history as well, but in typical Cubs fashion it was a rather dubious achievement. Chicago closed out the first half of the season in Pittsburgh against the Pirates and trailed, 4–3, with two outs in the ninth inning when Cliff Johnson's pinch-hit homer tied the game. After that, the two teams traded zeros on the scoreboard for ten innings until Omar Moreno's single to right field scored Ed Ott from second with the winning run in the bottom of the 20th. Chicago pitchers threw 12⅔ consecutive no-hit innings in the game, but the Cubs couldn't come away with a win.

"I felt like the 12th pig at an 11-place trough,"[25] said Chicago pitcher Mike Krukow in a somewhat odd reference, especially considering that Krukow hails from Long Beach, California, where pig troughs are few and far between. "We certainly can't feel ashamed of that game," said outfielder Mike Vail. "We had our chances. It was just an exercise in futility."[26] "Time flies when you're having fun," said Ott, who in addition to scoring the winning run, caught all 20 innings. "I felt like dropping but they don't let you lay down out there."[27]

The Pirates/Cubs marathon was an exciting end to an interesting first half of the season. In the American League, the Yankees enjoyed a 7½ game lead in the East, while the Royals led the west by 8½ games. But the National League was a different story. Montreal held a slim one-game lead over the Phillies, with the Pirates close behind at 1½ games back. In the West, the Astros and Dodgers were tied atop the division with the Seaverless Reds still within striking distance at 4½ games out. Houston's 45–33 record was the best in the National League, while the Padres' 34–47 mark was its worst.

San Diego came into the National League in 1969 and had had exactly one winning season in their history. They showed signs of life in the late 1970s, winning a franchise-best 84 games in 1978, but then slipped to 68 wins in 1979. That prompted General Manager Bob Fontaine to fire manager Roger Craig and make the unprecedented move of replacing him with Padres broadcaster Jerry Coleman for the 1980 season.

Coleman had won four World Series titles as a player with the Yankees. He also flew 120 combat missions in World War II and Korea and earned two distinguished flying crosses, 13 Air Medals and three Navy citations. What he hadn't done was manage a Major League Baseball team. By July it was clear that the Coleman experiment wasn't working, and the Padres needed to make a change. But rather than part ways with Coleman, on the day before the All-Star Game they fired Fontaine instead. "I'm not in this business to lose,"[28] said team President Ballard Smith, who also happened to be owner Ray Kroc's son-in-law. "I don't need the heartache and my family doesn't need it. I've never failed at anything else I've done in my life and I'm not going to accept failure now."[29]

Amiable by all accounts, Fontaine was decidedly old-school. He was a product of the Brooklyn Dodgers organization and was signed in 1940 by Branch Rickey himself. His first contract was written on the back of an envelope. Fontaine had been under fire, so the move wasn't unexpected, but the circumstances were. Rumors had the Padres' AAA manager, Doug Rader, taking over in the dugout with Coleman moving up to GM, a situation Coleman didn't seem to relish. "I feel terrible, just terrible," he said. "I feel if I had done a better job, it might not have happened. I think Bob Fontaine is one of the finest people who ever lived."[30]

The next day, a story in the *Trenton* (New Jersey) *Times* quickly made the Fontaine situation and its aftermath seem insignificant. On July 8, the *Times* reported that numerous members of the Phillies, including Pete Rose, Mike Schmidt, Larry Bowa and Greg Luzinski, had illegally obtained amphetamines from Reading Phillies team doctor Patrick Mazza. Denials rained from the Phillies clubhouse to the All-Star Game in Los Angeles. Rose claimed that he didn't even know a doctor in Pennsylvania, while Schmidt was outspoken in feeling he had been falsely accused. "That the media would take the liberty they did to tarnish my name and those of my teammates basically floors me," Schmidt said. "I'm on the verge of trying to decide whether I'm going to join the ranks of Steve Carlton [who had stopped talking to the media years ago]."[31]

Bowa insisted that he wouldn't talk to the press, and Luzinski refused comment as well. Phillies President Ruly Carpenter also wasn't happy with the distraction. "We're in a pennant race and the No. One priority in our minds is tomorrow night's game. No one has been charged with anything, no one has broken any laws. It's all speculative."[32]

Except that it wasn't. The case went to trial in 1981, and Mazza testified that he prescribed Dexamyl, Eskatrol, Dexedrine and Preludin for pitchers Steve Carlton, Larry Christenson and Randy Lerch, as well as Rose, Luzinski, Bowa and former catcher Tim McCarver.

"The [prescriptions] were made at the request of the ballplayers and were done in good faith," Dr. Mazza told District Justice Albert Gaspari. "Greg had a chronic problem with excessive weight, and he wanted Dexamine to help keep it down.[33] ... Bowa said he was running out of gas ... that he needed something to pick him up. Steve, being a moody person and a loner, needed something to pep him up, and he asked, 'Doc, can you help me?'"[34]

Mazza also testified that both McCarver and Rose asked for help as well. In his 2006 book, *Clearing the Bases*, Schmidt all but admitted that the charges may have been true. "In my day, amphetamines ... were widely available in major league clubhouses," he wrote. "They were obtainable with a prescription but be under no illusion that the name on the bottle always coincided with the name of the player taking them before game time."[35]

The Phillies' drug scandal broke on the morning of the All-Star Game in Los Angeles and added a secondary storyline to the midsummer classic. The primary story was the dominance of the National League. The NL had won eight straight All-Star Games and 16 of the last 17 matchups. The lone AL victory during that span came in 1971 at Tiger Stadium, when Reggie Jackson's towering home run off Dock Ellis helped the AL to a 6–4 win. The National League's dominance was such that Early Wynn had been the winning pitcher the last time the AL won two straight midsummer classics.

The odds were stacked against the AL again in 1980 as three elected starters would miss the game due to injury. Paul Molitor (ribs), George Brett (ankle), and Jim Rice (wrist) were out of the lineup, and four other AL starters were battling injuries, including Boston outfielder Fred Lynn, who had sat out the final five games of the first half with a hamstring injury.

Injuries and all, the AL lineup was still impressive. First baseman Rod Carew (.337–1–35) was the leading vote-getter in the league. The rest of the infield consisted of New York Yankees with the exception of the catcher. Willie Randolph (.283–4–21) was at second base, replacing the injured Molitor, Bucky Dent (.251–4–20) earned the starting nod at shortstop, and Graig Nettles (.246–14–39) was at third base, replacing Brett. Boston's Carlton Fisk (.300–9–30) was behind the plate. The outfield had Reggie Jackson (.289–20–53), Lynn and his bad hamstring (.311–8–39), and Ben Oglivie (.320–21–56). Oglivie's 21 home runs were tops in the

AL, but they weren't enough to earn enough votes for a starting slot in the AL outfield. With Rice sidelined, American League manager Earl Weaver named Oglivie as his replacement in the starting lineup.

The NL starting lineup had a decidedly blue tint as the hometown Dodgers were the beneficiaries of some serious ballot box stuffing. Steve Garvey (.291–18–66) was the starting first baseman. LA second baseman Davey Lopes (.239–5–19) led all vote-getters with more than 3.8 million, and garnered nearly as many votes as the next three contenders combined. Lopes' double play partner, Bill Russell (.291–3–20), was the starting shortstop, the first time he was named a starter, and St. Louis' Ken Reitz (.282–4–33) filled in for an injured Mike Schmidt at third base despite the fact that he had 1.3 million fewer votes than the second-place finisher, Ron Cey. Johnny Bench (.277–11–33) made his 13th straight All-Star appearance behind the plate.

Pirates outfielder Dave Parker (.286–10–43) was flanked in the NL outfield by Reggie Smith (.328–15–51) and Dave Kingman (.264–10–33). Fans at Chavez Ravine were so proficient in stuffing the ballot boxes that of the 12 players in the NL to amass more than two-million votes, seven wore Dodger Blue.

The mound matchup was a study in contrasts. J.R. Richard drew the start in the National League over Steve Carlton, who had beaten the Cardinals on the final day of the first half. Carlton's eight-inning, seven-strikeout performance was good for his 14th win of the season, which was tops in the major leagues. It also kept Chuck Tanner from naming him the starter.

With Carlton out of the mix, Richard got the nod. The Astros righty entered the All-Star break with a 10–4 record and a sparking 1.96 ERA along with 115 strikeouts in 110⅓ innings thanks to his dominant fastball. Tanner was hoping to keep Richard's weapons a secret by offering up a counter-espionage scouting report of his starter.

"His screwball is really tough in the twilight and his palm ball is tough," deadpanned Tanner. "It comes right at you and then takes a big drop. He changes speeds very well and works in and out around the plate. Sorry to give away your secrets, J.R."[36]

The last time Steve Stone had pitched in an All-Star Game was in high school in 1965, and his starting shortstop was Thurman Munson. Since then he'd torn his rotator cuff and won exactly 11 more big league games than he'd lost. But now he was 12–3 and the starting pitcher for the American League.

Stone was a fourth-round draft selection in 1969 out of Kent State University, where he was once again a teammate of Munson's, though by this time Thurman was behind the plate. Stone spent eight years with the Giants, Cubs and White Sox before ending up in Baltimore in 1979. After winning a career-best 12 games for the Cubs in 1975, he was hoping for a raise heading into 1976. Instead, Cubs owner Phil Wrigley proposed a cut of $2,500. Insulted, Stone didn't sign. Then he got hurt.

Cubs doctors couldn't diagnose his issue, but a kinesiologist at the University of Illinois named Tom Sattler eventually determined that Stone had a torn rotator cuff, a potentially career-ending injury. Rather than having corrective surgery, Stone decided to try a series of exercises to strengthen the shoulder. The rehab saved his career, but his once-potent fastball was now gone.

It was then that Stone began to rely more heavily on his curveball, and by 1980 it made him one of the top pitchers in the game. He opened the season with a record of 2–3 and then went on a tear. The curveball led him to ten straight wins from May 9 until the All-Star break.

So grateful for the honor was Stone that he wrote 31 different notes to his Orioles teammates and coaches, thanking them for their support. On the eve of the game, Stone visited a restaurant in Chinatown in Los Angeles and got a fortune cookie with his lunch. "The cookie said I would reach a high level of intelligence," Stone told the media. "What I wanted it to say was that that I was going to pitch three innings, allow no hits and strike out six."[37]

As it turned out, he wasn't far off. Stone turned in one of the best All-Star Game performances in recent memory, throwing three perfect innings against the best the National League had to offer. Even more impressive was that Stone went through nine hitters, stuck out three and only threw 24 pitches. Richard wasn't far behind, though he only threw two innings, per Houston manager Bill Virdon's request. Richard struck out three and gave way to Bob Welch, who was able to get himself out of a jam in the third inning. Willie Randolph led off with a single, but Welch picked him off first base. That turned out to be a big play, because Carew followed with a double that almost certainly would have scored Randolph. A walk to Reggie Jackson put two runners on, but Welch struck out Oglivie to get out of the inning.

In the top of the fifth, Welch retired Robin Yount and Randolph before Carew singled to right field, bringing up Fred Lynn. In the broadcast booth,

ABC color commentator Howard Cosell mentioned to Keith Jackson, "Something's 'gonna explode in this game, Keith."[38]

"Yup. You get that feeling," Jackson replied. "I suspect that Bob Welch would like very much to get Fred Lynn. Not have to go through the Reggie Jackson confrontation again."[39]

Welch and Jackson had a history that dated back to the 1978 World Series, when Jackson homered off the young Welch in an epic showdown. Two years later, the last thing Welch wanted was to face him again with two on in a scoreless All-Star Game.

Lynn worked the count full and on the payoff pitch, Welch missed his spot. Mets catcher John Stearns set up on the outside of the plate, but Welch's fastball was in, and Lynn smoked it into the right field stands. "You could sense something was about to happen and the explosion came," Cosell said. "Hamstring or no hamstring, Freddy Lynn did the job."[40]

The home run was Lynn's third in All-Star play and gave the AL a 2–0 lead. It wouldn't last long. AL skipper Earl Weaver brought Tommy John in, and he retired Garvey and Stearns, which brought up Kingman's spot in the order. In the National League dugout, Tommy Lasorda urged Tanner to pinch-hit Ken Griffey for Kingman. Lasorda was John's manager on the Dodgers and knew that John struggled to get Griffey out. As the Reds left fielder stepped into the batter's box, the ABC crew confirmed Lasorda's homework by flashing a graphic showing Griffey's numbers against John.

"An interesting graphic," said Cosell, as viewers reviewed the statistics. Griffey had a .422 career batting average against John in 45 at bats. John's next pitch was down and in, and Griffey jumped on it and sent it into the stands in right-center field. "See what I mean!" Cosell crowed. "He still owns Tommy John."[41]

The solo homer cut the AL lead to 2–1 but provided all the spark the National League needed. The Nationals scored two more in the sixth inning and one in the seventh, while the American League was completely shut down by a combination of Jerry Reuss, Jim Bibby and Bruce Sutter. The trio allowed just one hit over the final four innings of a 4–2 National League win.

The win further asserted the National League's dominance, much to the chagrin of players in the visiting clubhouse who were sick of hearing about it. "I'm not too proud of our record," said Bobby Grich. "You can't deny the fact that they've been winning the games. Sometimes you've got to go with what you see."[42]

"They've been getting the hits at the right time," said Rod Carew, who had played in 14 All-Star Games and been on the losing end of 13 of them. "I've never been one to believe they were superior. I hear we're not aggressive enough. That's a bunch of baloney as far as I'm concerned."[43]

"It might rattle some cages," Reggie Smith told the *LA Times*. "But I think the National League has better individual talent. It's a better league, a league with more talent. And that in itself makes better players."[44] The irony of Smith statement is that it came at a time when he was leading the National League in batting with a .328 average. That number would have placed him seventh in the AL batting race, and even further if Brett had enough at-bats to qualify, which his ankle injury prevented.

The game also marked the debut of something that would change forever the experience of attending a live sporting event. The 1980 All-Star Game was the first to feature the 560-square-foot video screen called "Diamond Vision." Manufactured by Mitsubishi, the video display board cost $3 million and showed instant replays to fans in the stands for the first time at a baseball game. The video screen was such a big deal that the *Los Angeles Times* sent Richard Hoffer to write a review of it. He wasn't impressed, citing the ability of the Dodgers to run ads to a captive audience a prospect he called "frightening."[45] He did concede that fans at the game enjoyed the idea of being able to see themselves on a giant TV screen in left field.

J.R. Richard stayed in Los Angeles after the All-Star Game and spent time with noted orthopedic surgeon Dr. Frank Jobe to try and determine what was causing his problems. After the meeting, Richard told the media and the Astros and Jobe had recommended that he not pitch for 30 days. The Astros disputed Richard's assertion, saying that two separate exams had found nothing wrong with Richard.

Something wasn't right, but Richard didn't know what it was and neither did any doctor he saw. He was trapped. He didn't feel like himself, but he was still getting big league hitters out. Just six days earlier, he had thrown two scoreless innings in the All-Star Game. He was 10–4 with an earned run average under 2.00. On July 14, he took the mound against the Braves. Things went okay for the first few innings. Richard struck out Glenn Hubbard to open the game and struck out the side in the top of the second. He doubled off Phil Niekro in the bottom of the third but didn't want to go out to pitch the fourth. Virdon, unconvinced that anything was wrong with him, coaxed him back out.

Richard walked Dale Murphy to lead off the fourth inning and got Chris Chambliss to ground out before pulling himself from the game with stomach problems. Atlanta won the game, 2–0, behind an outstanding performance by Phil Niekro, but the story, once again, was what was wrong with Richard. The answer depended on whom you asked. When asked about his ace's illness, Virdon was not in the mood. "Who's sick?" he asked. "That's not what he told me. He said his arm was getting tired."[46]

It was the tenth time in 17 starts that Richard had left complaining of some malady or another, yet no one could find anything physically wrong with him. It created genuine concern in some corners of the Astros clubhouse and genuine disdain in others. "We're in a pennant race and he pulls this?"[47] one anonymous teammate told the *Associated Press*.

When the media descended on Richard's locker after the game, they found him eating fried chicken and meatballs. He didn't do much to garner sympathy, saying, "I started feeling nauseated about the third inning."[48] When asked about Jobe's recommendation of 30 days' rest, Richard admitted that Jobe never said that. When asked why he lied, he said, "I just felt like it."[49]

Two days later, the Astros placed him on the disabled list after a 20-minute bullpen session. Richard said he had no pain but he could barely lift his arm above his head. In the heat of a pennant race, the Astros had lost their best pitcher to a mysterious malady. A *Sporting News* headline on Richard's situation trumpeted, "Houston has own JR Mystery,"[50] a play on the "Who shot JR?" mystery of the popular TV show, *Dallas*. It was an easy joke to make, but it was also a cheap shot.

In *The Sporting News* piece, Harry Shattuck wrote, "Pardon us Dallasites, but our JR saga may be as intriguing as yours ... and Houston's JR is real. Hard to believe, perhaps, but real."[51]

It was about to get much worse.

Johnny Bench had been squatting behind home plate since he was six years old. Over the next 26 years, he established himself as arguably the best catcher ever to play the game. He'd won Rookie of the Year, two MVP Awards, two World Series rings and ten Gold Gloves. But there was one record for catchers that had eluded him. On July 15, with the Reds leading the Expos, 7–4, in the bottom of the fifth inning, Bench stepped to the plate against Montreal's David Palmer and staked his claim.

Bench swung at Palmer's first pitch and knew immediately. As the ball headed towards the green seats in Riverfront Stadium's left field, Bench jumped out of the batter's box, raised his hands and began his joyous trip around the bases. The home run was the 347th of his career and his 314th as a catcher, moving him past Yogi Berra into first place on the all-time list among backstops. His teammates came out of the dugout to congratulate him, and Bench ran to the box seats behind home plate to give a kiss to his mom, Katie.

The home run may have rekindled the debate as to whether Bench was the best ever behind the plate, but he deftly deflected the question; sort of. "I think you're going to be judged by records and how people remember you," he told the *Cincinnati Enquirer*. "At least I think I'm in the top two. There's a lot of people in the Hall of Fame. None have hit as many homers as I have."[52]

The next day, Bench received the following telegram from Berra:

> Johnny,
>
> Congratulations on breaking my home run record last night. I always thought the record would stand until it was broken. It couldn't happen to a nicer guy. Best of luck the rest of the season, but take it easy on Dale and the Pirates. Maybe we'll see you in October.
>
> Yogi

At this point in the season, the prospect of the Reds playing meaningful games in October seemed unlikely. Bench's home run gave them a win over the Expos, but they were still in third place, 5½ games out of the National League West race, and they had just lost their best pitcher. But that didn't stop the Cincinnati front office from extending the contract of manager John McNamara through the end of 1981. Bench wanted a new deal, too, but Cincinnati president Dick Wagner wasn't budging. "The Reds have a contract with John Bench that has about two-and-a-half seasons to run," he said. "Both parties agreed to the contract in good faith in October 1977. At the time, it was one of the best [contracts] in the history of the game and even today ranks very high by all standards."[53]

The problem, as Bench and many other players saw it, was that the standards were changing quickly. Bench was a future Hall of Famer but he wasn't even the highest-paid player on his own team. That distinction belonged to George Foster, who signed a new contract in 1979 that paid him approximately $750,000 per season, nearly twice what Bench made. "I have the feeling I don't have to ask to have my contract renegotiated," he said. "Why should I? But I realize what happened in Kansas City when

George Brett wanted his contract renegotiated. Everybody else on the team wanted the same thing."[54]

Bench's assessment was dead on. But there was one major difference between him and the Royals star. Bench was nearing the end of his career, while Brett was enjoying the best season of his life.

George Brett was the hottest hitter in baseball when he went down on June 10 with torn ligaments in his ankle. In the 13 games prior to the injury, he had hit an amazing .491. For most players, missing a month would be tough to overcome, but Brett came back and began hitting like he hadn't missed a game. In the seven games after he returned to the lineup, he hit .586.

"When I was hurt, I spent … a lot of time thinking on hitting and fundamentals," he said after a 4-for-5 day against the Red Sox on July 16. "It has paid off."[55] Still, he insisted that hitting wasn't as easy as he was making it look. "Sure," said Boston manager Don Zimmer, under fire for a subpar season. "And I'm real popular in Boston."[56]

During Brett's 26-game absence, the Royals played .500 baseball, winning 13 games and losing 13. Fortunately for them, they actually added to their lead in the American League West, upping it from six games to 8½. Now that he was back, they were almost unstoppable. From July 10–25, the Royals went 12–4, outscored their opponents 105–61, and increased their AL West lead to 11 games.

In the National League, the Pittsburgh Pirates were nearly as hot as the Royals. Their marathon win over the Cubs earlier in the month helped, but they were still sputtering as they made their way to Philadelphia for a three-game series starting on July 12. The Phillies took game one of the series on Bob Boone's bottom-of-the-ninth single against Kent Tekulve. Pittsburgh evened the series the next day and sent Rick Rhoden to the mound in the series finale against Philadelphia's Randy Lerch. Neither was around very long.

Pittsburgh scored two runs in the top of the first inning, but the Phillies sent eight men to the plate in a four-run bottom of the first. From there the two teams swapped the lead back and forth until the top of the ninth inning, when Dave Parker's second home run of the game gave the Pirates a 13–11 win, a series victory that cut their deficit in the division to just 1½ games. Their second straight win over the Phillies was followed by five more. A 7–3 win over the Dodgers at home on July 19 moved them back into first place in the division.

On the day after they regained the lead in the NL East, the Pirates hosted the Dodgers for a doubleheader and special Willie Stargell Day ceremonies at Three Rivers Stadium. Despite temperatures nearing 100 degrees, more than 40,000 fans showed up to honor "Pops," who was on the disabled list with a knee injury. Both Stargell's teammates and the visiting Dodgers tried their best to ignore the heat and enjoy the love-fest for a man who was in his 19th season in Pittsburgh. Gifts included a mink cowboy hat and a solid gold Stargell Star. But what moved Stargell to tears was the surprise appearance of his parents. "The one thing I always wanted to do was play the game of baseball," he told the crowd. "I had the love and inner strength of my parents, particularly my mother, who was such a forceful individual in our family. I knew that with her love and guidance I would one day make her proud."[57]

Unfortunately the day wasn't a happy one for everyone. In the eighth inning of the first game, someone in the stands threw a 9-volt battery that narrowly missed Dave Parker in right field. It wasn't the first time someone threw something at him in his home ballpark, and he'd had enough. With Tanner's support, he left the game. "I could hear it go by me," he told the *Pittsburgh Press*. "It was too close for comfort. I wasn't going to stand there and give him another shot."[58]

Pirates Vice President Harding Peterson told the fans before the second game that he would not hesitate to pull his team off the field if it happened again, even if it meant forfeiting the game. Pirates fans' animosity towards Parker was difficult to understand. Certainly he made a lot of money, but he also produced. He was the MVP in 1978 and finished in the top ten in MVP voting in 1977 and 1979. He was poised to accept the torch from Stargell and lead the Pirates into the next decade. Yet fans didn't like him.

"I'm just not what the people of Pittsburgh want in right field," he said. "Whatever they want out there I hope they find it. I'll just go somewhere else."[59] He softened his stance a few days later and expressed hope that the situation with the fans could be worked out. The Pirates were playing good baseball, but all was not well within The Family.

Things were not going as planned on the other side of Pennsylvania either. In addition to the injuries on the pitching staff, Larry Bowa was banged up and Mike Schmidt was battling a slump and a hamstring injury. Tug McGraw hit the disabled list on July 2 with a shoulder problem, and three days later Greg Luzinski went down with a knee injury that eventually required surgery.

Then came the drug scandal. But in between, there was one bright spot. On July 6, Steve Carlton became the all-time strikeout leader among left-handed pitchers when he struck out Tony Scott of the Cardinals in St. Louis, fittingly on a slider in the dirt.

The moment had to be satisfying for Carlton, who began his career in St. Louis and was traded to the Phillies after a contract dispute in 1972. However, Carlton hadn't spoken to the media since 1976, so no one was certain about his feelings on the matter. But the fans in St. Louis hadn't forgotten his contribution to their team, nor were they unaware of the event they had just witnessed. After Scott's strikeout, the cheering didn't stop until "Lefty" emerged from the visitors' dugout to recognize the crowd.

"I've reflected on his achievements over the last 10 years and they're incredible," said Dallas Green. "At times he's been criticized for what he's done on and off the field but I think most of it is unjustified. In this game, production is the bottom line, and Lefty is a producer."[60]

That was certain, but the Phillies needed more than just Carlton to produce if they expected to reclaim the division title. After a red-hot May, the Phillies slipped back into mediocrity. They took three of four from the Braves at Veterans Stadium in late July before hosting the Astros in a big three-game series. Two straight victories, including a 17–4 win with Steve Carlton on the mound, had the Phillies feeling good. They felt even better knowing that they would face Gordie Pladson in the series opener rather than Richard.

Pladson entered his July 28 start against Philadelphia with an 0–2 record and ERA of 6.00. In his one previous start, the Expos had knocked him out in the second inning. But on this night he was masterful, allowing the Phillies just two runs in eight innings. Cesar Cedeno's tenth-inning triple off Ron Reed scored Jose Cruz to give the Astros a 3–2 win and drop the Phillies five games out in the division.

Perhaps sensing his team's fragility, Green passed on the opportunity to rip them publicly. "You guys think because [Pladson] has a big ERA he's out there to lose or get knocked around?" he asked the media after the game. "He's out there to earn his money, too. He had a good fastball and a good slider and he junked his curveball early when he couldn't get it over the plate."[61]

With two days to go in July, the Phillies were in third place in the NL East. They were running out of time to turn things around.

There was unrest in Chicago as well, and it came to a head on July 25 when the Cubs fired manager Preston Gomez. Chicago was 39–52 and in last place in the NL East, so the firing wasn't entirely unexpected, but Gomez went out guns blazing.

> Was I sent to war without any guns? I would say so. We had a lot of injuries and you can't run a horse with two legs. Besides the injuries, though, I think I was misled. When I talked to the general manager a few weeks ago, he told me that he thinks we should do this and we should do that for next season. Why would he say that to me if he didn't plan to keep me?[62]
>
> By the second day of spring training I could see the situation. More unhappy players than I've seen on any team. No kind of an organization. And I said to myself, "What in the hell am I doing here?"[63]

"I did this to shake up the club," said Kennedy. "I know it was sudden, but it was something that needed to be done. He was fired, he didn't resign."[64]

Among the players siding with Gomez was pitcher Bruce Sutter, who made no secret of his feelings about the Cubs' front office. "Three months ago, Bob Kennedy was saying what a smart baseball man Preston Gomez was; now he's fired. It's Kennedy's fault for not getting us more players. Preston did a good job with what we have. I don't think any manager we get will make much difference."[65]

After undergoing more extensive medical testing, J.R. Richard was released from the hospital and cleared for supervised workouts on July 26. Four days later, during a workout at the Astrodome, Richard collapsed in the outfield. He was rushed to Methodist Hospital, where doctors determined that he had suffered a stroke. He underwent emergency surgery to remove a clot from his neck to restore circulation to his brain, but the big man who had been questioned by many for asking to be taken out of games had nearly died. Then the doubters began to change their collective tune.

"Guilt has seized a lot of people in this town who believed in the weeks before his problem was diagnosed ... that Richard was playing his own kind of game,"[66] wrote columnist Mickey Herskowitz of the *Houston Post* on August 3. "Some wrote or said as much, and if anyone expressed any sympathy, or offered him the benefit of the doubt, no real notice was paid.... Our concern and shock were mixed with embarrassment, and we ought to admit it."[67]

6

August
Streaks, Suspensions and Spittle

"My wife, Bev, loved Ted Williams," said Duke Snider in his August 3 Hall of Fame induction speech. "I'd go 2 for 4; home run, 3 RBIs. I'd come home, she'd say, 'You had a good day, honey, but Ted got 3 for 4.'"[1]

Hall of Fame weekend in Cooperstown, New York, allows baseball to celebrate the past and take a breath before heading into the final two months of the regular season. Former Dodgers great Snider joined Detroit Tigers star Al Kaline, Boston Red Sox owner Tom Yawkey and Phillies slugger Chuck Klein as the newest members of baseball's most exclusive club. The next day it was one of Snider's former teammates taking center stage.

From their inception in 1977, the Seattle Mariners were not a good ballclub. In three seasons, Seattle's best finish was a 67–95 mark in 1979. But they had hope heading into 1980. In their first two seasons, the Mariners had exactly one pitcher win ten or more games. But in 1979 they had three, and they all returned for 1980. "The Mariners are the best young team at the major league level today," general manager Dan O'Brien told *The Sporting News* in February. "Pitching is the best part of the team."[2]

But by August, the Mariners were dismal once again. Seattle opened the second half of the season with a 35–45 record and then lost 23 of 27 games. O'Brien decided he'd seen enough. On August 4, he fired manager Darrell Johnson and replaced him with former Dodgers star Maury Wills.

"We regret having to dismiss Darrell after three years of continuous progress, but there seemed to be a definite need for a new direction," said O'Brien. "My hope is that Maury is the same as a manager as he was as a player—determined as hell and aggressive."[3]

Wills was definitely an aggressive player, especially on the base paths. In 14 major league seasons, he stole 586 bases, including a modern-day record 104 in 1962, earning him MVP honors. After retiring as a player in 1972, he spent time in the broadcast booth and managing in the winter leagues. He'd made no secret of his desire to pilot a major league club, but hadn't had the opportunity that fit until the Mariners called.

When they did, he became just the third African American field manager in baseball history, following in the footsteps of Frank Robinson, who managed the Cleveland Indians in 1975–1977, and Larry Doby, who managed the Chicago White Sox in 1978. "I don't look at myself as any kind of a pioneer," Wills told the *Associated Press*. "I don't know what's going to happen, but I didn't accept this position with any thoughts of paving the way for other former black players to become managers in the major leagues."[4]

As Wills took over in Seattle, more details were emerging about J.R. Richard's health, and they weren't good. "I think it's very possible that he will not be back this year,"[5] said Dr. Charles McCollum, who removed the blood clot from Richard's neck. He was still experiencing weakness in his left arm and leg, and while a return to the field in 1980 was perhaps overly optimistic, the big question was whether he'd return at all. "We have seen people with major strokes return to almost normal activities, and J.R.'s youth and tremendous physical conditioning should be in his favor,"[6] McCollum added.

The other thing that was now finally in his favor was public opinion. After enduring questions about his attitude and hearing whispers that he was faking an injury, Richard was now a sympathetic figure. All it took was a life-threatening stroke. *Sports Illustrated* ran a harrowing moment-by-moment account of Richard's collapse, along with an update on his condition. The article, titled "Now Everyone Believes Him," also addressed the role race may have played in the situation.

"Black and big, a big star," Richard's wife, Carolyn, told *SI*'s William Nack. "Other guys had problems on the Astros. Ken Forsch had problems. Ryan hasn't been pitching to his ability. I've never seen a player dragged through the mud like this. I don't know why, in 1980, they chose to do it to Rodney. But they did. It took death, or nearly death, to get an apology. They should have believed him."[7]

Los Angeles Times columnist Jim Murray addressed the race issue as well in his August 8 column.

J.R. Richard was on his way to the best season of his life before a stroke ended his season and his career (National Baseball Hall of Fame Library, Cooperstown, New York).

> There's a myth in baseball that certain classes of players are more susceptible to fits of "dogging" than others. This dread ballplayers' palsy is widely believed to affect blacks more than whites and Latins more than either. I have never seen anything to substantiate it.
>
> The word was that J.R. Richard wasn't sick, he was sulking. He didn't have any serious malady, he was just looking for sympathy.... When that theory saw print, J.R. Richard was about as popular as J.R. Ewing. Suddenly he was the black pitcher in the black hat.[8]

Richard's return was doubtful, but in Cincinnati a star pitcher was returning to the rotation at just the right time. The Reds were coming off a ten-game road trip in which they'd lost five of their last six games and needed a boost. They got it in the form of Tom Seaver. Cincinnati was 6½ games out of first place in the NL West when Seaver last pitched on June 30. Despite his absence, the Reds managed to trim two and a half games off their deficit when they began a seven-game homestand against the Padres and Dodgers at Riverfront Stadium.

Seaver pitched the first game of an August 4 double header against San Diego and looked like his old self again, allowing just four hits and one walk in six innings of a 7–1 Reds win. Cincinnati won game two, 11–2, behind Mario Soto and an eight-run seventh inning to complete the sweep. After a horrible June, the Reds' pitching staff stepped up in Seaver's absence, but his return would be a key to their repeating as division champs in 1980. "Ten days or even a week ago when we were having trouble Houston or Los Angeles could have buried us and they didn't," said manager John McNamara. "Now we're getting healthy with Seaver back and George Foster hitting the ball well, and we have a shot at it in August and September."[9]

While the Reds were battling back in the division, the Dodgers were battling each other. A day after Seaver's return, LA was in Atlanta taking on the Braves, and things weren't going well. The Dodgers took a 4–1 lead into the bottom of the ninth inning, when Atlanta scored five runs with two outs to pull out the win. The loss caused tempers to flare in the visiting clubhouse of Atlanta-Fulton County Stadium.

With Charlie Spikes up in the last inning, Dodgers manager Tommy Lasorda told center fielder Derrel Thomas to take a few steps back, and Thomas refused. His positioning didn't come into play in the outcome of the game, but it still didn't sit well with many Dodgers, or Lasorda, who confronted Thomas after the game. Thomas also exchanged words with

Reggie Smith, who became so incensed that he slammed his arm into a cooler and suffered a cut that required 60 stitches to close. Smith was already out of the lineup with a shoulder injury that would eventually cost him his season, but adding 60 stitches didn't help things.

The next day, it was the Braves who lost their tempers. Atlanta trailed 3–2 in the top of the ninth inning when Steve Garvey hit what appeared to be an inning-ending double play ball to second baseman Glenn Hubbard. But umpire Jerry Dale ruled that Hubbard's throw pulled shortstop Rafael Ramirez off the bag at second, and he called Dusty Baker safe. Instead of a double play, the Dodgers had two on and two out. Cox flew out of the dugout to confront Dale, and in the process more than words were exchanged between the two men. "Oh I did it," Cox said. "I spit in his face intentionally, but not until after he spit in my face first."[10]

"Cox spit tobacco juice in my face and all over my shirt," Dale said. "He spit right in my eye the first time. I've never had anyone do that. It's a disgraceful and cowardly act."[11] Cox's version of the story was that he sprayed Dale unintentionally at first, but when Dale spit on him, all bets were off. "I would never spit at an umpire intentionally. I would never spit in anybody's face. If a guy hits you in the jaw, you hit him back."[12]

National League President Chub Feeney wasn't interested in Cox's line of reasoning and suspended him for three games, along with a $300 fine. But the biggest machismo showdown in the NL West came on August 9, when the Astros and Padres faced off in the Astrodome. In the top of the first inning, Dave Winfield dug in against Nolan Ryan with two out and Ozzie Smith on second base. Neither Ryan nor Winfield was going to be intimidated. Ryan came up and in to the Padres' right fielder before eventually getting him to fly out to center field to end the inning.

On the bench, San Diego first baseman Willie Montanez suggested that pitchers would continue to pitch Winfield inside unless he did something about it. Winfield was in the final year of his contract, and negotiations with the Padres were not going well. It was a given that he would leave at the end of the season, and the Padres, having already fired their general manager, were going nowhere in 1980.

With all this going through his mind, Winfield led off the top of the fourth, and Ryan came up and in again. "Dammit, don't you ever throw at me!"[13] Winfield yelled and charged the mound. Once he got there he took a swing at Ryan, connecting with the back of his head as both benched emptied.

Once things settled down, Winfield was ejected, while Ryan remained in the game. Cesar Cedeno's two doubles and four RBI led Houston to the win, which kept them a half-game up over the Dodgers, who beat the Reds 9–4 that day.

"I don't know what's going on in a guy's mind to cause a display like that," Ryan calmly told the press afterward. "I was just trying to pitch inside, and I was wild. I was as surprised as anybody by the display he put on."[14]

Winfield viewed his actions more along the lines of self-preservation rather than a "display," saying, "He throws too hard to come that close that consistently. I don't dislike anybody and I rarely do that. It's hard to provoke me that much. Basically the pitcher is in control in that situation. If he wants to hit you, he can."[15]

There was a different kind of fight going on in the American League East. On August 1, the Yankees led the Baltimore Orioles by 7½ games. Then the Orioles got hot, trimming three games off their deficit in the first week of August before heading into Yankee Stadium for what was now a big three-game series.

More than 50,000 fans packed the Stadium for the series opener, which featured Baltimore ace Jim Palmer against the Yankees' Ron Guidry. Ruppert Jones' seventh-inning solo homer off Palmer gave New York a 2–1 lead, but the Orioles came back with four runs in the final two innings off Guidry and Goose Gossage and won the game, 5–2.

The next day, Ken Singleton's eighth inning triple off Tom Underwood gave the Orioles a lead, and Terry Crowley's pinch-hit single off Goose Gossage two batters later gave the Orioles a 4–2 win. "Gossage throws hard and you just have to prepare yourself and be ready," Crowley said afterwards. "I knew I hit the ball hard, but I just wanted to see it land in center field. Now I feel we've done our job here. Sunday is a bonus, we've already won the series."[16]

"I didn't feel any pressure," said Baltimore starter Steve Stone, who threw 136 pitches while going the distance for his 18th win. "If I had got knocked out in the first inning, I would've come in here and read my book."[17] Instead, his true crime book, "Blood Will Tell," about a Texas Oil baron accused of murder, sat idle in his locker while the Yankees were wondering how their lead had evaporated so quickly.

"They're playing hot right now," said Reggie Jackson. "If they play like this all the way through, they're going to beat us. But if we hang on like men, we'll be O.K."[18] The Yankees held on for eight innings in the series finale until Eddie Murray's two-out double off Tommy John gave the Orioles a 6–5 win and a series sweep. It was Baltimore's ninth straight win and their 20th in their last 25 games. They weren't dead yet.

"Can I remind everybody in New York that the Baltimore Orioles are the American League champions?" asked Earl Weaver. "I know exactly what they're saying over there [in the Yankees clubhouse]. They're saying, 'We're two and a half in front and we play Chicago and they've got to go to Kansas City.'"[19]

Weaver was correct about the schedule, but incorrect about the attitude in the home clubhouse at Yankee Stadium. There was genuine concern. "We're making too many mistakes," said shortstop Bucky Dent. "We're beating ourselves. You just can't keep doing that day in and day out."[20]

Once the Orioles left town, the Yankees and their fans were able to relax a bit and turn their attention to impending history. Reggie Jackson had been sitting on 399 career homers for a week, and if fans were getting anxious for him to get to 400, he wasn't. "Will I press to try and get my 400th homer?" he asked. "Hah, hah.... I got 50 more games to go get one homer. You figure it out."[21]

Number 399 came off the Rangers' Dave Rajsich on August 4 and was dedicated to George Steinbrenner's father, who was in the hospital. "I called him today," Reggie told the New York media after hitting the homer. "I told him to watch the game, and that if I hit 399 the ball would be his. When the kid who brought the ball in gave it to me, George gave the kid a TV."[22]

On August 11, Reggie Jackson stepped in against Chicago's Britt Burns in the fourth inning with no one on and sent number 400 into the right field stands to give the Yankees a 1–0 lead. With the crowd on its feet, he crossed home plate and headed straight to the box seats, where he hugged his father, Martinez. Once the hugs were complete, Reggie headed into the Yankees dugout but emerged twice to acknowledge the crowd. Chicago tied it in the sixth inning, but the Yankees scored twice in the top of the ninth inning to win the game, 3–1, and keep pace with the Orioles, who beat the Kansas City Royals, 2–1, on an Eddie Murray solo homer off Larry Gura.

Becoming just the 19th player in history to reach the 400-homer mark called for a celebration, and Jackson went out to sample the New

York night life. Shortly before 2 a.m., he exited Jim McMullen's, one of his favorite Manhattan haunts, when he was approached by a young kid with a large gun. "It was the biggest gun I ever saw," Jackson told the New York police. "He was pointing the gun at my head. I thought he was going to shoot me."[23]

The assailant lowered the gun to reach into Reggie's Rolls Royce and grab the keys. Jackson seized the opportunity to smack the kid with the door of the luxury car, causing him to run away. "Have you ever had a guy point a gun at your head and thought he was going to shoot you?" Jackson asked. "Let me tell you it's some trip."[24]

The Philadelphia Phillies began a trip of a different kind at the beginning of August, one that would go a long way toward deciding if they would be a factor in the NL East race. The Phillies trailed the Pirates by just two games when they began a four-game set that included a doubleheader on August 10.

Down 5–2 in the top of the seventh inning of the series opener, the Phils climbed back in it with back-to-back home runs off Pirates starter Rick Rhoden by the unlikely duo of Garry Maddox and Manny Trillo, and tied the game an inning later when Lonnie Smith scored on a ground ball. But a Lee Lacy sacrifice fly off Tug McGraw scored pinch-runner Matt Alexander, and the Pirates took game one.

They also took game two, behind John Candelaria, dropping the Phillies to 4½ games out and putting them in the tough position of needing a doubleheader sweep to salvage a series split. Making matters worse was that they had to beat Jim Bibby, who entered August 10 with a 13–2 record. Philadelphia sent 3–12 Randy Lerch to the mound. On paper, it was a terrible mismatch. It turned out to be one on the field, too, as the Pirates smacked Lerch around for five runs and eight hits in 5⅓, while Bibby allowed just a single run in a 7–1 Pittsburgh victory.

In between games, with the media waiting to get into the Phillies clubhouse, Dallas Green laid into his team. The doors were closed, but Green's voice had no trouble escaping, and the media gathered outside heard the entire tirade.

> This bleeping game isn't easy. But you guys have got your bleeping heads down. You've gotta stop being so bleeping cool. Get it through your bleeping heads! If you don't you'll be get so bleeping buried it ain't gonna be funny.[25]
>
> Get the bleep off your asses and just be the way you can be because you're a good bleeping baseball team. But you're not now and you can't look in the

> bleeping mirror and tell me you are. If you don't want to bleeping play, get the bleep in that manager's office and bleeping tell me because I don't want to bleeping play you.[26]

Green's speech was so inspiring that the Phillies promptly lost game two of the twinbill, 4–1, but not without incident. In the bottom of the seventh inning with the Pirates leading, 3–1, Green instructed relief pitcher Ron Reed to issue an intentional walk to Pittsburgh first baseman Willie Stargell. An obviously frustrated Reed kicked the dirt on the mound in disgust before following orders, but he was still upset when he returned to the dugout.

Words were exchanged, and suddenly Phillies players and coaches had to intervene before the 6'6" Reed and the 6'5" Green came to blows. In addition, some of the Pirates faithful were quite boisterous in their taunting of the Phillies, including one fan who climbed on top of the dugout to tell shortstop Larry Bowa exactly what he thought of the Phillies' chances to return to the playoffs. Philadelphia appeared to be unraveling. The headline in the next day's *Philadelphia Daily News* posed the question, "Beginning of the End?"[27] A star-studded roster had produced a record of 55–52, including ten straight road losses. They had 55 games to straighten out their season.

"I'm just not going to let them quit on themselves," Green said after the series finale. "The fans in Philadelphia haven't quit, so we're not going to let them quit either. I may not be doing it the right way, but I'm doing it the only way I know how."[28]

Emotions were running hot in the Phillies clubhouse, but Pete Rose caught the message behind Green's tirade and he agreed with it. "The meeting, I think, was absolutely right," he said. "I understood what he was saying, but I can't speak for the other guys. Just because we got beat 4–1, don't mean it didn't sink in because there's a good possibility it may have."[29]

There are certain players who transcend the game and endear themselves to the cities in which they play for years. The summer of 1980 saw the debut on one of those players and the final hurrah for another.

Joe Charboneau grew up Santa Clara, California, where he participated in bare-fisted fights in boxcars as a teenager to make extra money. He suffered multiple broken noses, one of which he set by himself using a pair of pliers. He also performed his own dental work, using a razor blade and a pair of vice grips, cut out an ill-conceived tattoo with a razor blade, opened beer bottles with his eye socket, had a pet alligator in the minor leagues that almost ate a teammate's kitten, and stitched himself back together after another fight using fishing wire.

Charboneau began his career in the Philadelphia organization but didn't fit in with the way the Phillies thought a ballplayer should conduct himself. In 1976, he hit .298 for the Phillies' Class A Spartanburg team and advanced to the Carolina League in 1977 with Peninsula. But after starting the season 3-for-17 at the plate, he found himself on the bench and on the outs with manager Jim Snyder and the organization. Fed up, Charboneau decided to leave the team and return home. But he was coaxed back, and in 1978 the Phillies loaned him to the Minnesota Twins, who assigned him to Visalia in the California League. Given a chance to play regularly, Charboneau responded with a .350 batting average, 18 home runs and 116 RBI.

A spring training injury to Andre Thornton allowed Joe Charboneau to make the Indians' Opening Day roster, win the AL Rookie of the Year Award, and become a Cleveland icon (National Baseball Hall of Fame Library, Cooperstown, New York).

Following the 1978 season, the Phillies traded Charboneau to the Cleveland Indians, and his career took off in 1979. He was assigned to Cleveland's AA affiliate in Chattanooga, Tennessee, and dominated, hitting a Southern League-leading .352 with 21 homers and 78 RBI.

"I know what he did at Chattanooga," Cleveland manager Dave Garcia told the *Akron Beacon Journal* before spring training began. "I understand he's a good hitter. If he doesn't make the club as a regular, though, I don't think we keep him as an extra man. It wouldn't be fair to him."[30]

When the Indians'

camp opened, the rookie asserted himself right away by getting three hits in the team's first intrasquad game. A few days later, he made news not with his bat, but because of one of the more bizarre spring training injuries in baseball history.

On March 8, the Indians were in Mexico City to play a series of exhibition games against some Mexican teams. Charboneau and two teammates were waiting outside the hotel for the team bus when a man named Oscar Villalobos Martinez approached them and asked Charboneau where he was from. When Charboneau responded that he was from California, the man stabbed him with a ballpoint pen, going deep enough to strike a rib. "I just froze until we hit the ground," Charboneau said. "When we were on the ground, he pulled the pen out and was trying to get me in the eye. I'm just happy [teammate Tom] Brennan could pull him away."[31]

About 45 minutes later, an ambulance showed up to take Charboneau to the hospital, where the wound was stitched up. His assailant was tried and fined 50 pesos, about $2.25. Fortunately the injury didn't keep him out of the lineup long, but an injury to an established star proved to be just the break Charboneau needed. On March 25, Indians first baseman Andre Thornton injured his knee in a game against the Angels. What was originally thought to be a minor injury ended up costing Thornton his season, but it also opened up a roster spot for Charboneau, and he took advantage of the opportunity.

An Opening Day home run against the Angels got his season off to a good start, and by the end of April, Charboneau was batting .354. "Super Joe" had arrived. A local band, "Section 36," wrote a song called *Go Joe Charboneau*, which reached #3 on the charts in Cleveland, and everyone wanted a piece of the rookie from California. On August 4, "Super Joe" was signing autographs before a game against Toronto when he spotted a young girl with braces on her legs. As he signed a baseball for her, she asked him to hit a home run for her. Not really thinking, Charboneau said yes. Now the pressure was on. He was having an outstanding season and had become an icon in Cleveland, but hitting home runs on demand for stricken children was something else entirely.

Indians shortstop Toby Harrah walked to lead off the bottom of the second inning, and Charboneau stepped in against Toronto starter Paul Mirabella. On Mirabella's first pitch, Charboneau hit a line drive into the left field seats for his 16th home run of the season. "The first thing I thought of when I hit the ball was the little girl," said Charboneau in his 1981 autobiography, *Super Joe*. "I was so happy for her."[32]

He later learned the young girl had spina bifida, a birth defect affecting the spinal cord. After meeting her and learning her story, Charboneau became the local chairman of the Spina Bifida Association. Just another reason for Clevelanders to love him. It had been 26 years since Indians fans had seen their team in the post-season, and they were subjected to a lot of bad baseball over that period. Charboneau gave Cleveland fans hope and a bona fide Rookie of the Year candidate.

"The thing about Joe Charboneau is that major-league pitching doesn't intimidate him," said Indians hitting coach Tom McCraw. "A lot of rookies come up and say, 'Oh, gee, Gaylord Perry's pitching, Fergie Jenkins is pitching. I'll never hit them.' But this kid comes to the ballpark and hits like he's at (AA) Chattanooga.[33] ... I think if he keeps progressing, keeps disciplining himself, he'll be the best hitter in the game in two years."[34]

Four years earlier, there was even more hype for a different rookie. In 1976, Mark Fidrych was more than a baseball player; he was a phenomenon. Nicknamed "The Bird," Fidrych captured the country's attention on June 28 when he beat the Yankees on "Monday Night Baseball." It was the birth of "Birdmania" and an amazing run for the 21-year-old from Worcester, Massachusetts. By the end of the summer, he would hang out with Elton John, start the All-Star Game, grace the cover of *Rolling Stone* magazine, and be named Rookie of the Year.

Unfortunately for Fidrych, his success disappeared as quickly as it arrived. He injured his knee in spring training of 1977 and didn't make his first start until May 27. Though he lost the game, 1–0, he was outstanding, going the distance while allowing just one run on eight hits. The Bird was back, or so it seemed. But by July, his season was over. What was originally described as a tired arm was considerably more serious than that.

In his haste to return from the knee injury, Fidrych had injured his throwing shoulder. The injury was severe enough to limit him to just seven major league appearances over the next two seasons. By 1980, the once-promising pitcher and media darling was trying to salvage his career. The 1980 season also saw a different Mark Fidrych. Some of the boyish enthusiasm was gone, replaced by sharp words and criticism of the organization during spring training.

After being sent to AAA Evansville at the end of March, Fidrych was miffed when manager Sparky Anderson was not among those who showed up to watch him pitch in an intrasquad game. "I noticed Sparky wasn't there," he said. "I don't know, maybe he's off his feed. I could care less. All this is doing is cutting into my pension time. This thing is nothing but a business with them and it's costing me money. I might be wrong, but I'm pretty sure I haven't lost any money for the Detroit Tigers."[35]

When the criticism hit the newspapers, Anderson didn't hold back. "Evidently he drew big crowds when he pitched," Anderson said. "and he feels he made the Tigers money, correct? Then, if that's so, how many big crowds has he drawn in the last 2½ years? Have the Tigers paid him? Well, then, when does the balancing come out?"[36]

After going 6–7 at Evansville, Fidrych was recalled by the Tigers, and on August 12, made his first major league start in nearly 15 months against the Boston Red Sox. He made the Tigers money as more than 48,000 fans showed up at Tiger Stadium.

The Red Sox jumped on Fidrych early, scoring four runs in the first two innings, but "The Bird" bounced back, throwing five shutout innings before allowing a solo home run to Jim Dwyer in the eighth inning to break a 4–4 tie. Boston edged out Detroit, 5–4, but Fidrych's return had the Tigers, and their manager, excited. "I've been in four World Series," said Anderson. "And I was more excited tonight than I was for any of them. The way he's throwing, I don't think the hoopla will fall off. I was very, very excited. I don't think you can pitch any better the first time than that."[37]

"He's back for real," pitching coach Roger Craig told the *Detroit Free Press*. "I was impressed. If he keeps pitching like that he's going to win a lot of games."[38] But he didn't keep pitching like that. He was hit hard by the Texas Rangers in his second start, giving up six earned runs in 4⅔ innings. He surrendered 12 hits to the Minnesota Twins in a loss on August 22 and lasted just two innings against the Brewers six days later. Worse yet, he was booed at Tiger Stadium.

"That's life.... I deserved them," he said. "Right now I'm breathing with scuba gear. I look at my stuff and it was nothing. I'm not doing my job."[39]

While Fidrych was struggling, George Brett was having the best month of his career. After going 0-for-4 against the Boston Red Sox on July 17, the Royals' third baseman hit in 30 straight games. But unlike Ken

Landreaux's streak earlier in the season, Brett was getting multiple hits per game and, more importantly, his team was winning.

"The way George Brett is hitting right now, God could have him down no balls and two strikes and he'd get a hit," said umpire Steve Palermo. "I wouldn't go that far," replied Brett's teammate, Hal McRae. "If the Lord was up 0–2, He might get George out ... but God better hit the black."[40]

From mid–July until the streak was snapped on August 18, Brett hit .467 with six homers and 42 RBI while the Royals went 23–7. But the highlight of the month came on August 17 at home against the Toronto Blue Jays. In the bottom of the eighth inning with the Royals leading, 5–3, Brett stepped in against Toronto relief pitcher Mike Barlow and doubled to left field to score three runs. More than 30,000 fans stood to applaud their hero, who raised his arms above his head at second base to acknowledge their admiration. His 4-for-4 day brought his season batting average to .401.

"Goosebumps, just goosebumps," Brett told the media after the game. "It was electrifying to stand on second and hear the crowd. When I got to .399, I said to myself that if I hadn't chased a bad ball last night I'd be at .400 already. I told myself to wait and relax.... I was very relaxed today. I wanted that hit."[41]

No one had hit .400 for an entire season since Ted Williams, who hit .406 for the Boston Red Sox in 1941. The closest anyone had come in recent memory was Rod Carew, who finished the 1977 season at .388, but Carew dropped below the .400 mark on July 11 and never got back there. George Brett was at .401 with 45 games remaining in the season, and he was hitting better than he ever had in his life.

Brett's chase for .400 was the only unknown surrounding the Royals, who had built a 14-game lead over Oakland by mid–August, but the other races were still tight. After fighting their way back into the hunt in the AL East, the Orioles had another big chance to gain ground on the Yankees in a five-game series in Baltimore from August 14–18.

Steve Stone picked up win number 19 in the series opener by beating Tom Underwood, 6–1, thanks to home runs from Gary Roenicke, Rich Dauer and Ken Singleton. The victory cut the Yankees' lead to just 2½ games, but New York took the next two games behind Tommy John and newly-acquired Gaylord Perry to increase their lead to 4½ games.

Game Four featured Baltimore's 26-year-old Scott McGregor, sporting a 13–6 record with a 3.50 ERA against New York's Luis Tiant, who was 13 years older than McGregor with a lofty 5.13 ERA Tiant made his major-league debut against the Yankees in 1964, throwing a four-hit shutout against a lineup featuring Roger Maris, Joe Pepitone and Tom Tresh. Sixteen years later, he was nearly as good. Baltimore managed just one run against Tiant, but McGregor was just a bit better, going the distance while allowing five hits and no runs. The Orioles had won five of their last seven games against New York and had Jim Palmer going in the series finale against Yankees ace Ron Guidry. "If we win tomorrow it's a real race, said Dempsey. "If not, we're not out of it, but it will be tougher to catch them. We couldn't afford many mistakes."[42]

Steve Stone rode his curveball to a 25–7 record and the 1980 AL Cy Young Award (National Baseball Hall of Fame Library, Cooperstown, New York).

The anticipated pitchers' duel between former Cy Young Award winners Palmer and Guidry didn't materialize as Baltimore knocked the Yankees lefty out of the game after just 3⅔ innings en route to grabbing a 6–2 lead after five innings. The Yankees scored three runs in the eighth inning off Palmer and Tippy Martinez, but Tim Stoddard got Bucky Dent on a controversial called third strike with two on in the ninth to preserve the win and pull the Orioles to within 2½ games of the division lead.

"The ball was outside." said a flustered Dent after the game. "It was a slider away. It was outside. He [home plate umpire Rich Garcia] said it was a strike."[43] "That was a perfect slider," said Stoddard. "the kind of pitch you always want to make."[44]

The five-game series

drew a major league single-series record 253,636 fans, nearly as many as the Oakland A's drew in all of 1979, and showed that the Orioles were still a factor in the AL East. Baltimore had won 13 of their last 17 games, while New York had lost six of their last eight. "Psychologically, now, they know if they don't play good baseball, what we're going to do is pass them," said catcher Rick Dempsey. "I, for one, don't want to see them anymore. We'll take our chances."[45]

A day after the Yankees series, the Orioles headed west to face the Angels and jumped on them early, scoring single runs in the second, fourth, fifth, seventh and eighth innings while Steve Stone flirted with a no-hitter. California finally pushed two runs across in the bottom of the eighth, but the 5–2 lead was plenty for Stone as he became the major leagues' first 20-game winner and the 22nd and perhaps most unlikely in Orioles history. "Good defense, timely hitting and good relief work, that's what it takes. I'm not what you call a shutout pitcher, so I have to have some help to win 20 games. I think the ballclub is the major reason I've done it."[46]

Reaching the 20-win mark in mid–August definitely established Stone as the front-runner for the AL Cy Young Award, and the respect he had for his teammates worked both ways. "If he didn't handle things so well he'd be cocky," said shortstop Mark Belanger. "But Steve just does not believe he'll ever lose another game ... and he's throwing like he might not."[47]

That Stone might not lose another game was not lost on the Yankees, particularly their owner, George Steinbrenner. After the Orioles/Yankees series, Steinbrenner convened a "summit meeting" in Tampa with his baseball brass and then lashed out at his players in the press. "Reggie hit .120 in the Baltimore series," "The Boss" complained to the *New York Times*. "If that isn't tanking, I've never seen tanking."[48]

But he wasn't finished. "He's killed us," said Steinbrenner of Eric Soderholm, who went 2-for-15 in the series. "He's been ridiculously bad."[49]

Steinbrenner also had some advice for his manager, Dick Howser, who by 1980 had a mere 22 years of experience in professional baseball compared to Steinbrenner's eight. "Here's [Eric] Soderholm hitting .147," explained Steinbrenner, "and he lets him hit away with a runner at first base. Bunt him over and then you tie the game. But our guy is a freshman manager and he made some mistakes."[50]

Things were also tightening up in the National League West. The Ryan/Winfield fight was a win for Ryan and the Astros, but they'd struggled since. Bill Virdon's club began the month with a 1½-game lead in the division, but after a 6–5, 12-inning loss to the Giants on August 13, they found themselves in third place, behind the Dodgers and the Cincinnati Reds, who had won eight of ten to take over the top spot.

Ryan won the series opener against the Padres on August 14, 3–1, and managed to pitch to Winfield without incident. Game two pitted San Diego's Rick Wise against Houston's Gordie Pladson, who was returning to the mound after missing a start when his cat clawed the index finger of his pitching hand.

Craig Stimac's single off Pladson in the bottom of the second inning gave San Diego a 1–0 lead. The Astros tied it on an RBI groundout by Denny Walling in the top of the fourth, and from there, the two pitching staffs combined for 15 scoreless innings. Futility reigned as the Astros loaded the bases in the seventh inning and didn't score, had two runners thrown out on the bases in the eighth, and hit into a bases-loaded double play in the 11th.

But the Padres were even worse. They left the bases loaded in the 11th and stranded two runners in the 13th, 14th, 16th, 18th and 19th innings. Luis Pujols led off the top of the 20th with a ground ball to shortstop, but Ozzie Smith's throw was off the mark and Pujols was on board. Art Howe bunted to advance Pujols, but Padres pitcher Eric Rasmussen's attempt to get the lead runner at second failed as well. Two batters later, Terry Puhl lifted a fly ball to right field that bounced between Winfield and center fielder Jerry Mumphry for a three-base error. Houston's Dave Smith retired the Padres in the bottom of the 20th to wrap up the six-hour, 17-minute win, which also moved the Astros into a first-place tie with the Dodgers, who leapfrogged the Reds. Houston had found their way and went on a ten-game winning streak.

On the same weekend the Astros began to pull away in the NL West, two American League owners pulled out of the game completely. On August 22, White Sox owner Bill Veeck announced that he had a deal in place to sell his team for $20 million to a group headed by Youngstown, Ohio, real estate developer Edward DeBartolo Sr. Veeck was a beloved figure in Chicago for his fan-friendly attitude and his ties to the city. It was he, as the son of the owner of the Chicago Cubs, who installed the iconic ivy on the outfield walls at Wrigley Field in 1937, and it was also he who kept the Sox from leaving town when he bought the team in 1975. "The Sox were on their way to Seattle when we got here, so at least we saved them for Chicago," he said. "We neither made money nor lost money, but the hell with money."[51]

DeBartolo's purchase of the White Sox was the latest chapter in his family's dalliance with professional sports. He purchased the San Francisco 49ers and Pittsburgh Penguins in 1977 and had attempted to purchase the A's and move them to New Orleans in a potentially very lucrative deal. Veeck cited DeBartolo's pledge to keep the team in Chicago as a major factor in why he was chosen over groups with similar bids, but the rumors hadn't died down, and David Israel offered DeBartolo some advice in his August 23 *Chicago Tribune* column.

"First, you have to convince everyone that you don't intend to move this team," he wrote. "Don't come in here thinking you can play us for suckers like O'Malley did in Brooklyn. Play straight in this town and you'll get an even break. Remember always, it's not often that a rube from Ohio rolls a fellow from Chicago."[52]

Before DeBartolo's deal was even announced, another rumor had the White Sox moving to New Orleans and being replaced by Charley Finley moving his team to Chicago. Those rumors weren't helped by the fact that Finley announced that he, too, would be holding a press conference. Adding to Sox fans' angst was the statement of DeBartolo's chief advisor in professional sports, Vincent Bartimo, that "there are no restrictions on the flexibility of the corporation regarding the franchise. Mr. DeBartolo does not make deals with strings attached."[53]

The story provided another twist when, a day later, instead of announcing he was moving to Chicago, Finley declared that he had sold his team as well. The buyers were locally based Levi Straus executives, Walter A. Haas, his son, Walter J. Haas, and his son-in-law, Roy Eisenhart. For A's fans and the Oakland Coliseum, the sale to a local group meant the A's would stay in town, and Finley would walk away with nearly $13 million, a profit of nearly $9 million over his purchase price.

Finley had few friends in the game. He was constantly at odds with other owners, Commissioner Bowie Kuhn, and many of his players. But he also loved the game and built one of the best teams in history in the early 1970s. His teams won three straight World Series championships from 1972 through 1974 and probably would have won more had free agency not changed the baseball landscape. Once players were able to move about and auction off their services to the highest bidder, Finley's days in the game were numbered.

Over his 20 seasons at the helm of the team, the A's played in Kansas City and Oakland and were rumored to be moving to Milwaukee, Seattle, New Orleans, Denver and who knows where else. He went through 18 managers, won five AL West titles, lobbied unsuccessfully for the adoption of orange baseballs for better visibility at night, and referred to Commissioner Bowie Kuhn as "the village idiot."[54]

"The main reason I'm leaving baseball is because I can no longer compete financially," he told the media. "During the time when we were winning championships, survival was a battle of wits. We did all right then. But it is no longer a battle of wits, but how much you have on the hip."[55]

Finley and Veeck ruffled feathers in the baseball establishment, and there were many who were happy to see them go. But their contributions to the game can't be overlooked. In his *Chicago Tribune* column of August 24, David Condon praised the departing baseball mavericks.

> What the establishment chooses to ignore are the great things that Veeck and Finley did for a sacred game before the money-changers took over the temple. Veeck hired the first black in the American League [Larry Doby] ... saw that Satchel Paige had a major league opportunity and pitched in a World Series.[56]
>
> Finley introduced the designated hitter ... scorned baseball's prison gray and drab white uniforms ... and ... never forgetting the working man and kids in school arranged for World Series games to start on weekends, with midweek games at night.[57]
>
> Bill Veeck and Charlie Finley thought baseball was a game that should be fun for the fans. They became outcasts among their peers. This weekend, they said goodbye.[58]

No sooner did Finley and Veeck say goodbye than another baseball lifer departed the game. Gene Mauch signed with the Brooklyn Dodgers in 1943, spent two years in the Army Air Force during World War II, and had been in baseball ever since. By 1980 he was the senior manager in Major League Baseball, having been on the bench for the Phillies and Twins since 1960. But on August 24, after a loss to the Tigers that put his team 26½ games behind the Royals, Mauch decided to walk away. "For a lot of years, I threw around a lot of words to a lot of players," he said at his departing news conference. "They were words which meant a lot to me; words like pride, dedication and responsibility.[59] ... It's time for these players to hear some new words from a new voice. I hate the word quit and I don't think that's what I'm doing. I'm not satisfied that I'm making contribution enough to stay around and that irritated me."[60]

Mauch was being a good soldier, but those in the clubhouse and in the Minnesota media knew the real story of his departure. "This team is screwed up," outfielder Rick Sofield told the *Minneapolis Star*. "He said he was leaving because he couldn't motivate us. But if he can't, who can? There are some guys in this room who just don't seem to care."[61]

Star writer Doug Grow touched on what he felt was the real reason behind Mauch's departure: He'd simply had enough of Twins owner Calvin Griffith. Grow speculated that Mauch had grown weary of Griffith's tight-fisted ways. It was Griffith who let established (and expensive) stars like Rod Carew, Larry Hisle, Lyman Bostock and others get away rather than pay them.

Mauch successfully lobbied Griffith to sign veterans Jerry Koosman and Mike Marshall, but he knew he needed more talent to compete against the Royals in the AL West. He pressed for more veterans, while Griffith and others in the organization continued to tout "younger" (a.k.a. cheaper) players in the Twins system. In the end, he decided it simply wasn't worth it.

Third-base coach John Goryl was tapped to take Mauch's place, but it wasn't a job he necessarily wanted. "I tried to talk him out of it," Goryl told the *Star*. "I told him things would get better. It was a bombshell. But he said the decision was made."[62]

As the smoke cleared from Mauch's bombshell, another one appeared in Toronto. As the Texas Rangers prepared for their Monday game against the Blue Jays, members of the Royal Canadian Mounted Police appeared at Exhibition Stadium to arrest Rangers pitcher Fergie Jenkins and charge him with three counts of possession under the Narcotics Control Act.

A check of Jenkins luggage when Texas arrived in town revealed four grams of cocaine, two ounces of marijuana and two grams of hashish. Jenkins appeared in court and was released, but he was potentially facing six months in jail and/or a $1,000 fine under Canadian law. "I'm just as sick as I can be about it," said Rangers Chairman of the Board Eddie Chiles. "I'm sad and I'm disappointed and I'm very, very surprised."[63]

Jenkins was scheduled to pitch the second game of the series, but the Rangers skipped his start, saying that pitching under the circumstances represented too much pressure. Jenkins disagreed. "I've been pitching all my life. I know what pressure is," he said. "I think the ballclub wanted to take the easy way out."[64]

"So many people's names and faces have flashed in front of me since this happened, people who looked up to me and asked my advice. It's just a bad scene. I'm here in my own country, I'm kind of a hero here and have been a pretty good athlete. When I went down to the [hotel] lobby there were still some kids who wanted my autograph. It kind of shocked me."[65]

Jenkins returned to the mound on August 28 against the Royals and, pressure or no, he was simply awful. Kansas City knocked him out of the game in the first inning, but not before he allowed five runs on five hits and two walks in just one-third of an inning.

After Dallas Green's tirade, the Phillies began to play good baseball. Green's club won ten of their next 14 games, including a five-game sweep of the Mets at Shea Stadium, to climb back into the race. On August 25, they began a three-game series with the Dodgers at home before heading on a crucial 11-game West Coast road trip.

LA's Jerry Reuss faced Philadelphia's Nino Espinosa in the series opener and did some damage with his bat. Reuss' two-run homer off Espinosa gave the Dodgers a 3–0 lead in the top of the second inning. The Phillies went ahead 4–3 in the sixth on a Garry Maddox double off Reuss that chased him from the game. A Steve Yeager single in the eighth tied it, and then things got interesting in the top of the ninth.

LA took a 5–4 lead on Dusty Baker's double off Warren Brusstar. Two batters later, Ron Cey doubled to left to score Rudy Law and give the Dodgers a 6–4 lead. Tug McGraw came in to relieve Brusstar and face Joe Ferguson. McGraw's plan was to walk Ferguson to load the bases and set up an inning-ending double play. But Ferguson leaned into McGraw's second pitch and singled to right field, scoring Cey and Steve Garvey.

Bill Russell was the next man up, and McGraw's first three pitches came close to hitting the Dodgers shortstop. The fourth one finally did. Russell charged the mound and the benches emptied, leading to Russell's ejection, but McGraw remained in the game, which did not sit well with the Dodgers, who won the game, 8–4. McGraw was scheduled to hit with two outs in the bottom of the ninth, but Green sent Del Unser up to pinch-hit for him. "There will be a day when McGraw hits and he'll be dead, and you can put that in the newspapers," said Davey Lopes. "That was bush. He's got his day coming. I don't care if it's eight years from now. I thought he had a little more class. I guess he doesn't."[66]

"It's as plain as the nose on your face that McGraw was trying to hit him," said Dodgers manager Tommy Lasorda. "He should have been

Steve Carlton led the National League in wins, innings pitched and strikeouts en route to his 3rd Cy Young Award (National Baseball Hall of Fame Library, Cooperstown, New York).

thrown out and heavily fined. What gives him the right to throw four balls at a guy who had nothing to do with it?"[67]

The "it" he was referring to was Ferguson's hit that, while smart, may have violated one of baseball's sacred "unwritten rules." Ferguson didn't see it that way. "For 13 years I've been going to the plate in situations like that," he told the *Philadelphia Daily News*, "and every time it's gone through my mind that I might get a pitch I could hit. The first one tonight was fairly close, so I was cocked and ready when he threw the next one."[68]

McGraw was stoic as he sat in his locker, smoking a cigarette after the game. When asked if he was trying to hit Russell, he shook his head. "What do you want," he asked, "the gory details?"[69] Another writer tried a different line of questioning, asking how he was trying to pitch Russell. "C'mon, let it rest," he said. "What difference does it make? I'm not going to answer that. It's not a court of law here."[70]

The Dodgers took the second game of the series by an identical 8–4 score to push the Phillies back to 3½ games out in the East, while staying within striking distance of the first-place Houston Astros in the West. The series wrapped up on August 27 with Philadelphia's Steve Carlton facing LA's Bob Welch. Philadelphia took a 4–3 lead into the ninth inning, and McGraw got Russell to ground out to end the game. For the Phillies, it was a 4–3 win which, coupled with losses by Pittsburgh and Montreal, pulled them to within 2½ games of the lead in the division.

For Carlton, it was yet another milestone; the fifth time in his career he had reached the 20-win plateau. Carlton had no comments for the news media after the game, of course, but there were plenty of others to put the accomplishment into perspective for him. "I think if you saw him shaking all his teammates' hands and acknowledging the fans like that," said Green, "you wouldn't have to ask whether this meant something to him."[71]

Carlton became the first National League pitcher to reach the 20-win mark and established himself as the odds-on favorite to earn the Cy Young Award. "In terms of innings pitched [238 at the time] and strikeouts [232], what he's meant to his team, I don't think there can be anybody close,"[72] said Green.

The fact that the game came down to McGraw against Russell was not lost on either team. "I was still kind of a head case from the other night, when I was totally out of line," McGraw said. "I haven't been able to get that off my mind. I'm always hyped up when I pitch. I guess sometimes that's an adverse thing, too. There was definitely added pressure this time."[73]

The pressure would only increase. At the end of August, the Royals held an insurmountable 20-game lead in the American League West, but the remaining three division races were tight. The Yankees led Baltimore by 1½ games in the East, while the Pirates, Phillies and Expos were separated by just a half-game in the NL East. In the NL West, Houston held a slim one-game lead over the Dodgers, with the Reds lingering three games off the pace. The stage was set for an outstanding September.

7

September

Rookies, Royals and Racism

A chorus of boos rained down on Ed Farmer as he stepped from the visitors' dugout at Tiger Stadium and headed towards home plate on September 1. Moments later, Al Cowens emerged from the home dugout to meet him. The two shook hands, and just like that, the feud that began in June was over. "It was apologies, and let's forget about the whole situation," Cowens told reporters. "Both of us have been through a lot. I got it off my mind tonight and maybe everything is over with now."[1]

The meeting was arranged when Farmer told *Detroit News* columnist Joe Falls he'd be willing to drop the charges against Cowens he'd initially filed after their dustup at Comiskey Park. The message was relayed to Tigers manager Sparky Anderson, who persuaded Cowens to take the deal. "I told him I was sorry. He said he was sorry. I said, 'Thank you very much,'" said Farmer. "It was just a misunderstanding. You have those in any endeavor."[2]

There was no misunderstanding the message Phillies General Manager Paul Owens delivered to his team in San Francisco on September 1. Owens had been in the Phillies organization since 1956 and had worked his way up from player to general manager in 1972. After failing to advance in 1976, 1977 and 1978, the 1980 Phillies represented his best shot at a championship, and he wasn't about to let this team quit.

But his team was sputtering. After winning eight of ten games following Dallas Green's "inspirational speech" in Pittsburgh, the Phillies lost seven of their next twelve contests, including two straight losses to the woeful San Diego Padres, the last a 10–3 drubbing on August 31. "The Pope," as he was known, had seen enough, and he let his team know it. In contrast to Green's lambasting, Owens' speech was not delivered within earshot of the media, but word got out pretty quickly as to the content.

"He said we played the last five months for somebody else," said Pete Rose. "And now he wants us to play the last month for him and [owner] Ruly Carpenter. They're the ones who put this team together. They're the ones who stuck with this team over the winter."[3]

Owens called out veterans Larry Bowa and Garry Maddox specifically in front of their teammates, but it was a sign of how much Owens meant to the team that they didn't fire back. The volatile Bowa may not have liked the message or the manner in which it was delivered, but he respected the messenger. "The Pope's the general manager and he has every right to come down here and say what he said," admitted Bowa. "He jumped on Garry and me. We have not been playing well."[4]

It seemed that the Phillies were finally embracing the "We, Not I" attitude that Green espoused in spring training. It was an attitude that drew ridicule from many veterans, including Bowa, but now it was beginning to seep into the brains of some of the more stubborn players. Aiding the cause was that the message was delivered by someone other than Green. Inspired by "The Pope's" sermon, the Phillies beat the Giants, 6–4, behind Steve Carlton, while the Expos beat the Padres and the Pirates split a doubleheader with the Astros. The result was a three-way tie for first place in the NL East.

The Houston split tightened things up in the NL West as well. In St. Louis, the Reds knocked Cardinals starter Jim Kaat out of the game after just one-third of an inning en route to an 18-hit outburst and an 8–1 win. It was the fifth straight win for Cincinnati, and the hot bat of George Foster was a big reason why.

Since his breakout season of 1977, when he won the National League's Most Valuable Player Award by swatting 52 home runs and driving in 149 runs, Foster's production had dropped off precipitously. By 1979, his home run total had dropped to 30 and the RBI count fell to 98. Still good numbers, but not on par with those he'd put up just two seasons earlier.

It looked like the decline was continuing in 1980. At the All-Star break, Foster was batting an anemic .229 with nine home runs. But in the second half he'd been on fire, batting .323 with 12 homers and 47 RBI over his next 52 games. "The way George is swinging the bat now means the world," said third baseman Ray Knight. "He's the most destructive hitter in baseball. When he's hot, he can tear up a team single-handedly."[5]

The Reds' win brought them to within 2½ games of the Astros in the division, but to get to Houston, they'd have to get past the Dodgers, who were also playing good baseball. September 1 home runs by Ron Cey (22) and Dusty Baker (26) gave the Dodgers a 5–2 win over the Mets and brought them to within a half-game of the Astros.

Another positive sign for the Dodgers was the performance of pitcher Bob Welch, who went seven innings to get the win. Welch began the year 8–2 but had dropped seven of his last eight decisions. If LA hoped to compete against the pitching-heavy Astros, they'd need him down the stretch.

Rookie Steve Howe threw the final two innings to earn his 13th save of the season. The young lefty had been a godsend for a Dodgers bullpen that began the season in a bind. With veterans Doug Rau, Terry Forster and Don Stanhouse battling injury, Tommy Lasorda was forced to rely on Howe, Rick Sutcliffe, Bobby Castillo and Joe Beckwith. Sutcliffe was the reigning Rookie of the Year, but Howe, Castillo and Beckwith had fewer than 100 combined big league innings under their belts when the season began.

After a somewhat shaky start, Howe had emerged as a legit stopper at the back of the LA bullpen, and people were talking about the Dodgers boasting back-to-back Rookie of the Year Award winners, something that hadn't happened in the National League since 1962.

"I've never seen a young fellow who has the kind of poise he has," said Dodgers pitching coach Red Adams. "He's had adversity, but it doesn't seem to bother him."[6] "I'm cocky as hell," said Howe. "That's the way I am on and off the field. I believe in myself."[7]

That belief carried over to his teammates, who appreciated the fact that someone just over a year removed from pitching at the University of Michigan had stabilized their bullpen. Even when Howe experienced the inevitable ups and downs of a rookie closer, the Dodgers had his back. That fact was evident in a late–July doubleheader against the Pirates. Howe earned the save in the first game but blew the save in the second game, and his teammates stood up for him publicly. "Don't anyone rap Steve Howe," said veteran outfielder Dusty Baker. "He's saved us all season."[8] "Without him we could easily be eight or 10 games back," added Reggie Smith.[9]

Things were tight in the AL East, too, as the Yankees and Orioles both opened September with sweeps of AL West opponents. In Detroit, the drama of the Farmer/Cowens saga was replaced with pure joy as Mark Fidrych beat the White Sox in the first game of a doubleheader on September 2. "The Bird" went the distance, allowing just two runs, both unearned, to pick up his first regular season win in more than two years.

Things didn't start off well as Chicago leadoff hitter Chet Lemon lined a single to center and Lamar Johnson ended the first with a hard-hit line drive. But Fidrych settled down and made it through the rest of the game with relative ease. The only blemish on his night was a two-run homer off the bat of Harold Baines in the fourth inning. The only other drama came in the eighth inning, when Fidrych faced White Sox catcher Bruce Kimm, who had caught most if his starts in 1976.

"It was pretty weird," said Fidrych. "I started laughing. I had to turn around. Then I said, 'Hey Mark, get serious, because this is a game.'"[10] Fidrych retired Kimm on the first pitch and wiggled out of a two-on, one-out situation in the ninth to finish the game, getting another former teammate, Bob Molinaro, to end it.

After recording the final out, Fidrych presented the game ball to the parents of his manager in Evansville, Jim Leyland, and then headed into the clubhouse before returning for a curtain call at the urging of a Tigers official. As he sat in his locker sipping a Stroh's Light, he reflected on his evening. "That feeling to me was great. It was the ultimate because it's been a long time since I've been able to satisfy the people in Detroit."[11]

A few days after Fidrych returned to the win column, George Bamberger announced his departure as manager of the Brewers, though he would remain with the team as a special assistant to General Manager Harry Dalton. Despite suffering a heart attack in spring training, Bamberger denied that health was the reason behind his decision. "I had signed through this year, and I thought the club could do a lot better, to be honest with you," Bamberger said. "I'm walking away from the game because George Bamberger wants to walk away."[12]

"Bambi" walked away with just 23 games remaining and was replaced by Buck Rodgers, who had filled in while Bamberger was recuperating from his heart attack. Rodgers' promotion and his previous stint as Brewers skipper helped ease the transition for the players. "I'm glad Buck got it," said second baseman Paul Molitor. "I never really expected George would be back next year, although I thought he might stick out this season. But I think it's logical to make the move now to give Buck a look at the young players."[13]

Bamberger stepping aside marked the latest episode in a busy summer of managerial and front-office changes. The Brewers were the fifth team to announce a manager switch, but they wouldn't be the last.

It didn't take long for cracks to appear in the deal Edward DeBartolo had agreed to in buying the White Sox. Rumors were swirling that DeBartolo had plans to move the team to New Orleans, and they wouldn't go away. On top of that, DeBartolo didn't live in Chicago, and his offer to purchase a home and spend at least 20 percent of his time there didn't seem to appease those who objected to his purchase of the team. Others had issues with his ownership of horse racing tracks and their ties to gambling.

"Don't sell [Jerry] Reinsdorf short," a White Sox investor told the *Chicago Tribune* in early September. "[William] Farley and Reinsdorf are still around and probably better set up to make a more firm bid if it again comes to that."[14]

It did come to that. DeBartolo's deal with Bill Veeck was eventually rejected by Veeck's fellow American League owners, and one factor was their attitude toward Veeck. There were some within the game who viewed this as a final chance to stick it to the maverick owner, and they leapt at the chance. The sale needed 12 "yes" vote to pass. It got eight.

"I think I can safely say that the vote that went so strongly in numbers against Mr. DeBartolo was, in fact, a vote against Bill Veeck and not Ed DeBartolo," said George Steinbrenner. "I think if Bill Veeck was applying for membership today in the American League he would find it hard to get one vote."[15]

Once the DeBartolo deal was dead, Reinsdorf pounced. He celebrated his purchase in true Chicago style, dining at Pizzeria Due and a hearty round of baseball trivia with a healthy dose of nostalgia. "When we went to law school at Northwestern, we lived in Abbott Hall on Chicago Avenue, and nobody had much money," Reinsdorf said. "When we got some money together, this was our treat, to come here for dinner. I haven't been here in 20 years"[16]

Every year someone gets hot at just the right time. A team that is struggling finds its way and vaults itself back into the race. In the National League East, the Phillies, Expos and Pirates alternated between small winning streaks and losing streaks, while the Reds and Astros did the same in the West. The Dodgers led the division in mid–August, but a miserable five-game homestand against Atlanta and Cincinnati put them in third place.

From there, Tommy Lasorda's team caught fire, winning 17 of their next 20 games to regain the lead in the division before heading into a big two-game series with the Astros in Houston. "What's gratifying is that we passed Houston when they were playing super baseball," said Lasorda. He was right. The Astros had won 14 of their last 20 games and lost ground in the division. Asked if he thought that might demoralize Houston, Lasorda said, "I think so. I hope so."[17]

"I know it's a cliché, but we're getting a 25-man effort," said second baseman Davey Lopes. "We've shown more togetherness this year. The next five games [two against Houston & three against Cincinnati] will be the five most emotional of the season. It sure looks good for the Dodgers."[18]

Any thoughts the Dodgers had of seizing control of the division quickly evaporated, however, as Lopes kicked Joe Morgan's ground ball to open the bottom of the first inning, one of six Dodgers errors in the game, leading to three unearned runs and an eventual 6–5 Houston win to cut LA's lead to one game. "We just played lousy," said Lopes, who made two errors. "I was lousy. The whole defense was lousy. It was due to catch up to us."[19]

Lopes' reference was to the fact that the Dodgers infield had made just one error in the last 25 games. Lopes was riding an errorless string of 43 straight games heading into the contest, while Derrel Thomas hadn't committed an error in 51 games. But on this day, third baseman Ron Cey was the only member of the LA infield who didn't commit an error. "Better to have them all in one game," Lopes said. "What makes you mad is that we still almost won."[20]

Dusty Baker gave the Dodgers an early lead in the second game of the series with a first-inning homer off Nolan Ryan. LA extended the lead to 3–0 after three innings, but the Astros tied it after seven, and the game stayed tied into the 11th inning.

With runners on 2nd and 3rd, Lasorda sent Gary Thomasson up to pinch-hit for catcher Steve Yeager, and Thomasson delivered a single to center off Houston's Dave Smith to plate both Bobby Mitchell and Derrel Thomas. But Houston rallied in the bottom half of the inning. Pinch-hits by Danny Heep and Gary Woods each drove in a run, and the game was tied again, this time at 5–5, before Rick Sutcliffe induced Enos Cabell to hit into a double play to end the inning.

Houston's Bert Roberge, their fourth pitcher of the evening, retired the Dodgers in order in the top of the 12th, and with one out, Jose Cruz stepped in against Sutcliffe in the bottom of the inning. Sutcliffe started Cruz off with a fastball, and Cruz jumped on it. "I told Deacon [hitting coach Jones] I was going to go deep," Cruz said. "I knew it was gone as soon as I hit it. We're tied now for first place. Now we have to go to LA and beat them there."[21]

Playing nearly .800 baseball for 25 games in September had earned the Dodgers nothing more than a tie, and they had reason to be concerned. The Astros were a confident bunch, and taking two straight from LA had only added to that. "Now they know that we can beat them even when they play well," said Cruz. "We stayed with them all the way and I hope they remember that."[22]

Not only were the Astros gaining confidence, the Dodgers were losing players. Outfielder Bobby Mitchell pulled a hamstring during the game, forcing Lasorda to use pitcher Bobby Castillo in the outfield in extra innings. The Albuquerque Dukes, LA's Triple-A team, were in the Pacific Coast League World Series, which had delayed some late-season call-ups and left Lasorda short-handed. That was about to get worse.

Following the Astros series, the Dodgers headed to Cincinnati to face the Reds for three games. Cincinnati was coming off a sweep of the Atlanta Braves and a 10–4 road trip. They trailed the Dodgers and Astros by 2½ games with 21 remaining, and their mission was simple. "We have to win two out of three at least," said outfielder Dave Collins. "We can't put any added pressure on ourselves by losing. We definitely can't let them sweep."[23]

Except that's exactly what happened. Strong pitching performances by Don Sutton, Bob Welch and Jerry Reuss held Cincinnati to just five runs over the three games and pushed the Reds 5½ games out in the division. But the sweep of the Reds came at a very high cost for the Dodgers.

In the first game, a Mike LaCoss fastball rode in on shortstop Bill Russell and shattered his right forefinger. For a team already missing Reggie Smith and others, losing their starting shortstop for the rest of the season was a devastating blow. Russell's loss made Derrel Thomas the starting shortstop, a position he hadn't played regularly since 1973. "I have confidence that I can play anywhere they need me," Thomas told the *Los Angeles Times*. "I think shortstop and second base are my second best positions. With Billy out, I'll be playing every day. That's my goal, to play every day for a pennant winner."[24]

Marty Bystrom should have been with the Phillies all season. They had been high on him since they signed him as an 18-year-old free agent out of the Miami area. He dazzled Dallas Green and Paul Owens in the Florida Instructional League in 1978 and sped rapidly through the Phillies' minor league system. But a freak accident during spring training resulted in a severely torn hamstring and delayed his arrival in the big leagues. By the time the leg finally healed, the Phillies sent him to Triple-A Oklahoma City to pitch himself back into shape. He made his major league debut on September 7 against the Dodgers, and three days later made his first start, in the middle of a pennant race, against the New York Mets at Shea Stadium.

Bystrom was the latest addition to the Phillies' youth movement championed by Green, the former farm director. He knew the talent the Phillies had in their system, and he intended to use it. Young players like Bob Walk, Lonnie Smith, Keith Moreland and Dickie Noles had replaced the likes of Jim Kaat, Bud Harrelson, Dave Rader and Jim Lonborg. So far, it had paid off.

Walk had ten wins, Smith was hitting .337 with 28 stolen bases, Moreland checked in at .339, and Noles showed he wasn't intimidated by big league hitters. Now it was Bystrom's turn to step up, and he did just that against the Mets, throwing a shutout while allowing just five hits. "How'd you like the kid?" asked rookie catcher Ozzie Virgil. "I've caught him for about three seasons in the minors and now you know why I've been saying Marty's a special pitcher. It was a mismatch, really"[25]

"This was my goal, ever since I was a kid," said Bystrom. "I never dreamed I'd pitch a shutout, though. I just wanted to get here and take it from there."[26] But as good as Bystrom was, his performance was overshadowed by that of another NL East rookie.

Bill Gullickson grew up in the Chicago suburb of Joliet, Illinois, and quickly established himself as a baseball star. By his senior year at Joliet Catholic High School, he was considered the top prep pitcher in the country. The Chicago White Sox held the number one pick in the 1977 draft and, though they liked Gullickson, they decided to choose Harold Baines instead, allowing the Montreal Expos to snap Gullickson up with the second choice. A little more than two years later, he was in a pennant race, and on September 10, he faced the Cubs at home and turned in a record-setting performance.

Gullickson began the game by striking out Chicago shortstop Ivan DeJesus. He got two more in the second, and struck out the side in the third inning. By the end of the fifth, he had already set the season high for a Montreal pitcher with 11, and after striking out the side in the sixth, he had set an Expos team record. "I was trying to keep the strikeout record out of mind," Gullickson said. "I was aware of what the crowd was doing and it was wonderful, but I was trying to concentrate on the game."[27]

By the time Gullickson got Jim Tracy looking to end the game, he had a 4–2 win and a rookie record of 18 strikeouts, just one off the major league record, held collectively by Tom Seaver, Nolan Ryan and Steve Carlton, all future Hall of Famers.

"He was just awesome," said his catcher, Gary Carter. "With that performance, he's up there with the Koufaxes and the Drysdales and any other strikeout pitcher. The thing that's so great about it is that he's just a rookie, but he acts like a veteran out there."[28] That veteran attitude showed through when the 21-year-old Gullickson was asked about his performance and stepped back to look at the big picture. "I'm actually more excited about getting the win than I am about the strikeouts," he said. "I feel like I'm contributing now. We needed a complete game victory and I did it. It was a big game for us."[29]

Unfortunately for the Expos, left fielder Ron LeFlore injured his wrist the next day when he crashed into the bleachers wall trying to catch a foul ball off the bat of Cubs slugger Dave Kingman. At the time of the injury, LeFlore had combined with Rodney Scott to become one of the top base-stealing duos in the game. Between the two of them, they had swiped 149 bases and were causing major headaches to opposing defenses.

LeFlore was also causing headaches in his own clubhouse. In the September issue of *Inside Sports* magazine, he got himself in trouble with his teammates and the city of Montreal all in the space of a few thousand words. In an interview that spared few, LeFlore expressed displeasure that he and other black players didn't get the support he felt they should from the hometown fans. "This town is 80, 90 percent white," he said. "Regardless of how many blacks are on the team, you still feel you're a nigger here. I don't think there's been too much concern for the black players around here. The fans didn't vote for me for the All-Star game, and didn't for the other blacks having great years like Warren Cromartie."[30]

LeFlore also said that former Expos outfielder Ken Singleton was traded because he married a white woman and that pitcher Rudy May signed as a free-agent with the Yankees because someone put sugar in the gas tank of his van. Then he turned his sights on his teammates. "Some of these guys are from the South, and all Southerners are rednecks," he was quoted as saying. "They've been brought up to hate niggers."[31]

Needless to say, the comments didn't sit well in the clubhouse, and his teammates shot back with some of their own accusations. "He called us all racists," said pitcher Steve Rogers. "The nucleus of this team has been together for four years. If suddenly there is any racial tension, consider the source."

"The problem isn't racism," said third baseman Larry Parrish. "The problem is different rules for different players. Some guys aren't showing up until 7 o'clock for a 7:30 game and don't even take infield. That breeds dissension."[32]

The dissension wasn't just between LeFlore and the rest of the team. Many of the players didn't care for Dick Williams and his gruff attitude, most notably pitching ace Steve Rogers, who didn't speak to his manager unless absolutely necessary. Then there was Bill Lee, who had an opinion on virtually everything and was not shy about sharing it, often to the detriment of team chemistry. "The basic problem is that articles aren't written and edited by the people they're about. And Ron, he's a heck of a guy."[33]

LeFlore later backed off some of his statements, but the damage had already been done at a time when the Expos could least afford it. The East Division title was within their grasp, and they didn't need any distractions.

By contrast, New York is a city full of distractions, and the Yankees had shown a tremendous ability to push them aside and just win baseball games, even when the distraction was caused by their owner. In early September, American League President Lee MacPhail sent a letter to all AL teams, reminding them that playing young players against contending teams could potentially alter the outcome of the season. It was something Yankees owner George Steinbrenner took to heart.

On September 16, the Yankees hosted Toronto for a three-game series while the Orioles enjoyed an off-day before taking on the Detroit Tigers. The Blue Jays were buried in last place in the AL East, 30 games back, when the series began, but they took two of three from New York behind two of their best pitchers, Dave Stieb and Jim Clancy. Once the Jays left New York, they went to Baltimore for another three-game series and started rookie Paul Mirabella, just up from Triple-A, in game one. Toronto's pitching rotation didn't go unnoticed by Steinbrenner, especially after Mirabella allowed four runs on six hits in an inning and one-third, and he immediately called out the Jays essentially for tanking by throwing rookies against the Yankees' competition. The fact that the series were back-to-back and that pitchers need rest between starts seemed to be lost on Steinbrenner, who complained to MacPhail at a luncheon meeting. "The Yankees had gone to Toronto and faced Clancy and Steib," MacPhail said. "George only said that he hoped Baltimore faced the same pitchers the Yankees did."[34]

When word got back to Toronto that Steinbrenner was unhappy with their lineup, the Jays went on the offensive and fired off a telegram to Bowie Kuhn that read:

> The Toronto club hereby requests the full investigation of comments, alleged to have been made by George Steinbrenner, to members of the New York and Boston media concerning the pitching rotation used by the Blue Jays against the Baltimore Orioles.[35]
>
> Based on your investigation, the very least we would expect is a full and complete public apology from George Steinbrenner, if not a substantial fine and suspension by your office.[36]

While Steinbrenner was making baseless accusations against other teams in the American League, his team was busy beating them. The Yankees began September by winning 15 of their first 16 games, thanks in large part to excellent pitching. The Yankees' streak allowed them to pad their lead over Baltimore in the AL East from 1½ games on September 1 to 6 games by the 16th. On September 17, the Orioles hosted Detroit, but Orioles manager Earl Weaver had an early evening thanks to a disagreement with first base umpire Bill Haller. Weaver's disdain for umpires was legendary, but Haller, the American League's senior umpire, held a special place on his list.

"We haven't gotten along too well, and it goes back to the incident when his brother played for Detroit and he umpired our games in the middle of a pennant race,"[37] Weaver explained after the game. With one out in the top of the first inning, Detroit shortstop Alan Trammell singled to right field and advanced to second when Haller called a balk on Orioles starter Mike Flanagan. That's when Weaver pounced out of the dugout to confront his nemesis.

It just so happened that a local television station had equipped Haller with a wireless microphone, and they were rolling when Weaver went after Haller. What ensued was an epic Weaver meltdown, complete with full audio.

WEAVER: You're here and this crew is here just to fuck us! (Haller ejects Weaver) You just couldn't wait to get me out of here!
HALLER: Ah.... You run yourself, Earl!
WEAVER: You're here for one Goddamn specific reason.
HALLER: What's that, Earl?
WEAVER: To fuck us!
HALLER: Ah.... You're full of shit.[38]

The showdown lasted several minutes, with Weaver walking toward the Orioles dugout multiple times only to return and give Haller another piece of his mind. Each man accused the other of touching him, each man called the other a liar, and each man said the game would be better off if the other weren't in it.

When Weaver told Haller to wait ten years and see which one of them was in the Hall of Fame, Haller had his response ready. "You're going to be in the Hall of Fame? Why? For fucking up World Series?"[39]

The argument took on another life when a highly edited version was replayed on both television and radio. It was an instant classic, but it also raised some eyebrows. The television station hadn't obtained permission to wire Haller for sound during the game, and neither the Orioles nor the Tigers knew Haller was wearing a microphone. It led to lots of questions and some conspiracy theories that Haller may have set Weaver up because of their long-running feud.

"I've voiced my displeasure and I sent a copy of the tape to the American League," said Orioles General Manager Hank Peters a few days later. "It's a sad thing that the American League has been put into this situation, and it's a disgrace in a sense that it was not meant to be heard by anyone other than who was on the field. It's totally wrong for an umpire to be wired and for the managers and players not to be aware of it."[40]

The drama in the AL East, was in stark contrast to the lack of drama in the AL West. The Royals entered the month with a 19½ game division lead, making a fourth title in five years a foregone conclusion. The only question was when they would clinch. That question was answered on September 17 when Dennis Leonard threw a three-hit shutout in the first game of a doubleheader against the California Angels. The Royals lost the second game, but it didn't dampen the celebration in the Kansas City clubhouse at the end of the day.

It was especially sweet for manager Jim Frey, who had spent the last 16 seasons as a minor league manager and a big league coach. Now, in his first season as a major league manager, he had a division title and a chance to go to the World Series. "You know, I never was a good ballplayer," he said. "But I was on some good clubs that had a lot of good things happen, but this is the ultimate. There's only one thing that can top it, and that's winning the World Series."[41]

In order to do that, it appeared they would have to finally get through the Yankees, the team that had knocked them out of the playoffs in 1976, 1977 and 1978, and the Royals would have it no other way. "I would prefer to play the Yankees," said pitcher Paul Splittorff. "I think they are the best team in that division, anyway."[42]

Splittorff was one of eight players on the 1980 roster who had been ousted by the Yankees three times. Another one was George Brett, who won his first batting title in 1976 at age 23 and followed that up by hitting .444 in the ALCS loss to the Yankees. Now, four years later and on the brink of a second batting title, he wanted another shot at the pinstripes. "It's not vengeance, it's wanting to regroup and regain your pride and self-respect," Brett said. "We were in Chicago one day, and I saw a sign that said, 'Welcome Pennant Chokers.' I think it would be good for baseball, good for this team and good for this city if we beat the Yankees."[43]

With the division wrapped up, the only question surrounding the Royals was whether Brett could finish the year at .400. He had missed ten days with an injury to his right hand, but returned to the lineup in the second game of the doubleheader against the Angels and went 2-for-5 to put his average at .396 with 16 games left in the season. A 2-for-3 game on September 18 and another two-hit night against Oakland brought his average to an even .400. If he did manage to hit .400, the other question was whether he'd have enough plate appearances to qualify for the batting title.

The magic number was 502. But the hand injury, along with the ankle injury that cost him a month, had him at 461 plate appearances with 14 games to go. That's where rule 10.23 (a) came in. The rule, which had never been used before, stated, "If there is a player with fewer than the required plate appearances, whose average would be the highest if he were charged with the required number of plate appearances or official at-bats, then that player shall be awarded the batting championship."[44]

In other words, if George Brett finished the season with 492 plate appearances, he would have to take an 0-for-10 to qualify for the batting title, thus putting him in the odd position of potentially finishing the season with one batting average but winning the batting title with a different batting average.

His main competition for the batting title was Milwaukee's Cecil Cooper, who had the misfortune of having his best offensive season in the same year that Brett had one of the best seasons in history. Cooper finished play on September 19 at .354, good enough to win the batting title easily in most seasons, but not in 1980. "It's my tough luck that the man's having a hellacious year," Cooper said. "But what can I do? All I can do is go out there and keep doing what I'm doing."[45]

Cooper wasn't bitter, nor was he jealous. "I wish George every ounce of luck," he said. "The guy is hitting more than .400 and that's terrific."[46] It just seemed that no matter what he did, George Brett was the story. "I'm not complaining. I'm obligated to go out and play, but it does bother me a bit.[47] I mean, if I was in L.A. and having this kind of year, I'd be a celebrity. But then maybe I couldn't handle that either. As long as my teammates and the fans here know what kind of year I'm having, I have to take satisfaction in that and keep doing my job."[48]

Rick Langford's job was to finish baseball games, and he did it with aplomb in 1980. Langford threw six complete games in June, all losses, and six more in July, all wins, including a 14-inning complete game against the Cleveland Indians in which he walked just one and struck out four. But on September 17, Billy Martin strode to the mound at Arlington Stadium to talk to his starter and suggest that it was time for the streak to come to an end. The Oakland A's were up by two runs in the ninth inning with two outs, but there were also two men on. Langford was in a jam, and Martin felt he didn't have a choice. Reliever Bob Lacey got Buddy Bell to ground out, and it was over—both the game and one of the most remarkable streaks in recent baseball memory. For the first time in four months, Rick Langford hadn't finished a game he started.

The streak began with a 3–1 loss to the Texas Rangers on May 23, followed by a 6–3 win over the Royals five days later. Langford threw six complete games in June and six more in July, including a 14-inning marathon against the Cleveland Indians, during which he walked just one and struck out four. That was the key. In one June start, Oakland pitching coach Art Fowler said, Langford threw an eight-inning complete game on just 77 pitches. An informal tally in the press box had the total even lower. "I don't throw a lot of pitches, I don't walk many hitters. Billy Martin has

Rick Langford led an Oakland pitching staff that threw an amazing 94 complete games. Langford alone threw 28, including 23 straight (National Baseball Hall of Fame Library, Cooperstown, New York).

helped me a lot. He lets me pitch my own ball game, he lets me move my fielders around out there. It's all part of the success."[49]

Martin also didn't have a lot of faith in his bullpen, which was a major factor in Oakland's starters throwing as many complete games as they did. On September 5, the A's bullpen allowed six runs in the final two innings of a loss to the Orioles, and Martin wasn't about to let it happen again. The next day, Langford's streak reached 21, surpassing Robin Roberts, who threw 20 straight for the 1953 Phillies and establishing a modern-day record. "I wouldn't have taken Langford out of the game tonight if he had put seven guys on base in the ninth," Martin said. "Not after last night, I wouldn't. Rick was going for a record and I was not going to take that away from him."[50]

The day after Langford set the individual record for a season, Oakland set the modern day team record. On September 7, Steve McCatty went the distance against Baltimore, throwing 150 pitches along the way, to earn Oakland their 78th complete game of the season, breaking the record set by the 1968 San Francisco Giants. "It's ironic that I pitched the record-breaking game," said McCatty, "because I have the least amount of complete games on the staff. It would have been nice in Mike Norris or Rick Langford had done it. But I feel I contributed, too."[51]

After finishing the series with Baltimore, the A's returned home to face the Royals. On September 12, Langford surrendered 14 hits, but went the distance and picked up the win in a 9–5 game. His next start came against the Texas Rangers, the team against which the streak began. Martin stayed with his starter as long as he felt comfortable, but with the game on the line, he had to make a move. "He had his consecutive game going," said Martin. "That's why I went as long as I did with him. I've seen him pitch better, but he pitched well."[52]

In his streak-snapping start, Rick Langford went 8⅔ innings, allowed four runs on 11 hits, and got the win. "What happened on the field justified my coming out," he said. "Billy runs this show, and he's done an outstanding job, obviously."[53]

After the series against the Rangers, Oakland traveled to Kansas City to face Brett and the Royals. Brett's batting average was at .398 entering the series, and after going 2-for-4 with two RBI, he was back at the .400 mark with 14 games remaining. His plate appearances stood at 461. In order to win the batting title with a .400 average, Brett would need 41 plate appearances. He would also need to keep hitting. "I can't let my concentration lapse because if I don't do it [hit .400] I'm going to feel like I let a lot of people down," he said. "Not just myself but a lot of people."[54]

The pressure was mounting daily, especially with the division title sewn up. There was little else for Royals fans, or the media, to focus on other than Brett's quest to hit .400. At a time when he could have been

George Brett went 4-for-4 on August 17 to raise his batting average to .401. He finished the year at .390, the highest average since Ted Williams' .406 in 1941 (National Baseball Hall of Fame Library, Cooperstown, New York).

resting and getting ready for the playoffs, it was almost imperative that Brett play every day and get at least two hits. "I need to get some leeway, some breathing space," he said. "I'd like to get it up to .406 or .408. I go 2-for-4 tonight and it barely raises it two points."[55]

Unfortunately, the next week was very unkind. Over the next seven games, Brett hit just .148 to drop his season average to .385. It was a remarkable year by any standard, but the quest for .400 was over.

8

October

Bitterness, Bashing and Breakthroughs

As the 1980 season entered its final week, three of the four division titles were still up for grabs. In the American League, the Yankees and Orioles were still battling to see who would face the Royals in the American League Championship Series. New York held a 4½-game lead entering play on Monday, September 29, but things tightened up when Baltimore swept a doubleheader from the Red Sox while the Yankees were idle. Not only did the sweep pull Baltimore closer to the Yankees, they were also the final games Don Zimmer served as the Red Sox manager.

On October 1, Boston general manager Haywood Sullivan announced that he was firing Zimmer and replacing him with Johnny Pesky for the remainder of the season, all of five games. The move wasn't a surprise to anyone. In fact, Zimmer had called his mother to tell her he would probably be fired before he received the call from Sullivan making it official. The Red Sox skipper had been under fire the entire season, especially among fans who mercilessly booed him no matter what he did. It was a season in which the Red Sox expected to compete; by the time the move was made, they trailed the Yankees by 16 games in the division.

"Coming out of spring training, I said that we had no excuses," Zimmer told the media. "We stayed together and worked together during the strike, then from mid–April until the middle of May we played as badly as we can play. We made a little run in September and got within five games, and while I don't like excuses, losing Fred Lynn and Carl Yastrzemski really hurt us."[1]

The injuries to Lynn and Yaz weren't the only ones Zimmer had to deal with. Dennis Eckersley battled through back issues, and Chuck Rainey was American League "Pitcher of the Month" in May, but he missed the final three months of the season with an elbow injury. None of that mattered to the denizens of Fenway Park, however, who took delight in booing Zimmer whenever he emerged from the dugout. "In a crazy sense they [the fans] were giving him a compliment," said Boston catcher Carlton Fisk.

> They came to the park to boo him. It sort of became the cool thing to do.[2]
> You know, we're different from a lot of parks. We don't have a chicken or a marching band or a ball girl on the foul lines to keep people preoccupied. Maybe if we had kept their minds on baseball more they wouldn't have booed the man so much. You can't blame the manager for what has happened this year. He doesn't hit, throw or run. No way should he have been fired.[3]

Late-season baseball often produces heroes. But while players like Reggie Jackson add to their legacies in October, sometimes heroes emerge from obscurity for their big moments. Such was the case in Montreal on Monday, September 29. The Cardinals and Expos were tied, 2–2, in the bottom of the ninth inning, but Montreal had a rally going. With two on and two out, the pitcher's spot was due up. Expos manager Dick Williams scanned his bench and summoned backup catcher John Tamargo as a pinch-hitter.

Tamargo began his professional career seven years earlier after being drafted by the Cardinals in the sixth round out of Georgia Southern University. Since then, he'd logged fewer than 200 career at-bats while playing for St. Louis, San Francisco and Montreal, and had made a total of seven starts in 1980. Playing time was scarce for someone who backed up Gary Carter, and with Montreal in a pennant race, at-bats were even tougher to come by. He'd made just one start in the second half and was pulled as part of a double-switch in that game. Making matters worse, the change took place in the second inning. Not good for one's self-esteem.

Yet here he was in a key situation for the Expos in extra innings with the game, and possibly the season, on the line. St Louis pitcher George Frazier tried to sneak a fastball past Tamargo, but the Montreal catcher jumped on it and sent it over the wall in right field for a three-run, game-winning homer, his first of the season and just the fourth of his career. "It has to be the biggest hit of my career," said Tamargo. "I once won an opening game in San Francisco with a 10th inning home run, but I think this one here can help us win the division and I hope we can pull it off."[4]

The 5–2 win gave the Expos a brief one-game lead over the Phillies, who were locked in a battle with the Cubs at Veterans Stadium as well as a battle with the media and with themselves. Prior to the start of the game, outfielder Garry Maddox accused *Philadelphia Inquirer* writer Jayson Stark of being responsible for Maddox being benched after Stark wrote about Maddox losing a ball in the sun earlier in the week. Additionally, shortstop Larry Bowa tore into Dallas Green on his radio show for benching slumping veterans and plugging in rookies in the heat of a pennant race.

"Dallas has said he's going to let the veterans go to the hilt," Bowa said on WWDB-AM. "To me, this is not letting the veterans go to the hilt. He can't sit down [catcher Bob] Boone and [left fielder Greg] Luzinski for four days and then when we go to Montreal say, 'Okay, go get 'em again. Dallas is trying to shake things up, which is very understandable. But on the other hand, he's talking out of the side of his mouth when he says he wants to stay with his veterans."[5]

Green likely would have preferred to play veterans over rookies, but some of his veterans weren't performing. Luzinski was hitting .175 with two homers in September, while Boone was hitting .198. Between them, they'd hit two home runs (both by Luzinski) and driven in 11 runs. But whether it was a "benching" or a "rest," the Phillies were in serious danger of unraveling once again late in the season.

Once the grumbling ended and the game began, the Phillies scored two runs in the bottom of the third inning before Chicago added a single run in the fifth and two more in the seventh to take the lead. Philadelphia tied it in the bottom of the seventh on an RBI groundout by Pete Rose, and then the two teams traded zeros on the scoreboard for seven more innings. Chicago finally broke through with two runs in the top of the fifteenth on a sacrifice fly by Scot Thompson and a Carlos Lezcano double off Phillies reliever Kevin Saucier. But a Garry Maddox single off Dennis Lamp, the Cubs' seventh pitcher of the evening, tied the game again, and Manny Trillo won it three batters later with a single to center to score Maddox and mercifully end the evening. A hard-fought win, which should have produced relief in the home clubhouse at Veterans Stadium, instead produced more bitterness and harsh words. Bowa and Schmidt took verbal swipes at the media assembled in front of Rose's locker, but perhaps the strongest words came, not surprisingly, from Dallas Green. "I get the feeling we're not all together in this thing," he said, echoing a sentiment that had plagued his team the entire season. "I wouldn't be surprised if there aren't a few guys out there who aren't rooting against us ... not to win this thing."[6]

A silence fell over the manager's office as the media processed Green's statement. With less than a week to go in the season and his team just a half-game out of the division lead, Dallas Green was publicly questioning his team's will to win. "Hell, we're fighting for the pennant. This is a time where you need to put everything aside. I don't care if it's at home, if it's in the clubhouse, if it's the manager. You just gotta put it all aside and say, 'It's We, Not I.'[7] ... I'm not talking about every guy on this team. I'd say 90 percent of the guys care.... The rest ... well they can look in the mirror. They know if they care or not."[8]

When told of Bowa's pre-game radio remarks, Green fired back, pointing out that both Boone and Luzinski had played in a crucial series the week before against Montreal and saying, "I can't forget about every player on this team for the sake of a few veterans. I'm in this for one fucking thing and that's to win it. I'm beyond the point of caring about people's feelings. ... I'm not going to get into a pissing contest with Larry Bowa. If I ever were to open up on Larry Bowa, he'd never play another inning of baseball in Philadelphia—and that's official.... We've got six games left and I'm going to battle like hell to win those six games."[9]

The next night, the Phillies scored 14 runs on 15 hits, more than enough for Marty Bystrom, who allowed just two runs in seven innings to earn another win. Since his debut on September 10, Bystrom had been a key to keeping the Phillies in the race. His win on the final day of the month brought his record to a perfect 5–0 with a sterling E.R.A. of just 1.50.

On the same night Bystrom scored a key win for the Phillies, another rookie emerged on the West Coast. The Dodgers trailed the Giants, 3–1, in the top of the ninth inning when RBI singles by Pedro Guerrero and Steve Garvey tied the game, 3–3. An inning later, Guerrero's three-run homer gave LA a 6–3 lead, and a lefty from Mexico named Fernando Valenzuela finished off the Giants for his first win. "He has done a very, very outstanding job and we've put him in some very tough spots," said Tommy Lasorda. "Heck, he's just 19 years old!"[10]

The pressure of the pennant race was lost on Valenzuela who, in addition to beginning his major league career with 11⅔ scoreless innings, had finished his minor league season with another 35 scoreless innings. He was also battling a language barrier. Valenzuela didn't speak any English, which made things that much more difficult. When asked a lengthy question about the gravity of the situation he found himself in at such a young age, if he realized how much was on the line on days he pitched, and was he really that cool, his answer was succinct. "Sí."[11]

The win over the Giants gave the Dodgers an 88–69 record, but they trailed the Houston Astros by two games in the NL West with five to play. The two teams had traded the lead all month and were tied on September 24, but the Astros won four of their next five to take control. As October began, Houston finished a three-game sweep of the Atlanta Braves while the Dodgers took two of three from the Giants. But a 3–2 loss on October 2 put LA three games out with three to play. The two teams were set to finish the season with a three-game set at Dodger Stadium, and the Dodgers needed a sweep to force a playoff or their season would be over. "I think we can do it, I really do," said Dodgers outfielder Dusty Baker. "But I'm sure the Astros think they can, too."[12]

Dusty Baker was right if the quotes coming from the Houston clubhouse were any indication. "I feel a lot better about having to win only one game out there instead of two,"[13] said Astros infielder Art Howe. Relief pitcher Fran LaCorte was even more confident. "If we can't win one out of three, there's something wrong."[14]

Back in the NL East, the Phillies built on Bystrom's performance to finish a sweep of the Cubs behind Steve Carlton, who won his 24th game against nine losses, and Bob Walk to set up their showdown in Montreal with the Expos, who swept the Cardinals in a mid-week series. The two teams entered the weekend tied for first place with three games remaining. Whoever won the series would win the division, and the fact that the games were in Montreal had the Expos excited.

"It's going to be a three game series for the championship," said outfielder Andre Dawson. "But they'll have to take it away from us in our own park. We are loose and confident and we'd just as soon get it over in the first two days of the series."[15] "The people will be out there having a few brews.... I'll tell you, they'll be tearing down the cement,"[16] said catcher Gary Carter, who was coming off a September in which he had hit .336 with seven homers and 23 RBI, which earned him National League Player of the Month honors.

The Yankees had control of the AL East but had trouble wrapping up the division. On September 30, New York held a 9–8 lead over the Indians in the eighth inning with Goose Gossage on the mound looking for his 32nd save of the season.

Five singles and a walk later, Cleveland had put four runs on the board to take a 12–9 lead. Yankees bats couldn't put anything together in the top of the ninth, and the New York lead in the division was suddenly down to 2½ games with five to go.

The loss was the third in a row for the Yankees, while Baltimore had won three straight. But there was no panic in the Yankees clubhouse, at least not from their manager. "We're still three up on them [Baltimore] in the loss column," said Dick Howser. "They have to come and get us. We can win tomorrow, but if we don't we still have four at home."[17]

The four at home were against the Detroit Tigers, but the Yankees had one more game against Cleveland, and they won handily, 18–7, behind Gaylord Perry, whom they acquired in August from the Rangers. The win was Perry's tenth of the season and the Yankees' 100th, the third time they had reached the 100-win mark in the past four seasons.

New York clinched a tie for the division title the following day with a 3–2 win over the Tigers. Ron Guidry went 7⅓ strong innings, and Gossage rebounded from the Cleveland debacle by throwing 1⅔ scoreless innings. Just one more win, or an Orioles loss, would give the Yankees another AL East crown. But rain on the East Coast wiped out both the Friday night Yankees/Tigers game and Baltimore's game against Cleveland, forcing doubleheaders on the season's next-to-last day. Far from ideal for teams hoping to conserve pitching for the post-season.

Rain wasn't an issue as the two big series in the National League got underway. In Montreal, Pete Rose led off the game with a single off Expos starter Scott Sanderson, moved to third on a double by Bake McBride, and scored on a sacrifice fly by Mike Schmidt to give the Phillies a 1–0 lead. A sixth-inning Schmidt homer, his 47th, gave Philadelphia a 2–0 lead, and the Phillies' bullpen took over from there. Newly acquired Sparky Lyle threw a scoreless seventh, and Tug McGraw struck out five of the six batters he faced to preserve the win. The Phillies were one win away from their fourth division title in five years, but the normally ebullient McGraw did his best to keep his cool. Just a week earlier, in Philadelphia, the Phillies had won the first of a three-game set against the Expos, only to drop the next two, and McGraw knew there was still work to do. "Last Friday we got all keyed up and then we went out and lost Saturday and Sunday. So I thought maybe we should change our program a little bit—not get too emotional about winning tonight and it'll be easier getting it together tomorrow."[18]

"It's very simple now," said Expos manager Dick Williams. "We win or we have to face the winter with the knowledge that we were only a second place ball club."[19]

The Los Angeles Dodgers needed a sweep to avoid being a second-place ball club, and they faced a simple message as they entered their clubhouse prior to the first game of the series. A sign on the wall read: "For you guys who don't think we can win four in a row, do us a favor. Don't get dressed."[20]

Despite the inspiration, the Dodgers were in trouble late in Friday's opener. Alan Ashby's eighth-inning sacrifice fly gave the Astros a 2–1 lead, and LA had just two at-bats left to save their season.

Houston starter Ken Forsch, whose second-inning single off Don Sutton gave the Astros a 1–0 lead, set LA down in order in the bottom of the eighth and was scheduled to lead off the top of the ninth. Astros manager Bill Virdon opted to let Forsch hit for himself against Valenzuela, who had still not yielded a run on the season, and Forsch lined out to second baseman Davey Lopes.

Rafael Landestoy, who entered the game as a defensive replacement for Joe Morgan, struck out, but Enos Cabell and Terry Puhl put together back-to-back singles before Valenzuela got Jose Cruz to ground out to end the inning.

Being pulled late in games was becoming commonplace for Morgan, and he didn't care for it. He also thought it was personal. When Houston was slumping in August, Morgan had called a players-only meeting and challenged his teammates to play for the team rather than for themselves. Coming from a guy like Joe Morgan, the words sank in, and the Astros immediately went on a nine-game win streak which thrilled everyone in the Houston clubhouse except Virdon, at least according to Morgan.

In his book, *Joe Morgan: A Life in Baseball*, Morgan stated that his relationship with Virdon changed after that meeting. Apparently feeling that Morgan had overstepped his bounds, Virdon began removing him from games in the late innings under the guise of a defensive upgrade. Morgan was livid. Part of the reason he came to Houston was to help them get over the top. Now his manager was removing him from games at key moments for, according to Morgan, spite.

That strategy was on display when Landestoy hit for Morgan in the ninth inning on October 3 and struck out. Having let Forsch hit for himself, Virdon sent him back out for the ninth inning, despite the fact that

Houston had three pitchers—Joe Sambito, Dave Smith and Frank LaCorte—who would finish the season with double-digit save totals.

Forsch got Jay Johnstone to ground out to open the ninth, but a Rick Monday single was followed by an error by Landestoy, Morgan's defensive replacement. Two batters later, Ron Cey singled to left field to tie the game.

Valenzuela again set the Astros down in order in the top of the tenth inning, and Virdon again sent Forsch out in the bottom half of the frame. Former Astros catcher Joe Ferguson sent Forsch's first pitch into the stands over a leaping Cesar Cedeno in left-center field for a walk-off homer, giving the Dodgers new life. Ferguson celebrated his game-winning homer by throwing his batting helmet into the air as he rounded third base and, after crossing home plate, picked up Lasorda in a bear hug before being mobbed by his teammates and blowing kisses to the fans. "Sometimes we don't look pretty out there," said Ferguson, "but this team has shown more heart than any team I've ever played on."[21]

The two teams squared off the following afternoon with LA's Jerry Reuss, author of the season's only no-hitter, facing Houston's Nolan Ryan, author of four no-hitters to that point. He would add three more before he was finished.

LA took a 1–0 lead in the bottom of the second inning when Derrel Thomas singled to left to score Steve Garvey. Art Howe's RBI single in the fourth tied the game at 1–1, but Garvey led off the bottom of the fifth with a home run, his 26th, and Reuss shut out the Astros the rest of the way for his 18th win.

"I've never seen him more aggressive," Lasorda said of his starter. "I've seen him throw better, but he went after every batter today."[22] "I loved every minute of it," said Reuss. "I loved the excitement of the fans. I even stopped to look at it, to experience it. I enjoyed it as much as they did."[23]

The win meant that Houston's lead was down to just a single game with one game remaining. A Dodgers win on Sunday afternoon would force a one-game playoff in Los Angeles, while a Houston win would secure the division title.

"The fact is this: We can win it tomorrow. They can't," said Morgan. "We win tomorrow and it's all over. The percentages are in our favor. The Dodgers haven't beaten us four straight all year and I don't see them doing it."[24]

While the Astros would have to wait until at least Sunday to wrap up their division, the Yankees had a chance to win the American League East on Saturday against the Detroit Tigers at Yankee Stadium. Rudy May took the mound in the first game of a doubleheader and allowed Detroit to grab a 2–1 lead after four innings, but the Yankees came roaring back. Once again, Reggie Jackson provided the big blow, a three-run homer off Detroit's Roger Weaver in the bottom of the fifth inning that gave the Yankees a lead they wouldn't relinquish. After a torrid start, Jackson cooled off in August. But from mid–September through the clinching game, he caught fire when the Yankees needed him the most, batting .429 with four homers and 12 RBI in 11 games. "It's been a struggle all along and Reggie did it," said Howser. "It couldn't happen to a better guy. October looks like it's going to be a very good month for him."[25]

The win was not only big for the Yankees as a team, but also for a number of individual players. Jackson's home run was his 41st, which moved him into the lead in the American League home run race, though Milwaukee's Ben Oglivie would hit one on the season's final day to tie him. Jackson would also record two hits in his final four at-bats to hit an even .300 for the season, the only time in his career he did so.

Additionally, Rudy May's seven-inning, two-run performance lowered his ERA to 2.46, best in the American League, and Goose Gossage picked up his 33rd save, which capped a tremendous second half. From the All-Star break until the end of the season, Gossage converted 20 of 22 save chances while posting a 1.84 E.R.A. and striking out 60 in 53⅔ innings. The 33 saves established a career high and led the American league.

There was one other milestone for the Yankees that day. In the second game of the doubleheader, third baseman Graig Nettles returned to the New York lineup after missing nearly 70 games while fighting infectious hepatitis. Following doctors' orders, Nettles refrained from all physical activity for seven weeks before resuming baseball workouts near the end of September. Once the division was clinched, both Nettles and the Yankees decided it was time to see if he was ready to return to action. In his first game back since June 23, he went 2-for-5 with a double before leaving the game in the ninth inning.

"I expect to be a little stiff [tomorrow] but I expect to play," Nettles said after the game. "I hope to remain on the active list for the playoffs. I want to play in Kansas City. I didn't come all the way back here not to play."[26] "We'll see how he feels on Sunday," said Howser. "We'll see how his timing is and ultimately, I will have to make a decision. His fielding seems to take care of itself. It's one of the many decisions I have to make before Wednesday in Kansas City."[27]

The American League was set. For the fourth time in five years, the Royals and Yankees would play each other for a shot in the World Series. New York had dealt KC painful losses in 1976, 1977 and 1978, and the Royals were ready for another shot at their nemesis. "The fans would like to see us play the Yankees," said outfielder Willie Wilson. "You know, the revenge factor or something like that. I think most of the players feel the same way."[28]

"New York isn't as good as they used to be," said pitcher Larry Gura, a former Yankee who left New York under unfriendly circumstances. "They don't have Roy White, Thurman Munson, Sparky Lyle or the Catfish—Jim Hunter—anymore. Baltimore would have been tough."[29]

The final Saturday game with playoff implications took place in Montreal. The Phillies held a one-game lead in the NL East with two to play, but Montreal had their hottest pitcher on the mound. Steve Rogers had started on Opening Day against the Phillies but was bested by Phillies ace Steve Carlton in a 6–3 final. Since then, Rogers had gone 16–10, including a complete-game win against Philadelphia in his last start, on September 28 at Veterans Stadium.

The win gave Montreal a lead in the division and poked holes in the prevailing wisdom that said Rogers wasn't a big-game pitcher. If Rogers truly wanted to shed the choker label, he'd need to do it in October, and this was his chance. If he won, the Expos' season continued. If he didn't, it didn't. He faced the biggest start of his career, and aside from the Phillies, he had one more thing to worry about. An October storm pummeled Montreal with rain, and the start of the game was delayed by more than three hours. When the weather finally cleared, he faced a Phillies lineup with a few surprises. Veterans Garry Maddox and Bob Boone were replaced by Del Unser and rookie Keith Moreland as Dallas Green once again sat struggling regulars. Later in the evening, both Maddox and Boone would factor into a very strange baseball game.

The oddities began in the bottom of the first inning, when Montreal's Rodney Scott hit a ground ball to second, where it was fielded by Manny Trillo, who made a wild throw to Pete Rose at first base, which allowed Scott to advance to second. Trillo was charged with an error, just his tenth on the season. Phillies starter Larry Christenson attempted to pick Scott off second, but his throw was off the mark and skipped into center field for another error, allowing Scott to advance to third.

Rowland Office hit a ground ball to Trillo, who threw to Rose for the out, but Scott took off for home and got there ahead of Rose's throw. Moreland had the plate blocked and was able to tag the speedy Scott to end the inning.

Montreal threatened again in the second inning when Andre Dawson and Gary Carter reached with no one out. After a Warren Cromartie fly out, Larry Parrish blooped a ball to center field that dropped in front of Unser. It's a ball Maddox likely would have caught, but not from the bench. The single loaded the bases, but Chris Speier grounded into an inning-ending double play to get the Phillies out of the jam.

Rain began to fall again as the game headed into the third inning, and Bake McBride could see his breath as he stepped into the batter's box with one out to face Rogers. McBride smacked a hard ground ball down the first base line and beat Cromartie to the bag for an infield single. Mike Schmidt then hit a ball off the wall in left field and McBride rounded third on his way home. But Andre Dawson made a perfect relay throw to Speier, who threw to Carter to nail McBride to keep the game scoreless.

Philadelphia's spirits were not lifted when Christenson walked Rogers to lead off the bottom of the third and made another errant pickoff throw, which allowed Rogers to go to third. Jerry White homered on a 1–2 pitch, and Montreal had a 2–0 lead. "You expect a lot of people to hurt you in this Montreal lineup but you don't expect much from Jerry White,"[30] said Phillies broadcaster Richie Ashburn.

It was 2–1, Montreal, in the top of the seventh when the Phillies loaded the bases for Greg Luzinski. In the Phillies broadcast booth, Ashburn remarked that the impending showdown would be the biggest at-bat in a season of frustration for Luzinski. Once one of the game's most feared sluggers, "The Bull" was limping to a horrible finish to 1980. He'd hit just .167 since the beginning of September with three homers and nine RBI en route to posting the worst batting average of his career.

Rogers ran the count to 3–0, Green gave Luzinski the green light, and he took advantage, smacking a single to center to score Pete Rose and Bake McBride. But Mike Schmidt got caught in a rundown and once he was tagged out, the Expos nabbed Luzinski when he strayed too far off first base. It was the fifth double play of the night for the Expos, but it also gave the Phillies a 3–2 lead. It was short-lived.

In the bottom of the seventh, Speier lifted a pop-up to Trillo, who saw the ball pop out of his glove for his second error of the game. Dick Williams brought Ron LeFlore in to pinch-run for Speier. LeFlore's wrist injury had proven costly as the Expos were without both him and Ellis Valentine for the crucial season-ending series. The wrist hampered LeFlore's ability to handle the bat, but not to run.

With Ron Reed on in relief and a rookie catcher in Moreland, everyone at Olympic Stadium knew that LeFlore would be on the move, including Dallas Green, who called a pitch-out. But Moreland's throw was low and skipped into center field, allowing LeFlore to advance to third on the Phillies' fifth error of the game. Three batters later, Rodney Scott doubled to left to score rookie Tim Raines, and the Expos had a 4–3 lead.

It stayed that way until the top of the ninth. With two out and Bake McBride on second base, Bob Boone came to the plate to face reliever Woody Fryman with the game on the line. Like Luzinski, Boone was struggling through a tough season offensively. He was hitting .228 and riding a 2-for-24 skid when he poked Fryman's second pitch into center field to score McBride and tie the game.

Green summoned his closer, Tug McGraw, for the ninth inning to shut down the Expos. McGraw was making his 57th appearance of the season and had been virtually unhittable in the second half. The previous night, he had fanned five of the six batters he'd faced in nailing down his 20th save. He breezed through the inning by striking out Parrish and Jerry Manuel and getting Tim Wallach to foul out to the catcher.

Dick Williams turned to Stan Bahnsen, who was also making his 57th appearance of the season, for the top of the tenth inning, and like McGraw he breezed through the Phillies' lineup. But things got interesting in the bottom of the tenth inning.

Jerry White led off with a single and moved to third base on a sacrifice bunt and a groundout. That brought Dawson to the plate with the winning run on third base and two out. Dawson had hits in 15 of his last 16 games and was perhaps the last person McGraw wanted to face at the time. But three straight screwballs had Dawson heading back to the dugout to get his glove, while McGraw skipped off the mound, pounding the maroon script "P" on his chest with his pitching hand and slapping his right thigh with his glove hand. "Tugger" had come through again.

Rose led off the top of the eleventh with his third hit of the day to bring up McBride. Conventional wisdom called for McBride to bunt Rose to second, but if Green did that, Williams would surely walk Schmidt with a base open and pitch to Don McCormack, who had replaced Boone and had a total of zero big-league at-bats. McBride swung away and popped out on the first pitch to bring Schmidt to the plate. Bahnsen ran the count to 2–0 and threw his next pitch right down the middle. Schmidt unloaded on it.

"Long drive, watch that baby!" yelled Phillies play-by-play man Harry Kalas as the ball made its way deep into the left field seats. "Way, way outta here. Home run Mike Schmidt, Phillies lead 6–4! Pete Rose scores in front of him. Home run #48 for Schmidt, I have never seen Mike as excited as this."[31]

He wasn't the only one. The Phillies dugout erupted in joy as scores of men in powder blue pants and maroon jackets leapt up and down and hugged each other before greeting Schmidt near the on-deck circle to slap him on the back. McGraw came out for his third inning of work and shut down the Expos to wrap up the game and the division. The Phillies were back in the playoffs.

As the players filed into the Phillies' clubhouse, Ashburn stood on a picnic table, trying to grab players for the live post-game show. Among the first to approach him was Bowa, who poured champagne on Ashburn's head. It wasn't the first time the Phillies had won the National League East, but there was a different feel to this championship. "This is better because of all the controversy," Bowa told Ashburn. "We made some mistakes today but.... I tell you what, Rich, Schmitty is unbelievable. If he's not most valuable player ... and Tug.... Fireman of the Year and Carlton the Cy Young. I tell you what—those guys have been unbelievable all year."[32]

He was right. Winning championships requires big seasons from big players, and the Phillies had gotten exactly that. Schmidt's division-winning home run was his 48th of the season, which not only established a career high, but also set a National League record for third basemen. Carlton finished the season 24–9 with a 2.34 ERA, and McGraw went 5–1 in the second half of the season with 13 saves and an unbelievable 0.52 ERA.

For the third time in four seasons, the Royals, Yankees and Phillies advanced to the playoffs. There was one spot remaining, and the Dodgers and Astros would go head-to-head to decide who would face Philadelphia in the NLCS.

Mike Schmidt finally delivered the kind of season Phillies fans were hoping for, capturing NL MVP honors while establishing career highs in home runs (48) and RBI (121) (National Baseball Hall of Fame Library, Cooperstown, New York).

For game three of the series, Dodgers manager Tommy Lasorda started 14-game winner Burt Hooton, while Houston skipper Bill Virdon went with Vern Ruhle. In his seventh season in the big leagues, Ruhle had taken J.R. Richard's spot in the Astros' rotation and had been outstanding, posting 6–2 record win 13 starts with a 2.17 ERA. Unfortunately for him and the Astros, he also cut his right index finger on a nail in the dugout on Friday. The wound required two stitches to close and left Ruhle unsure how long he could go in the season's final game. "I don't think it's going to be a factor, but I'm going to let the trainer work on it," Ruhle said. "Obviously I can't pitch with a Band-Aid on, but I think I'll be all right. If I can't [pitch] I'm sure Joaquin will be ready."[33]

In addition to Ruhle, Joe Morgan injured himself in Friday's game sliding back into first base on a pickoff attempt. The Dodgers weren't faring much better, though, as Davey Lopes was battling a sore neck and both Ron Cey and Dusty Baker were dealing with hamstring pulls. But minor injuries wouldn't keep anyone out of a game of this magnitude.

It didn't take long for the Astros to get to Hooton or to practice a little gamesmanship. Cesar Cedeno led off the top of the second inning by testing Ron Cey's sore hamstring with a bunt down the third-base line that turned into an infield single. A stolen base and a Hooton error on Art Howe's sacrifice bunt attempt put runners on the corners with no one out. Alan Ashby singled to center to score Cedeno, and Craig Reynolds singled to right to give Houston a 2–0 lead and chase Hooton from the game.

Ruhle wasn't around much longer than Hooton, but it wasn't the Dodgers who knocked him out of the game, it was his finger. The stitches opened up early, and by the third inning he had to come out of the game. "I went as far as I could as hard as I could," he said afterwards. "It started breaking by the first inning, but it didn't start bleeding. It just started tearing downward and by the last two pitches I made, I just didn't see any point in going on. I would have been hurting the team."[34]

Houston increased the lead to 3–0 in the top of the fourth, but the Dodgers got one back in the bottom of the fifth on Davey Lopes' RBI single off Joaquin Andujar. The fact that Lopes was even in the lineup, let alone contributing, was a testament to his fortitude. The Dodgers' second baseman was playing despite a pinched nerve in his neck that caused severe pain, numbness and temporary paralysis in his hand. But he continued to make key defensive plays and deliver clutch hits, including the one to plate the Dodgers' first run.

Down 3–1, Lasorda once again called on Fernando Valenzuela to keep his team in the game, and once again, the rookie delivered, throwing two scoreless innings. When he was due to hit in the bottom of the seventh with two men on base, the 19-year-old Valenzuela was replaced by 42-year-old Manny Mota, whom the Dodgers activated as a pinch-hitter in

September. This presented a slight problem as Mota was also the Dodgers' first-base coach. Ever the strategist, Lasorda sent pitcher Don Sutton to take Mota's place in the coach's box while Mota took Valenzuela's place at the plate against Joe Sambito.

The two had faced each other on September 10, when Sambito induced Mota to ground into a double play in the ninth inning of a 6–5 Houston victory. This time, Mota stroked an RBI single to right field to cut the lead to 3–2 and end Sambito's afternoon. Bill Virdon summoned Frank LaCorte from the bullpen, and he retired Lopes and Dusty Baker to escape the inning.

LaCorte got Steve Garvey to hit a ground ball to third baseman Enos Cabell to open the eighth inning, but Cabell couldn't handle it and Garvey was safe at first base to bring up Cey. Conventional wisdom called for Cey to bunt, especially since he was nursing a sore hamstring, which not only prevented him from running well but also sapped a lot of his power. Cey squared around to bunt twice, but couldn't get it down. He worked the count full and, when LaCorte delivered his next pitch, Cey drove it straight into his left ankle. Now both legs were hurting, but the count was still full, and Cey looked to put a ball in the gap.

He fouled off two more pitches before LaCorte delivered a fastball that caught too much of the plate. Cey pounced on it, sending the ball deep to left field. "You gotta be kidding me," Sambito thought as the ball sailed into the left field seats.[35]

The two-run homer, Cey's 28th of the season, gave LA a 4–3 lead, but there was plenty of drama left. Houston put two men on in the top of the ninth, which brought Lasorda out of the Dodgers' dugout and drew a round of boos at the prospect of his removing Steve Howe, who had replaced Valenzuela in the eighth. But the boos turned to cheers when starter and ersatz first-base coach Don Sutton emerged from the Dodgers bullpen and trotted to the mound. Working on just one day's rest, Sutton told catcher Steve Yeager that he didn't have much, but what he did have moved a lot. Two pitches later, Sutton got Denny Walling to bounce out to Lopes to end the game and force a one-game Monday afternoon playoff at Dodger Stadium.

"I wouldn't mind sleeping here tonight," Lopes said. "Better than that, let's play another, the last game, right now. Let's do it while we're hot."[36]

In the opposing locker room, another second baseman was a bit more subdued. "We're just one man away from winning this thing," said Joe

Morgan. "And I'm that man. I haven't done anything for this team the last two days. But, I promise you, Joe Morgan will do something tomorrow."[37] There was similar optimism in other corners of the Houston locker room as well. "What we have to do," said LaCorte, "is go back to the hotel, have a couple of beers, relax and go out tomorrow and kick the bleep out of them."[38]

The other thing the Astros needed to do was not give up home runs in clutch situations. Dodgers homers were the difference in each of the three games, which promoted the *LA Times* headline "As Astros hit the wall, the Dodgers Clear it—Again." The headline was accompanied by a graphic:

Game No. 160: Ferguson
Game No. 161: Garvey
Game No 162: Cey
Game No 163: ???

"This team's going to grow up a lot tomorrow," said Morgan, "or it'll die. It'll be strong, I'll tell you that, one way or another, or it'll die."[39]

The man charged with staving off the Astros' death was knuckleballer Joe Niekro. In 14 big league seasons, Niekro had thrown more than 2,100 innings, and not one of them had come in the post-season. Whether or not that streak continued was up to him, but his two previous outings against LA had not gone well. "The challenge is out there, and I've got to go out and get it," Niekro said. "I accept it. If we had to have a playoff game, I wanted to pitch it."[40]

Niekro was gunning for his second straight 20-win season, while the Dodgers' starter, Dave Goltz, was trying to redeem himself after not living up to the free-agent deal he signed before the season. Goltz averaged 15 wins and more than 250 innings over his last five seasons in Minnesota, but fell on hard times in LA. Things got so bad that he asked Lasorda to remove him from the Dodgers' rotation after heading into the All-Star break with a 3–6 record and a whopping 5.68 ERA. Now the season was on the line, and Goltz was the man in charge of keeping the remarkable Dodgers comeback alive. "I'm excited about being given the chance to win it," Goltz said. "I've never been in a situation where a game meant so much. I'm really looking forward to this."[41]

So were the Dodgers faithful. Nearly 150,000 fans attended the three games over the weekend and they, uncharacteristically, made their presence known. "For the first time in my 15 years here, it feels like we have a 10th man,"[42] said Sutton.

Astros General Manager Tal Smith got caught up in the excitement as well, but he also could have lived without it. "It's just like a World Series," he said. "Three of the most exciting games you'll ever see, especially if you're an impartial observer, which I'm not."[43] Few of the 51,000 fans who showed up for the playoff game were impartial either, and there was another biased observer sitting on the Dodgers bench.

Ron Cey woke up on Monday morning with a badly swollen ankle, the result of the previous day's foul ball, and was in enough pain that Lasorda had no choice but to remove him from the lineup. For a team already missing Reggie Smith and Bill Russell, it was a big blow and the first sign of trouble for the Dodgers.

The next sign came when Terry Puhl led off the game with a ground ball to Lopes, who had the ball pop out of his glove for an error. Enos Cabell singled to center and stole second. After two batters, Houston had runners on second and third, and the Dodgers' bullpen began to stir. Two batters later, Jose Cruz hit a ground ball to Mickey Hatcher, who had taken Cey's place at third base. Hatcher came home with the throw, but Joe Ferguson couldn't hold onto it after Puhl collided with him. Cesar Cedeno's groundout gave the Astros a 2–0 lead despite their having only one hit.

While Goltz and the Dodgers looked a bit shaky in the early going, Niekro was anything but, retiring the first six batters he faced on the strength of an active and unpredictable knuckleball. In the top of the third, Art Howe faced Goltz with two out and a man, on and deposited Goltz's offering into the left field seats to give his team a 4–0 lead. For Howe, it was his tenth home run of the season and the 33rd, and most important of his career.

Houston added three more runs the following inning, and Niekro handled the rest. When Jack Perconte came up with two outs in the ninth inning and his team down, 7–1, the Dodger Stadium organist broke into the inspirational World War II tune, "We did it before and we can do it again." But there was no miracle comeback this time. Perconte popped out to Dave Bergman at first base, and the Astros, for the first time in their 19-year existence, were headed to the playoffs.

A few minutes later, the floor of the visitors' clubhouse at Dodger Stadium was a morass of beer, water, ice, champagne, tuna salad, milk, orange juice and who knows what else. It stank to high heaven, but it didn't stop the party. "This is the sweetest, best moment of my baseball life," said Howe. "All the trips to the minor leagues, all the frustration.... It was worth it a thousand times. We're champions now."[44]

The fact that Howe was even in the major leagues was a minor miracle. Ten years earlier, he was working as a systems analyst at Westinghouse when he went to a Pittsburgh Pirates open tryout on a dare. The Pirates were so impressed with his abilities that they took nearly a year to sign him. In the summer of 1971, Howe took a $700 a month pay cut to play in the Single-A Carolina League with the Salem Rebels, where he hit .348. Four years after that, he was the "player to be named later" in a deal that netted the Pirates 36-year-old second baseman Tommy Helms, whose best years were definitely behind him.

Not many guys go from player to be named later to hero, but Howe's 3-for-5 day with a home run and four RBI in a one-game playoff earned him the honor. "I said to my wife last night, 'this is something I've always dreamed about my while life,'" Howe told reporters in the soggy clubhouse. "Now everyone is going to be watching us."[45]

While Howe was addressing the media, catcher Bruce Bochy was doing a live radio interview with a reporter who thought he was Howe. "I didn't know if the ball was going out or not," said Bochy as Howe. "But when it did, I said hoo-ray, I did it. You know, these guys have been riding my back to the pennant all year."[46]

Bochy's impersonations aside, there was one factor that kept the Astros in the race, and it wasn't Howe's bat, or Bochy's, it was pitching. "No team beats us four in a row," said Joe Morgan. "No team does that to us. Our pitching is too good. The Dodgers learned that today, no matter what kind of momentum they thought they had."[47]

In the Dodgers' clubhouse, the mood was subdued, but not melancholy. The optimism of the last three days had given way to a feeling of acceptance and an odd sort of satisfaction with what they had accomplished despite falling short of their goal. "We're disappointed," said Davey Lopes, "but you can't look back and say, 'If we had won this game or that game.... When you come this far, you want to win. But if I had to sum up this season in a word, I'd have to say exciting."[48]

"Only one team could go to Philadelphia," said Lasorda. "It was Houston. That means this can't be a good season. It was exciting. The fans were excited and that excited us. But I don't like finishing second."[49]

The Astros were in the post-season for the first time in franchise history and were, indeed, headed to Philadelphia. The only problem was that they had to fly cross-country to get there, and Game One of the NCLS was scheduled to start less than 24 hours after the party in the visitors' clubhouse finally broke up. Still, tired but in the playoffs beats rested and watching the playoffs on TV, and the Astros had finally silenced some of the naysayers.

"Houston used to be considered a joke," said Nolan Ryan. "You look around this clubhouse, you think about this season, what all we've been through. You know one thing. Houston isn't a joke in baseball anymore."[50]

9

The Postseason

Goose, Garry and Georges

"I think you have to agree we match up better against Houston than Los Angeles," said Pete Rose once their opponent was certain. "Houston's pitching is a little more out of rotation and I'd rather play in the Dome."[1]

Dallas Green concurred, citing the fact that his team beat Houston nine times in 12 regular season matchups, and the fact that Houston's Astrodome didn't have the late-afternoon shadows of Dodger Stadium.

The bigger question for the Phillies was who would be on their post-season roster. Lefty reliever Sparky Lyle was not eligible because he wasn't on the roster before September 1, having been acquired in a September 13 trade with the Texas Rangers. Lyle pitched well down the stretch and, perhaps more importantly, gave the Phillies another left-hander out of the bullpen to spell Tug McGraw.

But that was known. What wasn't known was the status of Marty Bystrom, without whom the Phillies may not have even made the playoffs. Since Bystrom was added to the roster on September 1, he was not eligible either. But after an intense back and forth with the National League office, which included examination of Phillies pitcher Nino Espinosa's medical records, Philadelphia was allowed to add Bystrom to the playoff roster after Espinosa was declared unable to pitch due to chronic bursitis in his pitching shoulder.

Bystrom wasn't needed for Game One of the National League Championship Series on October 7 because the Phillies had ace Steve Carlton available. "Lefty" had thrown 304 innings, the most since his outstanding 1972 season, but was also working on extra rest, having not pitched since October 1. Houston countered with Ken Forsch, working on three days' rest. The short rest didn't seem to bother the Astros righty as he cruised through the first five innings without allowing a run, while his teammates scored a single run off of Carlton in the top of the third.

Mike Schmidt had enjoyed a breakout season in 1980 after years of frustration. He was on his way to his first MVP Award, but post-season success had been tough to find. Through 46 playoff at-bats, Schmidt had managed just eight hits and 4 RBI, including an 0-for-2 in Game One when he stepped to the plate in the bottom of the sixth inning with Pete Rose aboard. A big hit here could set the tone for the rest of the Series for both him and the team.

Schmidt fouled Forsch's first pitch off the mask of Houston catcher Luis Pujols, and after a ball, Forcsh came back with another fastball. Schmidt just got under it and sent a fly ball to center field, where it was caught by Cesar Cedeno. The Phillies' slugger returned to the dugout amid a chorus of boos from his hometown crowd.

Rose was in danger of being stranded on first base when Greg Luzinski strode to the plate. In contrast to Schmidt, Luzinski had enjoyed post-season success in the past, but had just endured his worst regular season of his career. His .228 batting average was a career-low and he had racked up more strikeouts than hits. "The Bull" ran the count full, and after a foul ball straight back, Forsch came with a fastball, but he missed his spot. Pujols wanted the ball up and in, but the pitch was too low, and Luzinski crushed it. "Forget it!"[2] exclaimed Howard Cosell on the television broadcast as the ball sailed into the seats in left field.

Like his Opening Day home run, Luzinski's two-run shot in the first game of the playoffs gave his team the lead and, as on Opening Day, it was a lead they wouldn't relinquish. Carlton didn't allow another run, and Tug McGraw pitched the final two innings to earn the save. The Phillies led the series, 1–0. "I can't even tell you when the pitch was, to tell you the truth," Luzinski said. "I know it was down and in. The ump told [catcher Bob] Boone later it was about a foot inside. It was one of those pitches where I was just short and quick."[3]

"I thought I pitched pretty good, but I didn't want to hang ... one ... to Luzinski and I came with a fastball," Forsch said after the game. "He hit it out. We got that early lead and we had our chances. If we had jumped on Carlton ... well, who jumps on Carlton?"[4]

The answer was very few, but Houston did have Carlton in trouble throughout the game. Astros hitters reached base in six of the seven innings Carlton pitched, but they could never put together the big inning they needed. Still, it was a testament to the season, and career, Carlton had put together that allowing one run in seven innings of work and giving his team a post-season lead could be viewed as an off-night.

Temperatures reached nearly 90 degrees the following afternoon in Kansas City when the Yankees and Royals faced off in Game One of their series. It was the fourth time in the past five seasons the two teams had faced each other in the ALCS, but this year there was an entirely different feel. Both teams had new managers, Jim Frey in Kansas City and Dick Howser in New York, and there had been turnover on the rosters as well, particularly with the Yankees.

Mickey Rivers, Catfish Hunter, Chris Chambliss and Thurman Munson were no longer there, and five of the nine Yankees starters in Game One were not on the roster on October 7, 1978, when New York knocked Kansas City out of the post-season for the third year in a row.

The man charged with stopping this new lineup was Royals lefty Larry Gura, who won 18 games during the season but was terrible down the stretch. In his final seven starts, Gura went 0–5 with a 6.46 E.R.A. But this was the post-season and, more importantly for Gura, it was the Yankees, a team he loved to beat.

Gura pitched for the Yankees in 1974 and 1975, but one day during spring training, manager Billy Martin saw him going to play tennis with a teammate and flipped out. In Martin's mind, Gura wasn't pitching well and should have been working to get better. In Gura's mind, he was staying in shape. Martin hated tennis and decided he was going to get rid of Gura. A few months later, the Yankees traded him to the Royals for backup catcher Fran Healy, who played 74 games over three seasons for the Yankees, hitting .250 with 16 RBI before retiring to go into the broadcasting booth.

Free from Martin, Gura went to Kansas City and won 59 games in his first five seasons. As luck would have it, Billy Martin was in the ABC broadcast booth for the ALCS, along with Al Michaels and Orioles pitcher Jim Palmer. Martin took another shot at Gura, saying he had to choose between him and Catfish Hunter and went with Hunter, then downplayed the incident, calling it a misunderstanding and saying that he and Gura got along just fine.

Whether or not that was true was anyone's guess, but Gura was not sharp early, allowing a leadoff double to Willie Randolph before retiring Reggie Jackson on a foul out to left field to escape the inning. In the top of the second, he wasn't so lucky.

Eric Soderholm grounded out to lead off the inning and bring catcher Rick Cerone to the plate. In the booth, Martin spoke about how important it was for the Yankees to have a good catcher to take over after the tragic death of Thurman Munson. Palmer was more focused on how to get Cerone out, noting that while Cerone wasn't a home run hitter, he did have home run power. Soon, Cerone put that power on display, hitting a 2–1 change-up down the left field line and sneaking it just inside the foul pole for a solo homer to give the Yankees the lead. An ABC camera showed a disgusted Gura seemingly chastising himself on the mound before cutting back to Cerone slapping hands with third base coach Mike Ferraro. Next up was left fielder Lou Piniella, who had won Rookie of the Year honors in 1969 as a member of the inaugural Royals team.

Gura quickly got Piniella down in the count, 0–2. But Piniella fought back to even it before leaning on an outside pitch and hooking it down left field line, just fair. The ball landed a few feet to the right of where Cerone's did, and got Frey to the mound and Renie Martin up in the KC bullpen. When Aurelio Rodriguez doubled to right field, the Yankees looked like they might be on their way to a blowout.

The Royals fought back in the bottom of the frame. Amos Otis led off with a single off Yankees starter Ron Guidry and stole second. John Wathan walked, and Willie Aikens struck out to bring up Darrell Porter, who hit a sinking line drive to Piniella in left. Piniella made a great catch on the ball but hurt his leg in the process. He stayed in the game, but it was obviously bothering him, and it took all of one batter to find out how much.

Second baseman Frank White hit a shallow fly ball to left field, and Piniella charged it, but it dropped in front of him, allowing both Otis and Wathan to score. There was some question as to whether Piniella's leg was bothering him or he lost it in the sun. Either way, the ball should have been caught, and it cost the Yankees two runs. Kansas City loaded the bases an inning later, and Willie Aikens took a Guidry fastball on the inner half to left field to score Brett and Otis, giving the Royals a 4–2 lead.

It was still 4–2 in the bottom of the seventh inning when Brett faced relief pitcher Ron Davis. Davis was 6'4" and had gone 23–5 with 16 saves out of the Yankees bullpen over the past two seasons, the kind of guy championship teams can count on in the late innings. He got in front of Brett, 0–2 in the count, before wasting a pitch on the outside corner, trying to get Brett to chase. He didn't. On the next pitch, Cerone again set up outside, and Davis hit his spot. It was a thigh-high fastball on the outer edge of the plate, and Brett sent it over the wall in center field, just left of the Royals Stadium fountain to give the Royals a 5–2 lead. They added two more in the eighth, and Gura coasted to a 7–2 win. "Larry Gura," mused Reggie Jackson after the game. "The man had his day in the sun. He beat Reggie Jackson and the New York Yankees. No, he didn't just beat Reggie Jackson, he kicked my ass. He made me look like a 46-year-old man at the plate."[5]

Gura struck Jackson out on a slow curveball with two on in the fifth inning and then, in the seventh, again with two on, got him to ground out to Frank White. Those two at-bats, both coming in a 4–2 game, were crucial, and Gura emerged on top both times. On the afternoon, Jackson was 0-for-4 and stranded six men. "I didn't pitch any differently today than I have in the past," Gura said after the game. "I really don't pitch differently against the Yankees. They know what I can do."[6]

What he did was to own the Yankees. The playoff win brought his record against New York to 4–0 in 1980 and 8–1 in his career. The win also gave the Royals an emotional boost against a team that had definitely had their number. "It was very important, especially if we can go on and win tomorrow," said Brett. "Today was a confidence builder. We were down 2–0 after they hit back-to-back homers and we came back."[7]

In the visitors' clubhouse, Howser was left wondering about missed opportunities. Gura allowed two runs in a complete-game win, but the Yankees had runners on base in all but one inning. "We had a good opportunity there, but he really did the job when he had to," Howser said of Gura. "All of our opportunities during the game seemed to come with two out, and we didn't get the key hits when we needed them."[8]

A few hours later in Philadelphia, the Phillies and the Astros headed into the bottom of the ninth locked in a 3–3 tie, and Frank LaCorte had a tough task ahead of him. "If you had to stack the deck, you couldn't ask for it to turn out any better than this,"[9] said Don Drysdale in the ABC broadcast booth. "Not for the Phils, you couldn't,"[10] added Howard Cosell.

Pete Rose led off the inning, having already reached base four times on two hits and two walks. LaCorte's first pitch was right down the middle, and Rose swung so hard his helmet flew off. But he missed. He flied out on the next pitch, but Bake McBride and Mike Schmidt followed with singles. The winning run was on second base in the form of Bake McBride with one out.

Lonnie Smith, who had run for Luzinski in the eighth, worked the count full against LaCorte before fouling a ball straight back to the backstop. As the crowd began to rise in anticipation, Smith fouled off five more pitches, seemingly in an attempt to increase the drama.

LaCorte's next pitch was on the outer half of the plate, and Smith went with it, slapping it to right field. As the ball floated toward Terry Puhl, the crowd broke into a fever pitch, sensing the game-winning run. Puhl came in and played the ball on a short-hop, wheeled and fired a strike home to Alan Ashby, who instinctively caught the ball and dropped to one knee to brace for the collision he knew was coming. McBride would have been off at the crack of the bat and, with a full head of steam, this was going to hurt. But when Ashby looked up, McBride wasn't there. Phillies third base coach Lee Elia had held him. As Ashby breathed a sigh of relief and flipped the ball back to LaCorte, ABC cameras cut to McBride at third, who slumped his shoulders and shook his head in disbelief.

It was right there. The game should have been over.

Replays showed that McBride was, indeed, off with the crack of the bat, but he slowed down as he approached third base. The mistake was compounded by the fact that had Puhl caught the ball, McBride surely would have been doubled up anyway. His only option was to keep running. But he didn't. Still, the Phillies were in great shape. They had the bases loaded with just one out. All they needed was a fly ball to take a 2–0 Series lead. Instead they got a strikeout from Manny Trillo and a foul out from Garry Maddox. In the bottom of the ninth inning of a tie game, the Phillies strung together three consecutive hits and had nothing to show for it.

Things got much worse when the Astros plated four runs in the top of the tenth, the last two on a triple by Dave Bergman to score Jose Cruz and Cesar Cedeno. LaCorte and Joaquin Andujar allowed one run in the bottom of the tenth, but it wasn't enough. The Series was tied and heading to Houston.

As the media filed into the jubilant Astros clubhouse, shortstop Craig Reynolds strutted around wearing a pair of rubber glasses with a fake nose, saying, "We had it all the way. And if you believe that, you'll believe anything."[11]

The mood was quite different in the home clubhouse, where Elia stood up to take the blame for the baserunning gaffe that cost the Phillies the game. "The fact that there was one out kept standing out in my mind," said Elia. "I wanted to make sure it was a run. That's why there was that hesitation. It was no fault of Bake McBride. He could have scored had I sent him."[12]

The win was crucial to the Astros, who couldn't afford to go down two games to none in the best-of-five Series. But their fortitude, and the Phillies' ineptitude, evened the Series and made it a best-of-three, with the final three games at the Astrodome.

"When we've had to win we've come through," said Joe Morgan. "Maybe people will stop underrating us if we do it a few more times."[13]

In addition to respect, the Astros needed rest, and they finally got some as both NL teams took October 9 off to travel from Philadelphia to Houston. The Astros' flight arrived at Houston's Intercontinental Airport shortly before 4 a.m., when they were greeted by about 100 hearty fans. Since September 1, the Astros had played 35 games in 38 days in eight different cities, including both coasts, and they needed down time.

The day off for the Phillies and Astros allowed the ALCS to take center stage on October 9. Fifteen-game winner and AL ERA champion Rudy May got the call for the Yankees against 20-game winner Dennis Leonard of the Royals.

This time it was Kansas City that jumped out in front early. The Royals put up three runs in the bottom of the third inning on Willie Wilson's two-run triple and a double off the bat of shortstop U L Washington. But the Yankees cut the lead to 3–2 on a Graig Nettles' inside-the-park homer and an RBI double by Willie Randolph. It was still 3–2 Kansas City in the top of the eighth when Bob Watson came to bat with Randolph on first base and two out. Still in the game, Leonard played cat and mouse with Randolph at first, throwing over multiple times to keep the tying run close to the bag.

A check-swing foul ball put Watson behind in the count, 1–2, and the crowd rose to their feet, anticipating an inning-ending strikeout and an end to the threat. Instead, Leonard hung a curveball and Watson smoked it into left field. "There's a base hit," said Phil Rizzuto on the Yankees' television broadcast. "Willie might score on this one."[14]

The ball bounced three times and took a clean hop off the base of the wall and right to Wilson, who turned and threw back toward the infield. His throw sailed over the head of Washington, the cutoff man. Fortunately for the Royals, Brett was positioned about 20 feet behind Washington, and the ball came right to him. He turned and threw to catcher Darrell Porter, who caught it just before Randolph arrived at the plate in a combination head-first dive and off-balance face plant.

Baserunner and catcher did a pirouette on top of home plate and came to a rest with Randolph lying on his back, legs spread, facing third base with Porter hovering just above him. On-deck hitter Reggie Jackson was crouched behind the plate in anticipation and looked over at umpire Joe Brinkman, who pointed to Randolph and threw a sideways punch towards the backstop, indicating the out as the crowd went crazy. Inning over.

Porter walked toward the pitcher's mound and received an enthusiastic high-five from Brett and Washington, then turned and headed to the first-base dugout. Jackson continued standing behind the plate, unable to believe what just took place as television cameras showed Royals fans standing and applauding before cutting to George Steinbrenner, who was beside himself.

Clad in a blue shirt, blue tie and a white sweater-vest, Steinbrenner angrily pulled on his navy blue blazer and sneered, his frustration and anger on display for everyone to see. The Yankees again threatened in the ninth, putting two men on, but Royals fireman Dan Quisenberry got Nettles to ground into a game-ending double play, and the Royals were up 2–0 in the Series.

"Let's get dressed," barked Steinbrenner in the Yankees' locker room after the game. "I want to get this team out of here. I want this team to get home and get some rest. We can win this thing."[15]

But despite his outwardly positive attitude, "The Boss" was seething. In his mind, there was one person responsible for the loss: third-base coach Mike Ferraro. It was Ferraro who sent Randolph home on the play, therefore it was Ferrero who was at fault. "I thought it was a bad play," said Steinbrenner. "These players didn't lose the game. We got taken out of this one."[16]

"I was sending him home the whole time," said Ferraro. "We had to take a chance. When they missed the first cutoff man, I thought he'd score."[17] "When you see the ball thrown high or off-line you send the runner," said Howser. "That's what you look for."[18] "Nonsense," said Steinbrenner. "He never should have gone. I was sitting in the stands. I saw everything. He never should have gone."[19]

For the second straight day, a decision by a third-base coach had potentially cost his team the game, but the similarities ended there. There were no incendiary quotes from Phillies owner Ruly Carpenter regarding Lee Elia's decision, but Steinbrenner couldn't wait to blast Ferraro. It was the culmination of a season's worth of animosity between Steinbrenner, Howser and Ferraro. Steinbrenner was a meddler, and he needed people who obeyed orders. Howser wasn't that guy. He began refusing to take Steinbrenner's calls to discuss strategy, especially during games. That didn't sit well with The Boss and would ultimately lead to Howser's departure.

After a day of rest, the Phillies and Astros resumed their Series in front of a sellout crowd in the Astrodome. It was the first home playoff game in the team's 19-year history, and Houston was ready. The team staged a pep rally at the Hyatt Regency on Thursday afternoon while Astrodome crews prepped the playing surface. Game Three had a scheduled start time of 2 p.m. on a Friday, perfect for Houstonians to take a half-day at work and head to The Dome, or if they couldn't get a ticket, call in sick, pop open a Lone Star, and enjoy the game from the comfort of their own home.

What they saw was either a tremendous pitcher's duel or a tremendous display of offensive ineptitude, depending on your perspective. The Phillies had runners in scoring position in each of the first three innings but couldn't push a run home. Houston had runners in scoring position in the first, third and fourth innings and couldn't get a run home. Each time the Phillies threatened, Joe Niekro's knuckleball helped him escape the jam. Each time Houston looked to break through, Larry Christenson shut them down.

Third baseman Enos Cabell led off the home half of the sixth inning with a single to center field and advanced to second on a groundout. With a base open, Dallas Green elected to walk Jose Cruz to bring up Cesar Cedeno in hopes of inducing an inning-ending double play.

In his first 11 seasons, Cedeno had emerged as an offensive force and had continued that trend in 1980, batting .309 with 10 homers and 48 stolen bases. But Cedeno hadn't been hitting in the Series, or the game. He'd popped out to Larry Bowa at short his first time up and grounded out to Bowa his second time up.

On Christenson's first pitch, Cedeno hit another ground ball to Bowa, who scooped it up and flipped to second baseman Manny Trillo for the first out. Trillo avoided Cruz's attempt to break up the double play and threw to Rose at first. As Cedeno approached the bag, he lunged like a sprinter trying to break the tape and landed awkwardly, his right foot hitting the outside of the bag, then fell face-first into the turf down the first base line.

As was his habit, Rose spiked the ball into the turf in celebration of the inning-ending play, but to add gusto, Rose turned and spiked the ball behind him, towards the Houston center fielder, who lay sprawled on the Astrodome turf. Keith Jackson remarked that Cedeno might be injured, but that didn't stop Cosell from continuing to point out Cedeno's failures in the post-season. Cedeno had suffered a compound fracture of his right ankle and would be lost for the rest of the Series. Despite his struggles, Philadelphia still had to respect Cedeno as an offensive threat. Without him, their offense would have even more difficulty scoring runs.

An ambulance took the Houston center fielder to Methodist Hospital, the same hospital where J.R. Richard went after his stroke. Before being wheeled into the operating room, Cedeno called the Astros dugout. "Keep it going for me," he said. "I'll see you in the Series."[20]

The game remained scoreless through ten innings, but the Phillies put something together in the top of the 11th. Garry Maddox doubled off Dave Smith with two out, forcing Virdon to walk Larry Bowa and pitch to Bob Boone. Green countered with left-handed pinch-hitter Del Unser, with the pitcher's spot due up next.

Smith got ahead of Unser, 0–2, and the crowd came to their feet. The Astrodome scoreboard flashed, "Strike Him Out!" and the rookie did just that, getting Unser to swing over a forkball to end the inning.

Tug McGraw came out in the bottom of the 11th for his fourth inning of work. He'd relieved Dickie Noles in the eighth and retired seven of the nine batters he'd faced, allowing an intentional walk to Jose Cruz and a tenth-inning single to Enos Cabell, who pulled a groin muscle in the process. In the Houston dugout, Cabell limped over to Joe Morgan, who was due to lead off the inning and said, "Do something. I can't play anymore."[21]

Morgan wasn't feeling much better. The sprained ligaments in his left knee had been bothering him for more than a week, so much so that he sat out the first game of the Series. But he took McGraw's third pitch and stroked it into the gap in right-center field. Jackson, thinking the ball was gone, went into his home run call, "Way back! Going, going...,"[22] but the ball bounced off the top of the wall and caromed back toward the infield as Morgan limped into to third with a triple. "One of the greatest professionals of our time in major league baseball, Joe Morgan," said Cosell. "And now the stage is set."[23]

Indeed it was, but not before Virdon lifted the gimpy Morgan for pinch-runner Rafael Landestoy. Two batters later, Denny Walling lifted a fly ball to Greg Luzinski in left field. His throw home was hopelessly off-line, and the Astros had a thrilling 1–0, extra-inning win and a lead in the Series. "I've waited 14 years to pitch a game like that," said Niekro. "If I was gonna get beat, it was gonna be with my best pitch—my knuckleball. I made a few mistakes here and there, but I got away with them. Why? You know why. We're playing in the Dome."[24]

The Astrodome was an equalizer. Balls that would get out of nearly any other ballpark were outs in The Dome, and the Astros knew how to use it to their advantage while the Phillies were left shaking their heads and counting the lost opportunities. "We should be drunk on champagne right now," said Pete Rose. "We should have swept this thing and been looking forward to the World Series. All we had to do was hit a sacrifice fly the last two games and we win them. It's just a fact that when you get a man to third with less than two outs, you gotta get him in."[25]

Rose was right. The Phillies stranded McBride on third in Game Two, and Rose, himself, was unable to score from third in Game Three. They'd stranded runners in scoring position in five different innings in Game Three alone. Instead of being drunk on champagne, they were facing an elimination game on Sunday evening on the road. Their only saving grace was the fact that Steve Carlton would be on the mound. "They have to beat the best pitcher in the world tomorrow to win the pennant," said Rose.[26]

The Yankees were also facing an elimination game with a lefty on the mound, but at least they were at home. Tommy John had just finished his second year in pinstripes, and he'd already won 43 games. But his lone start of against the Royals in 1980 hadn't gone well. On July 27, John had surrendered eight runs in 3⅓ innings in a 15–4 Kansas City win. Fortunately for John, his mound opponent, Paul Splittorff, had been even worse in two starts against the Yankees, allowing ten runs on 11 hits in just 2⅔ innings, good for a tidy 33.75 ERA.

John and Splittorff traded zeros on the scoreboard through the first four innings and sat through a 32-minute rain delay before Kansas City came up to hit in the top of the 5th inning. John struck out Clint Hurdle to lead off the inning, but his first pitch to Frank White came in fat, and White jumped on it.

"Oh, uh and that's gone," said Phil Rizzuto on WPIX-TV. "It's a 1–0 ballgame."[27]

Splittorff put up another scoreless frame in the fifth, but things began to change in the bottom of the sixth. Bob Watson led off with a shot towards White, who leapt and barely snared it. After Reggie Jackson sliced a double down the left field line, Jim Frey went to his bullpen, summoning Dan Quisenberry. Dick Howser countered with pinch-hitter Oscar Gamble, who hit a dribbler up the middle that White was able to track down. With his momentum carrying him toward left field, White saw that he didn't have a play at first base and tried to catch Jackson rounding third. But his throw sailed over the head of George Brett and into the Royals' dugout, which allowed Jackson to score and sent Gamble to third. Rick Cerone lined a single to left to score Gamble and give the Yankees a 2–1 lead. Frey's move had backfired.

John came back out in the top of the seventh, but Howser wanted to be prepared should his starter falter, and he got Goose Gossage up in the bullpen. John retired the first two batters he faced, but a Willie Wilson double brought Howser out to the mound to make a change.

In the Yankees' bullpen, Gossage fired one last fastball and then got in the front seat of the bullpen car for the short trip to the mound. "GOOOOOOSE!" cried the Yankees fans as Gossage met Howser and Cerone. "Let's Go!"[28] implored a departing John.

Standing 6–3, weighing just shy of 200 pounds and possessing a 100mph fastball, Gossage was the embodiment of intimidation on the mound, his Fu Manchu–style mustache adding to the persona. He glared in at his catcher to get the sign, kicked his left leg out to begin his delivery, then exploded in a flurry of arms and legs before falling off toward first base after he released the pitch.

Gossage ran the count full to Kansas City shortstop U L Washington, who hit a two-hopper up the middle. Randolph fielded it cleanly to the left of the second base bag, but Washington was too quick and beat it out for an infield single. The next man up for the Royals was Brett, who was 0-for-3 in the game and just 2-for-10 in the Series. It was the matchup the fans had come to see.

Gossage began his delivery, and Brett leaned back in his stance, looking for Gossage's signature fastball. He got it. It came in thigh-high at 98mph, and Brett sent it into the third deck down the right field line. He took nearly 30 seconds to round the bases.

"We had wanted to keep the ball down and away to Brett during the series," Dick Howser explained after the game. "With Goose, we wanted it up and away. But the ball apparently was down the middle."[29] "I knew it was out," said Frey. "I didn't even get up. I started thinking about who was going to pitch the next inning."[30]

Brett's three-run homer gave the Royals a 4–2 lead. Quisenberry wiggled out of trouble in the eighth inning and retired the side in order in the ninth to complete the sweep. For the first time in franchise history, the Kansas City Royals were going to the World Series, and the fact that they beat the Yankees, the team that had knocked them out of the playoffs three of the past four seasons, made it all the better. "For us to beat New York is the ultimate for [Kansas City]," said Brett. "There was no real revenge from past years. The Yanks are a great team. I respect them and I hope they respect us. But for the city of Kansas City, it's a very special moment."[31]

The moment was made more special because of the drama of Brett beating Gossage—two greats going head-to-head with the season on the line. Post-season heroes are often role player who come up big at opportune moments. This moment was different. It was the top hitter in the American League facing the top relief pitcher in the American League. Strength against strength.

"When Rich Gossage is pitching, you don't look changeup," said Brett. "He throws his slider 94 miles per hour and his fastball at 98. I know it's 309 or 310 [feet] to the wall. I just tried to pull it and get it in the air."[32] Gossage was more succinct in his assessment, saying, "He's the best and I'm the best—and he just beat me this time."[33]

The win also gave the Royals a luxury they'd enjoyed since midsummer, the opportunity to rest and see who they would face next in their quest for a championship. The answer could come as soon as the next day, when the Phillies and Astros faced each other in Game Four of the NLCS. It turned out to be one of the most controversial games in playoff history.

The fun began in the top of the fourth inning. With Vern Ruhle on the mound, Bake McBride and Manny Trillo delivered back-to-back singles, putting runners on first and second with no one out. Then it happened.

Garry Maddox hit a soft line drive up the middle that Ruhle caught at his feet. Or did he? Not taking any chances, Ruhle threw to Art Howe at first, who touched the bag, then looked around and saw McBride standing at third and Trillo at second. While Howe was assessing the situation, Joe Morgan, Ruhle and catcher Luis Pujols convened in front of the mound with home plate umpire Doug Harvey to argue that Ruhle caught the ball. As they discussed the play, Howe ran to second and tagged the bag. Moments later, Harvey ruled that Ruhle had, indeed, caught the ball, and because Howe had caught Ruhle's throw on the first base bag and then tagged second base, the Astros had just turned a triple play. It was then that all Hell broke loose.

Members of the Phillies' front office were sitting near the third base dugout. They could clearly see that Ruhle had short-hopped the ball, and they were hopping mad. General Manager Paul Owens was so incensed that team owner Ruly Carpenter had to physically prevent him from running on the field to argue the call. Owens couldn't reach Doug Harvey, but Dallas Green, Larry Bowa and the rest of the Phillies could, and they let him have it.

As the argument raged on, ABC replays showed that the ball had, in fact, bounced before Ruhle caught it. Three different groups of Phillies personnel argued with three different umpires on the Astrodome infield as Houston manager Bill Virdon tried to stay calm in the home dugout. Harvey and members of his crew then consulted with National League President Chub Feeney, who was sitting in front row next to the Astros' dugout, smoking a cigar. Once that meeting adjourned, Harvey made his way to the Houston dugout to speak to Virdon. Now it was Virdon's turn to lose it.

The call had changed. It was now a double play, and the Phillies were still batting. Larry Bowa, who was on-deck when the play took place, was still in the middle of the infield, bat in hand, arguing the play, while contingents of Astros and Phillies personnel pled their respective cases to whoever would listen.

After a delay of more than 15 minutes, order was restored and the line drive was officially ruled a double play. Trillo was out, and McBride returned to second base. Both teams protested the game, which was somewhat futile since the man who would eventually rule on the protest was Feeney, who had already rendered his decision. Bowa eventually stepped into the batter's box and bounced Ruhle's first pitch to Morgan for the third, or fourth depending on your point of view, out of the inning.

The game was still scoreless, but not for long. Perhaps hurt by the delay, Carlton surrendered single runs in the fourth and fifth innings before Philadelphia bounced back with three runs in the top of the 8th to take a 3–2 lead. But Houston tied it in the ninth against Warren Brusstar. For the third straight game, the NLCS was headed to extra innings.

Pete Rose got the Phillies going in the tenth with a one-out single and, after a Mike Schmidt line-out, Green sent Greg Luzinski up to pinch-hit for McBride. Luzinski turned on Joe Sambito's second pitch and drove it into the left-field corner, where Jose Cruz fielded it cleanly and came up firing to Landestoy.

When Landestoy caught the ball, Pete Rose, trying to score from first, had just rounded the third-base bag. Houston had him. But the throw bounced in front of catcher Bruce Bochy and Rose, reminiscent of the 1970 All-Star Game, plowed into Bochy, delivering a forearm to his cheek to score the go-ahead run.

Manny Trillo followed with a double of his own to give the Phillies a 5–3 lead. Tug McGraw pitched a 1–2–3 tenth, and the Phillies had new life. The Series was tied 2–2 and headed to a deciding fifth game on Sunday.

As thrilling as Game Four was, it had nothing on the Series finale played a day later. Bill Virdon tapped Nolan Ryan as his starter, while Green went with Marty Bystrom. The contrast couldn't have been much more striking. Ryan was 33 years old and, including the post-season, had 179 major league wins and had thrown more than 2,000 innings. Bystrom was 21, with five wins and 36 innings pitched.

Houston jumped on Bystrom in the bottom of the first. Terry Puhl, who seemingly was incapable of making an out, led off with a single and scored on a Jose Cruz double, but Bob Boone's two-out, two-run single in the top of the second gave the Phillies a 2–1 lead. Ryan settled in after that and held the Phillies scoreless for the next five innings while his teammates scored one run in the sixth inning and three more in the seventh, giving Houston a 5–2 lead.

In between innings, as he had done since mid–August, Bill Virdon sent Deacon Jones to tell Morgan that his night was over and that Rafael Landestoy would be replacing him. Morgan protested, telling Jones that if they made it to the World Series, Virdon would need another second baseman because he would never play for him again. But the decision was made, so Morgan and Art Howe, who had been pinch-run for in the previous inning, went to the clubhouse to watch the rest of the game on television.

The Phillies' dugout was a mixture of optimism and despair, but there was still competitive fire, too. Rose approached Larry Bowa, who was set to lead off the eighth, and told him that if he got on base, the Phillies would win the game. Bowa did just that, singling to start things off. Bob Boone hit a chopper up the middle, a sure double play ball. But the ball deflected off Ryan's glove and rolled harmlessly toward second base. Instead of two out and no one on, the Phillies had runners on first and second with no one out. With Morgan and Howe out of the game, no one went to talk to Ryan, something Morgan, in his book, *Joe Morgan: My Life in Baseball,* claims he would have done.

> In ... big games, pitching is the loneliest job on the team. All the pressure the position players feel is double that for the guy on the hill. You're standing there in front of 50,000 people and sometimes—even if you're Nolan Ryan—you need someone to go out there and pat you on the back, let you know you really aren't alone, that the magic circle you're in is protected by the guys behind you.[34]

Instead of calming Ryan, Morgan picked up the clubhouse phone, called Astros General Manager Tal Smith, and told him no matter how the game played out, he was done playing for Virdon. In Morgan's mind, Smith and the Astros had brought him to Houston to provide veteran leadership and now, when the team needed it the most, he was unable to provide it because he wasn't in the game.

After the botched double play ball, Greg Gross laid down a perfect bunt towards third and the bases were loaded, setting up another great matchup. It was Ryan against Pete Rose, with the bases loaded and both teams' seasons on the line. Rose took a big cut at Ryan's first offering but fouled it off. As the drama increased, so did Rose's showmanship. He watched each pitch as it left Ryan's hand and followed it into the catcher's mitt, then snapped his head back around to stare at Ryan. The count went full and Rose fouled off another pitch, this one a 99mph fastball, then took ball four and defiantly threw his bat toward the Phillies' dugout as Bowa trotted in to score.

Ryan was replaced by Joe Sambito, who got Keith Moreland to ground into a fielder's choice, which scored Boone to cut the lead to one at 5–4. The Astrodome crowd, so raucous just ten minutes earlier, was a bit more subdued as Virdon made another move, replacing Sambito with Ken Forsch. Forsch struck out Schmidt, but a Del Unser single tied it, and Manny Trillo's triple gave the Phillies a 7–5 lead.

But Houston wasn't about to give up. They strung together four hits off Tug McGraw to tie the game 7–7 and send it to extra innings once again, prompting another Cosell platitude. "You're watching maybe the most incredible championship baseball series ever played. Emotions are stripped bare on both teams."[35]

With one out in the top of the tenth, Unser hit a chopper to first base. But instead of being a routine out, the ball hit a seam in the Astroturf and bounced over Dave Bergman's head, giving the Phillies a man on second with one out instead of no one on with two outs. Two batters later, Garry Maddox hit a sinking liner to center field that fell in front of Puhl, and the Phillies had the lead once again. This time they held it. Dick Ruthven retired the Astros in order in the bottom of the tenth, and the Phillies were headed to the World Series for the first time since 1950.

"They aren't the same old Phillies, they are the 1980 Phillies," said Cosell. "They did it with a controversial manager ... openly disliked by many of his players, but they did it. They did it because somewhere within them there was a spirit that will not be quelled."[36]

The World Series

"I'm picking up heavy positive vibrations on the Phillies," said noted psychic Jeane Dixon. "I hope it's not just because I'm here."[37]

During a press conference at Philadelphia's Warwick Hotel, Dixon predicted that the Phillies would win the World Series in six games. She was definitely in the minority. Many in the national media felt that the Royals were the team to beat, citing their superior pitching and team speed. Even computers were picking the Royals. The *St. Louis Post Dispatch* noted that a computer that had correctly picked the Pirates to win in 1979 liked the Royals in six. Reds pitcher Tom Seaver, who joined the NBC broadcast team as a color analyst, was among those picking Kansas City. Not surprisingly, he liked their pitching as well.

Despite chilly temperatures, more than 65,000 people showed up to cheer on their teams. Among them was Army staff sergeant Craig Burns, from Pennsauken, New Jersey. A die-hard Phillies fan, Burns was stationed in Aschaffenburg, Germany, but that didn't stop him from requesting a three-day pass to take in Game One. His commanding officer willingly signed it. Not because he knew how much it meant to Burns, but because he didn't think Burns would go. He was wrong. Before Burns hopped on an army transport for the 3,153-mile trip home, he slipped a note on his commander's desk that read, "Phillies Number One, See You Later."[38]

But not even Craig Burns could have liked the pitching matchup. By virtue of their three-game sweep of the Yankees, Kansas City had the opportunity to set up their rotation and start 20-game-winner Dennis Leonard in Game One, while the Phillies were forced to start rookie Bob Walk, who hadn't pitched in 12 days. Walk was the first rookie to start the opening game of the World Series since the Brooklyn Dodgers' Joe Black in 1952. But Black went 15–4 and won the Rookie of the Year Award that season. Walk was a pedestrian 11–7 for the Phillies. He was also the only fresh arm Dallas Green had, and he struggled early in the game.

KC took a 2–0 lead in the second inning on an Amos Otis two-run homer and made it 4–0 an inning later when Willie Aikens added a two-run shot of his own as a 26th birthday gift to himself. But the Phillies got something going in the bottom of the fifth. Larry Bowa started the rally with a single off Leonard, but the big blow came from right fielder Bake McBride, who was batting cleanup despite hitting just nine homers all season. McBride had struggled in the NLCS, batting just .238, including an 0-for-5 in the critical Game Five. But a pre-game session with Phillies hitting coach Billy DeMars did the trick. After watching a handful of swings, DeMars told McBride that he was overstriding. McBride made the adjustment and, in his second at-bat of the game, hit a three-run homer to give Philadelphia a 5–4 lead. Their lead swelled to 7–4 before Aikens hit another two-run homer to make it 7–6, but that's as close as they got. The Phillies had a 1–0 lead and their first World Series win since 1915.

"We've been through a very nice kind of hell the last 10 days," said Green, reflecting on the do-or-die nature of the recent past. "We've played the types of games that have prepared us for any eventuality. Tonight was a piece of cake compared to some we played before. It's the first game we've played in some time where if we lost it our backs wouldn't be against the wall."[39]

Before Game Two, Royals manager Jim Frey issued a statement unlike any other in World Series history, saying, "The lineup will have George Brett at third base. The proctologist and the team physician both examined him and assured me that there was no real danger of a lasting, serious problem. It's simply a case of: How much pain can he stand?"[40]

The proctologist?

George Brett had been battling a severe case of hemorrhoids since the Royals had clinched the American League pennant. The condition had become so painful that there were serious doubts as to whether he could even play in Game Two. Not only did he play, but he singled in his first at-bat off Phillies starter Steve Carlton, prompting Pete Rose to fake a congratulatory slap on the rear end, much to the delight of all who witnessed it.

By the sixth inning, the pain became too great and Brett was forced to take himself out of the game. He tried to get comfortable in the Royals' clubhouse as his teammates scored two runs off Carlton in the seventh inning to take a 3–2 lead. But once again, the Phillies fought back.

Bob Boone led off the bottom of the eighth against Royals closer Dan Quisenberry with a walk, and pinch-hitter Del Unser drove him home with a double. Two batters later, McBride hit a chopper over a drawn-in infield to tie the game, 4–4. Needing an out, Quisenberry went with his sinker, and Mike Schmidt drove it off the wall in right-center. Bake McBride slid home just ahead of Frank White's relay throw, and the Phillies had the lead. "It was like it was on a tee," said Quisenberry. But he didn't mean a hitting tee, he meant a golf tee. "The pitch was like where you pull your socks up. He must be awfully tough on the driving range."[41]

"I didn't want to get behind him," said Schmidt in explaining why he uncharacteristically swung at Quisenberry's first offering. "Also, he's kind of a one-pitch pitcher. He's got 33 saves on the best sinker in the American League. It ain't like Tug McGraw, where he's got a scroogie, a slider, a fastball and a changeup. I guarantee you he's gonna throw me a good hard pitch, first pitch."[42]

Quisenberry was far more succinct in assessing his performance, saying that instead of his sinker having "pop," it was simply "poop."[43]

After Schmidt drove home McBride, Keith Moreland's single capped the four-run eighth inning, and Ron Reed, giving McGraw a much-needed day of rest, shut the Royals down in the ninth to give the Phillies a 2–0 lead in the Series, while the Royals were suddenly longing to play in front of their home crowd. "We've won a championship, we've done what our fans wanted more than anything in the world, and we haven't heard one cheer yet," said catcher Darrell Porter. "We need to hear some cheers. We need that more than anything."[44]

But the Phillies' 2–0 Series lead was almost secondary to the George Brett hemorrhoids story. All jokes aside, and there were many, all of them bad, no team could afford to lose its best player in the World Series to any malady, especially when down two games to none. "We're going to put him directly in the hospital tonight in Kansas City," said Royals team doctor Paul Meyer, who also said that surgery might be the best remedy for Brett's condition, but added, "It doesn't mean he'd be out for the whole Series."[45]

Brett wasn't the only key player who wasn't feeling well. Phillies slugger Greg Luzinski missed Game Two with a fever of 103 degrees as a result of an intestinal virus. "The Bull" watched the game from home, and his status for Game Three was also unknown. Center fielder Garry Maddox was sent to the hospital for precautionary x-rays after fouling a ball off his knee in the second inning.

The October 16 off-day proved to be perfectly timed, especially for Brett and the Royals. After further examination, Brett did, in fact, require surgery for his condition, and the procedure was performed in time for him to return to the lineup for Game Three at Stadium in Kansas City.

As he had done all season, whether it was coming back from an ankle injury in June or a hand injury in September, Brett picked up right where he left off. With two outs in the bottom of the first inning, Brett came to the plate against Phillies starter Dick Ruthven and homered to right field to give the Royals a 1–0 lead. "I felt a lot of eyes looking at me," said Brett after the game. "I don't think they were looking at my head or my toes, though. The pain is all behind me."[46]

Pete Rose tied the game at 3–3 in the eighth inning with a single off reliever Renie Martin and, once again, the Phillies were headed to extra innings in the post-season. In the top of the tenth, Philadelphia put two men on with one out with Mike Schmidt up. Schmidt had homered earlier in the game, his first in 19 career post-season games, but this time he lined out to Frank White, who scampered over to the bag to double up Bob Boone and end the threat. "You could have hung the wash out on it," said Schmidt. "I hit is as hard as I could hit it. He made a great play. If it's six inches the other way, we win the game."[47]

The double play was part of a frustrating day offensively for the Phillies, who stranded a World Series-record 15 runners, and for Schmidt, who was personally responsible for eight of them. That frustration grew when Willie Aikens singled to left field off Tug McGraw in the bottom of the tenth to score Willie Wilson and give the Royals a walk-off, 4–3 win.

Aikens was making the most of his chance on the national stage. Through the first three games, he was 5-for-12 with two homers and five

RBI. He was driven by what he felt was a lack of respect from the media and his opponents. He cited a newspaper article that gave Pete Rose and the Phillies the edge in the first base matchup in the Series and also brought up Tigers manager Sparky Anderson's comments from April about how he'd face Aikens a thousand times rather than pitch to Hal McRae. "I feel like I proved something to a lot of people tonight," said Aikens. "I proved I'm a major league hitter; I can hit anybody. I proved it to the whole world."[48]

Saturday, October 18, was officially declared Kansas City Royals day in Missouri, and the Royals and their fans were feeling much better after their Game Three win, especially since they had their ace, Dennis Leonard, back on the mound for Game Four, while the Phillies countered with Larry Christenson.

Leonard handled the Phillies with relative ease in the top of the first, yielding only a single to Rose, but the same couldn't be said for Christenson, who faced six batters and had five of them reach base before being pulled. In the Phillies' bullpen, Dickie Noles and Kevin Saucier had only thrown a handful of pitches between them when the call came from the dugout asking if they were ready. The answer was no, but Noles feared this might be his only chance to pitch in the World Series and said yes anyway. A bit rusty, he loaded the bases but managed to escape the inning without any further damage.

In Noles' second inning of work, Willie Aikens, who had homered in the first inning, unloaded again, sending the ball off the back wall of the Kansas City bullpen. When Noles finished watching the flight of the ball, he turned back toward the plate and saw Aikens still standing there. The home run hadn't bothered the Phillies' reliever, but the showboating did. At the end of two innings, the Royals had a 5–1 lead, and Noles heard from multiple teammates that it was time to send the Royals a message. Aikens needed to go down.

The Royals' first baseman was on deck when George Brett came to bat with one out in the fourth inning. Noles' first pitch was a fastball that Brett swung through. His next one was fouled off. Amped up on the mound, Noles wanted to retire Brett to get to Aikens and exact his revenge, but Brett began kicking dirt off the plate with his cleats and then stepped out of the batter's box. As he was leisurely getting back in the box, Noles yelled that he'd better get ready to hit. Brett finally stepped back in and crouched in his stance. Given time to think about it, Noles decided the target of his rage would be Brett instead of Aikens, and his next pitch sailed directly at Brett's chin at about 90mph. Brett flipped backwards towards the Royals dugout, his feet seemingly trading places with his head, and landed on his left side, facing his stunned teammates, his legs draped across home plate. "That's a message right there," said play-by-play man Joe Garagiola. "There's a message."[49]

Transmission didn't take long as Royals manager Jim Frey charged out to confront home plate umpire Don Denkinger. "Stop it right now!" he implored Denkinger. "Stop it right now. Go out [to the mound] and stop it! Stop it right there. Go out and tell him!"[50]

As Frey was talking to Denkinger, Pete Rose began jawing at Frey, telling him to get back in the dugout. Frey accused Noles of throwing at Brett, which he absolutely had. But Rose responded that Noles couldn't have been throwing at Brett because if he had wanted to hit the Royals star, he would have done it. Rose looked in the Royals dugout and yelled to Noles to pitch his game, and if he wanted to hit someone there was a dugout full of guys wearing white.

Kansas City would win the game, 5–3, but the Phillies had the tying run at the plate in the top of the eighth inning, and the Royals managed just one hit after Brett was knocked down. The Series was tied at two games apiece, but a shift had taken place, and Frey was still steaming afterwards. "I think it was a knockdown pitch," he said. "With a team hitting the ball as hard as we were, with a good hitter up there and an 0–2 count ... the situation was there. He threw the ball at his head."[51]

"I didn't see a knockdown pitch," said a coy Dallas Green. "Was there one today? The only guy who got upset about it was Jim Frey. Brett didn't."[52]

The pivotal Game Five took place the next day, and the Phillies jumped out to an early 2–0 lead thanks to Mike Schmidt's second homer of the Series. But Amos Otis led off the bottom of the sixth with a homer of his own to tie the game, 2–2. U L Washington's sacrifice fly gave Kansas City a 3–2 lead and brought Willie Wilson to the plate with one out and Darrell Porter on first base. Wilson hit Ron Reed's second pitch over McBride's head in right field, but McBride fielded the short-hop and threw a strike to Manny Trillo. "The minute the ball hit the wall, I turned around and saw that [Porter] was barely standing on second base," said Trillo. "I thought we were going to have a shot at him."[53]

They did. Trillo caught McBride's relay throw and threw another strike to Bob Boone at home to nail Porter. Frank White fouled out on the next pitch, and the Royals had run themselves out of a potentially big inning. "It's easy to coach third base from the press box,"[54] said Frey in an effort to defend his coach. But the fact of the matter was that Porter had been thrown out at the plate twice in the Series.

By the seventh inning, both starters were gone and the game had been turned over to each team's respective relief ace. Both of them had been outstanding during the regular season, and both of them were out of gas. Including the post-season, Tug McGraw had pitched in 24 of the Phillies' last 29 games. Dan Quisenberry led the American League in appearances and had pitched in two of the Royals' three ALCS games and every game of the World Series. Both had clean eighth innings, but the ninth would be a different story.

As the Phillies prepared to hit in the top of the ninth inning, Frey pulled George Brett aside and told him to play in on the man set to lead off the inning. Mike Schmidt led the major leagues in home runs during the regular season and had homered earlier in the game, but he also had laid down bunts in Games Three and Four. With Brett playing in, expecting a bunt, Schmidt jumped on Quisenberry's offering and hit a shot down the third-base line that a diving Brett couldn't handle. Had Frey told Brett to play at normal depth, the ball likely would have been a groundout; instead, it was a leadoff single. "No way I was gonna bunt in that situation," said Schmidt. "Not one run down in the ninth. My job there is to get a good pitch and try to drive it. No way would I think of trying to get on base with a bunt."[55]

Del Unser came through again, this time with a pinch-hit double down the right field line to score Schmidt and tie the game at 3–3. After a Keith Moreland sacrifice bunt, Trillo hit a shot up the middle that Quisenberry couldn't handle. Unser came in to score the go-ahead run as the ball rolled harmlessly towards shortstop U L Washington.

The Royals weren't finished yet, though. McGraw walked Frank White to lead off the bottom of the ninth and, after striking out Brett, walked Aikens and Otis to load the bases and bring former Phillies outfielder Jose Cardenal to the plate with two out. McGraw got ahead in the count, and NBC cameras broke away after every pitch to show his wife, Phyllis, in the stands. She couldn't bring herself to look at the field. She simply stared at her hands in apparent prayer. McGraw's 1–2 pitch came, and Cardenal swung through it. "They knew what they were doing," said

McGraw. "Jose has always worn me out with men on base. I always got him out with nobody on, but he got a lot of base hits off me with men on base when he was with the Cubs."[56]

"The important thing is that we won," said Schmidt. "[We] got out of here with one win after we lost our first two games here. We did it in our old fashion. We were unable to hold the lead. I'm just looking forward to that 1–2–3 ninth inning one of these days. Maybe Lefty will give it to us Tuesday night."[57]

The Phillies did indeed have their ace going for Game Six, but he was far from fresh. Steve Carlton threw 157 pitches in his Game Two start and had racked up nearly 320 innings since the season began. "He's tired, there's no question about it," said Dallas Green. "He has every right to be tired. But he's also got the quality of a champion who's able to come back and get it one more time. All we need from him is one more time."[58]

For their season to continue, the Royals needed a solid effort from Game Three starter Rich Gale, who lasted just 4⅓ innings and was fortunate to escape without a loss.

"They should have scored more runs off me for all the opportunities they had," said Gale the day before Game Six. "It's not like I'm the only person who matters out there. Obviously if I don't perform well, my teammates will not have the opportunity to make the big plays or clutch hits. If I don't do well and we lose, the sun will come up tomorrow."[59]

Dan Quisenberry got right to the point in his assessment, saying, "Our backs are against the wall. The Berlin Wall.... East side."[60]

Nearly 66,000 fans, more than the stadium's stated capacity, packed Veterans Stadium for Game Six while a record television audience tuned in to watch the game on NBC and saw former Phillie Tony Taylor throw out the ceremonial first pitch. Taylor played 1,669 games in a Phillies uniform, amassing more than 1,500 hits and stealing 169 bases, but he never played in the postseason as a Phillie. Now he was on hand to see many of his former teammates on the brink of a championship.

Despite having thrown more than 320 innings since the season began, Steve Carlton was as sharp as ever, facing just one over the minimum over the first three innings, including back-to-back strikeouts of Willie Wilson and U L Washington to open the game. Controversy crept in in the bottom of the third inning. Bob Boone led off with a walk, and Lonnie Smith hit a bouncer to Frank White between first and second base. White was thinking double play, but his throw pulled Washington off the bag, at least according to umpire Bill Kunkel, who ruled Boone safe. Frey disagreed and came out to plead his case.

"The ball pulled him off the bag,"[61] said Kunkel.

"The ball didn't pull him off nothin'!" said Frey. "What's goin' on for cryin out loud! How can you call a play like that, Bill? You don't see that twice a year, Bill. Come on ... for cryin' out loud."[62]

With two on and no one out, Frey approached Brett on his way back to the dugout, telling his third baseman that he anticipated a bunt from Rose and Brett should play in. But when Gale ran the count to 3–1, Brett crept back, even with the bag at third. Spotting the change, Rose laid down a perfect bunt down the third-base line. Brett initially moved to cover his base for a force play but then charged and bare-handed the ball and threw to first base. Living up to the nickname "Charlie Hustle," the 39-year-old Rose beat the throw, loading the bases with no one out and Schmidt coming to the plate.

The Phillies' slugger was mostly a non-factor in his previous three post-season series, batting a combined .163 in the NLCS in 1977, 1978 and 1980. But the World Series had brought the best out in Schmidt. He'd gone 7-for-18 in the first five games, and now he had a chance to put his team that much closer to the title he and the city coveted. Gale's third pitch was a fastball on the outer half, and Schmidt drove it into right center field for a single to score Boone and Smith and give the Phillies a 2–0 lead.

There was vindication in that line drive. Years of frustration, some of it self-induced, had led to the moment where Schmidt gave his team a lead in a deciding game. As the Phillies third baseman headed back to first after rounding the bag, he punched his right fist triumphantly in the air, a signal of relief for both him and the crowd.

Schmidt's punch also served as a metaphorical knockout blow to Gale, who was replaced immediately after the play. It was the third time in the Series that a Kansas City starter had failed to last five innings. Reliever Renie Martin was now charged with pitching some of the most important innings in franchise history.

Meanwhile, Steve Carlton kept putting up zeros, allowing only a John Wathan single over the next three innings. He took a 4–0 lead into the eighth when he began to tire, and the call went out to the Phillies bullpen to get McGraw up. In anticipation of the Phillies potentially winning the game and securing the Series, the Philadelphia police department had begun to work their way onto the field with trained dogs to control the crowd. When the order came for him to get ready, McGraw looked for his glove and saw it underneath a resting German shepherd who had taken up temporary residence in the Phillies' bullpen. When he went to reach for it, the dog expressed his displeasure at the thought of losing his pillow but, with the aid of the dog's handler, eventually relented.

As McGraw got loose, Carlton walked Wathan and Jose Cardenal singled, which brought Dallas Green out of the dugout to remove his ace starter and replace him with his ace reliever. In typical fashion, McGraw retired the first batter he faced, then walked Willie Wilson to load the bases. The Royals pushed one run across before McGraw escaped by inducing Hal McRae to ground out to end the frame. It was in the top of the ninth that things got really tense for the Phillies and their fans. McGraw got leadoff man Amos Otis on strikes, but he walked Aikens and allowed a single to John Wathan. "He seems to thrive in these kinds of circumstances," NBC broadcaster Tony Kubek said of McGraw. "He creates his problem, then somehow wiggles out."[63]

His problem got bigger when Cardenal singled to load the bases. Philadelphia was two outs away from its first championship, and McGraw was running on fumes. In seven innings of work in the World Series, McGraw had allowed 15 baserunners, and now Frank White was at the plate, representing the go-ahead run.

Known far more for his glove than his bat, White had hit a torrid .545 during the American League Championship Series en route to winning the MVP Award. But his bat had gone cold against Philadelphia. As he stepped in against McGraw, he was just 2-for-24 in the Series. It was a battle of attrition. Sore arm vs. ice-cold bat.

McGraw stepped onto the mound, fired the ball into his glove a few times, and looked in for a sign from catcher Bob Boone. Fastball. He delivered a belt-high pitch that by all rights should have been sent over the fence in left-center for a grand slam. But White got under it. The ball shot up and to the right, toward the Phillies dugout. Boone raced after it, as did first baseman Pete Rose. As the ball came down, Boone reached up to grab it but the ball popped out of his glove. In what became one of many signature moments in his career, Rose grabbed the ball milliseconds before it hit the ground, then nonchalantly bounced the ball off the turf like he was dribbling a basketball and flipped it back to McGraw, who was joined on the mound by Boone.

Dallas Green now had a decision to make. Should he stick with the obviously tired McGraw, or go to a fresher arm? Green called down to the bullpen and told coach Mike Ryan to get Dickie Noles up in case he was needed. But the hero of Game Five refused. This was history in the making, and Noles didn't want to miss it. When Ryan yelled at him to get up and throw, Noles responded, "Yeah, right. Like Dallas is really going to take Tug McGraw out and put me in this game."[64] He had a point. Being one out away from a World Series title is probably not the best time to bring in a rookie pitcher. Ryan agreed, and Noles took a seat.

The only thing standing between the Phillies and their first World Series title was Willie Wilson, who had struck out 11 times in the Series at that point, but had serious speed. He also hit .326 during the season, amassing a major-league-leading 230 hits. Any ball on the ground could turn into a hit and, potentially, a big inning.

After 97 years of misery, the Phillies and their fans finally got a chance to celebrate a championship (National Baseball Hall of Fame Library, Cooperstown, New York).

Wilson stepped into the batter's box while the Philadelphia police brought McGraw's favorite guard dog and his friends as well as a bevy of horses on the field in an attempt to quell a potential riot should McGraw hold on. Philadelphia Mayor William J. Green wanted to wait as long as possible before deploying the horses so he wouldn't get blamed for jinxing it if the Phillies lost. McGraw glanced to the side and saw a horse lift his tail and make a deposit on the field. He thought to himself, "If I don't get out if this inning, that's exactly what I'm going to be in this city."[65]

With a 1–2 count, Boone signaled fastball. McGraw threw it, and Wilson swung through it. Game over. McGraw threw his hands up in the air and turned toward third base to see Schmidt making a beeline for the mound. When Schmidt got there, he dove on the pile and was the central figure in a photo any Phillies fan will remember for the rest of their lives. For the first time in franchise history, the Philadelphia Phillies were World Series Champions.

Epilogue

In a moving scene in September of 2003, Tug McGraw, who was dying of brain cancer, made one last appearance at Veterans Stadium. For the final game at the stadium before moving into Citizens Bank Park, a special ceremony was held, emceed by long-time Phillies broadcaster Harry Kalas.

"When it's time to get one last out, who do you call on?"[1] Kalas asked the crowd, who roared as a black Lincoln sedan made its way down the right field line and parked by first base.

Out stepped McGraw, in full uniform, glove on his right hand.

Over the PA system, Kalas boomed, "Now pitching for the Phillies ... #45 ... Tug McGraw!"[2] The crowd went wild, and Kalas recited a call no Phillies fan will ever forget.

"The 1–2 pitch to Willie Wilson, struck him out! Phillies are the World Champions of baseball!"[3]

On the mound in 2003, McGraw

Tug McGraw took to the mound one final time when Veterans Stadium closed in 2003 (Mike Apice Photo, Willow Grove, Pennsylvania).

reenacted his leap and made his way to the plate, where he was greeted by Bob Boone.

They were older now, and they all knew Tug didn't have much time left. Boone and McGraw embraced at home plate. Next came Dickie Noles, then Manny Trillo, then Dallas Green and many other members of the first World Series championship team in Phillies history.

The music blared, the crowd cheered, and for just a brief moment, it was 1980 again.

Chapter Notes

Introduction

1. Bruce Webermarch, "Ruth Ann Steinhagen Is Dead at 83; Shot a Ballplayer," *New York Times*, 24 March 2013, A22.
2. Joseph Durso, "Phils, with Carlton, Confident but Wary," *New York Times*, 21 October 1980, C15.
3. Peter Abraham, "Baseball Lost a Character in McGraw," *Bridgewater (NJ) Courier Times*, 11 January 2004, E9.
4. "Agony of Victory," *Arizona Republic*, 14 January 1995, C2.
5. "Phils Find Out How to Win," *Odessa (TX) American*, 21 October 1980, 15.

Chapter 1

1. *Dallas—A House Divided*, directed by Irving J. Moore (1980; Hollywood, CA), YouTube, https://www.youtube.com/watch?v=9YPQARBgHS8
2. Larry Hagman and Tom Gold, *Hello, Darlin': Tall (And Absolutely True) Tales About My Life* (New York: Simon & Schuster, 2001), 195.
3. Charley Feeney, "Bucco Bonanza Awaits Hassler," *Sporting News*, 15 March 1980, 50.
4. Bill Giles and Doug Myers, *Pouring Six Beers at a Time and Other Stories from a Lifetime in Baseball* (Chicago: Triumph, 2007), 141.
5. *Ibid.*
6. Hal Bodley, "Phillies End 30 Years of Frustration," *Sporting News*, 25 October 1980, 8.
7. Hal Bodley, "Bull Hears Rumors, Sheds Suet," *Sporting News*, 12 January 1980, 43.
8. "McBride Spent the Winter Waiting for Phone to Ring," *Asbury Park (NJ) Press*, 11 March 1980, 25.
9. Hal Bodley, "'Get Set to Sweat,' Green to Phillies," *Sporting News*, 16 February 1980, 38.
10. Andre Dawson and Tim Bird, *Hawk: An Inspiring Story of Success at the Game of Life and Baseball* (Grand Rapids, MI: Zondervan, 1994), 73.
11. Herschell Nissenson, "Bucs Will Be Hard-Pressed to Repeat," *Woodstock (IL) Daily Sentinel*, 1 April 1980, 5.
12. Ian MacDonald, "Fans Salute Second-Best Expos," *Sporting News*, 9 February 1980, 37.
13. *Ibid.*
14. Don Baylor and Claire Smith, *Don Baylor—Nothing but Truth: A Baseball Life* (New York: St. Martin's Press, 1989), 159–160.
15. *Ibid.*
16. Dick Miller, "Ryan Raps Bavasi ... Again," *Sporting News*, 2 February 1980, 43.
17. *Ibid.*
18. Joe Morgan and David Falkner, *Joe Morgan: A Life in Baseball* (New York: W.W. Norton, 1993), 224.
19. Bob Rathgeber, "Red Machine's Morgan Motors into 'Dome,'" *Cincinnati Enquirer*, 1 February 1980, C1.
20. *Ibid.*
21. Bob Runyon, column, *Longview (TX) News Journal*, 22 February 1980, 17.
22. Earl Lawson, "Keystone No. 1 Question Mark for Reds," *Sporting News*, 9 February 1980, 38.
23. *Ibid.*

24. Bruce Brothers, "The Twins Are Still Goltz's First Love," *Minneapolis Star-Tribune*, 13 March 1980, 43

25. *Ibid.*

26. Gordon Verrell, "Sutton Appears Done as Dodger," *Sporting News*, 29 March 1980, 45.

27. Gordon Verrell, "Sutton Update: No Trade and No Hostility," *Sporting News*, 5 April 1980, 42.

28. Jeff Merron, "I Hate You Like a Brother," ESPN.com, http://www.espn.com/page2/s/list/teammatefeuds/031103.html.

29. "Lasorda—Lefebvre: 1-Punch-and-Done," *Binghamton (NY) Press and Sun-Bulletin*, 18 February 1980, 18.

30. Ken Nigro, "Williams Joins Talks on Palmer," *Baltimore Sun*, 10 March 1980, C5.

31. "Billy's Marshmallow Man Talks About 'The Punch,'" *Odessa (TX) American*, 31 October 1979, 14.

32. "Reggie: He Takes Charge of NY," *Miami News*, 5 July 1980, 53.

33. Will Grimsley, "Millionaire Jackson Decides 3 Days Worth a $2,000 Fine," *Fort Myers News Press*, 4 March 1980, 25.

34. "Jim Frey Replaces Herzog as Royals Manager," *Minneapolis Star-Tribune*, 25 October 1979, 49.

35. *Ibid.*

36. Del Black, "KC Counting on the Kids," *Sporting News*, 9 February 1980, 36.

37. Del Black, "White, McRae Stir Up Some Royal Ripples," *Sporting News*, 19 April 1980.

38. *Ibid.*

39. *Ibid.*

40. *Ibid.*

41. Darrell Porter and William Deerfield, *Snap Me Perfect: The Darrell Porter Story* (Nashville: Thomas Nelson, 1984), 169.

42. *Ibid.*, 185.

43. "One Against 971 ... Religious Decision?" *Binghamton (NY) Press and Bulletin*, 3 April 1980, 25.

44. "Angry Autry Would Cancel Baseball Season," *Wilmington (DE) News Journal*, 3 April 1980, 21.

45. *Ibid.*

46. "Miller Fires Charges at Owners," *Sayre (PA) Evening Times*, 1 April 1980, 13.

47. "Deplane Cabell," *St. Louis Post-Dispatch*, 4 April 1980, 14.

48. *Ibid.*

Chapter 2

1. "He Walked All the Way to a Very Special Game," *Hartford Courant*, 10 April 1980, 107.

2. *Ibid.*

3. Ken Picking, "Braves Ticket Murphy for Left Field Post," *Sporting News*, 5 January 1980, 51.

4. *Ibid.*

5. Larry Granillo, "Wezen-Ball: The Drawbacks and Demise of a Stat," Baseball Prospectus, February 16, 2012, https://www.baseballprospectus.com/news/article/16054/wezen-ball-the-drawbacks-and-demise-of-a-stat/.

6. "Richard Proves Sambito Right," *Columbus (IN) Republic*, 11 April 1980, 14.

7. "Richard Throws Fastballs by Dodgers," *Poughkeepsie (NY) Journal*, 11 April 1980, 13.

8. "Richard Proves Sambito Right," 14.

9. *Ibid.*

10. Mike Littwin, "Dodgers Go Down Swinging in Opener," *Los Angeles Times*, 11 April 1980, 59.

11. Mike Littwin, "Lasorda Makes Cey, Ferguson, Monday Angry," *Los Angeles Times*, 11 April 1980, 59.

12. *Ibid.*

13. Randy Coppersmith, "Vuckovich Is Loose After 'Another Game,'" *Springfield (MO) News-Leader*, 11 April 1980, 29.

14. *Ibid.*

15. Doyle Dietz, "Bull Rocks Expos' Boat," *Reading (PA) Eagle*, 12 April 1980, 6.

16. *Ibid.*

17. Tom Cushman, "Luzinski's Launching Is a Smash," *Philadelphia Daily News*, 12 April 1980, 39.

18. Doyle Dietz, "Bull Rocks Expos' Boat," *Reading (PA) Eagle*, 12 April 1980, 8.

19. Jim Hawkins, "Kirk Gibson: It's Hit or Whiff," *Detroit Free Press*, 11 April 1980, 45.

20. Warren Mayes, "Morris Gives Royals 0–1 Mark," *Springfield (MO) News-Leader*, 11 April 1980, 27.

21. "Al's Advice Gets Gibson Off to Fast Start," *Detroit Free Press*, 12 April 1980, 29.
22. "Demoted!" *Hattiesburg (MS) American*, 22 April 1980, 11.
23. Tony Schwartz, "It's Captain Courageous Vs. the Boy Wonder," *Honolulu Star-Bulletin*, 29 April 1980, 45.
24. *Ibid.*
25. Bob Verdi, "With 161 Games Left, Cubs Already Are Playing Dead," *Chicago Tribune*, 11 April 1980, 45.
26. *Ibid.*
27. *Ibid.*
28. Richard Dozer, "Kingman Slam Is a Real Blast," *Chicago Tribune*, 20 April 1980, 62.
29. Bob Verdi, "Ex-Teammates Found Kingman a Giant Puzzle," *Chicago Tribune*, 13 April 1978, 57.
30. Thomas Rogers, "White Sox Defeat Yanks in 12th, 8–7," *New York Times*, 27 April 1980, S1.
31. "A Few Hot Ones," *Pittsburgh Press*, 28 June 1904, 13.
32. Nick Coleman, "Griffith Spares Few Targets in Waseca Remarks," *Minneapolis Star Tribune*, 1 October 1978, 1.
33. *Ibid.*
34. Bob Fowler, "Landreaux's Lofty Goals," *Sporting News*, 22 March 1980, 41.
35. *Ibid.*
36. Scott Papillion, "'I Don't Feel Sad; It's All Right' Says Landreaux as Hitting Streak Ends," *Minneapolis Star Tribune*, 1 June 1980, 39.
37. *Ibid.*
38. "Padres' Ozzie Smith Runs Part-Time Ad," *Philadelphia Daily News*, 25 April 1980, 76.
39. Charley Feeney, "'Happy' Blyleven Bids Bucs 'Bye," *Sporting News*, 17 May 1980, 5.
40. *Ibid.*

Chapter 3

1. Bruce Weber, "Betsy Palmer, 88, Dies; from TV Panelist to 'Friday the 13th' Villainess," *New York Times*, 15 June 2015, B19.
2. Rick Groen, "Suspense Grist Mill Churns Out Clunkers," *Toronto Globe and Mail*, 4 May 1980, B16.
3. Michael Blowen, "Bloody 'Friday' Is Nauseating," *Boston Globe*, 13 May 1980, B12.
4. Groen, "Suspense Grist Mill Churns Out Clunkers," B16.
5. *Today* (television program), 23 May 1980, YouTube, https://www.youtube.com/watch?v=Ht8OXIJC9g4
6. Janet Maslin, "Film: Nicholson and Shelley Duvall in Kubrick's 'The Shining,'" *New York Times*, 23 May 1980, C8.
7. William Wilson, "Riding the Crest of the Horror Craze: Horror," *New York Times*, 11 May 1980, SM11.
8. Charley Feeney, "'Happy' Blyleven Bids Bucs 'Bye," *Sporting News*, 17 May 1980, 5.
9. Charley Feeney, "'Umps Almost Boycott Because of Madlock," *Pittsburgh Post-Gazette*, 3 May 1980, 5.
10. Gerald Eskenazi, "'Disputes Mark 10–1 Yank Rout," *New York Times*, 5 May 1980, C1.
11. *Ibid.*
12. *Ibid.*
13. "Right on for White Sox 'Lefty' Catcher," *Lafayette (IN) Journal and Courier*, 7 May 1980, 23.
14. *Ibid.*
15. *Ibid.*
16. "Brawl Two! Bad Rap, Says Proly," *Tampa (FL) Tribune*, 7 May 1980, 65.
17. *Ibid.*
18. Bill Jauss, "Sox Rip Brewers—It's a Riot," *Chicago Tribune*, 6 May 1980, 49.
19. Charley Feeney, "Madlock Booted for 15 Days," *Pittsburgh Post-Gazette*, 6 May 1980, 9.
20. *Ibid.*
21. "Billy's A's Going on Stealing Show (and Home)," *Binghamton (NY) Press and Sun-Bulletin*, 29 May 1980, 10.
22. *Ibid.*
23. "Marshmallow Barrage Leaves Unpleasant Taste in Billy Martin's Mouth," *Tampa Times*, 26 April 1980, 17.
24. *Ibid.*
25. "New Baseball Agreement May Only Delay a Strike," *Chicago Tribune*, 24 May 1980, 21.
26. Bob Verdi, "Settlement Gives Buckner

Insomnia," *Chicago Tribune*, 24 May 1980, 21.

27. *Ibid.*

28. "'Craftsman' Jenkins Seeks 250th Victory," *New York Times*, 18 May 1980, S8.

29. *Ibid.*

30. *Ibid.*

31. Ross Newhan, "Angels Punched Out on a Holiday for Swings," *Los Angeles Times*, 27 May 1980, 43.

32. *Ibid.*

33. *Ibid.*

34. Charley Feeney, "Phillies Wrestle First Place Away from Bucs," *Pittsburgh Post-Gazette*, 27 May 1980, 5.

35. *Ibid.*

36. *Ibid.*

37. Frank Dolson, "Are Phillies Taking Up Where the Flyers Left Off?" *Philadelphia Inquirer*, 27 May 1980, 19.

38. Tom Cushman, "A Fight Without a Decision," *Philadelphia Daily News*, 27 May 1980, 79.

39. Steve Howe and Jim Greenfield, *Between the Lines: One Athlete's Struggle to Escape the Nightmare of Addiction* (Grand Rapids, MI: Masters Press, 1989), 77.

40. Mike Littwin, "Welch Is Near Perfect in 3–0 Win," *Los Angeles Times*, 30 May 1980, 172.

Chapter 4

1. Richard Pryor, *Richard Pryor: Live on the Sunset Strip* (Los Angeles: Columbia Pictures, 1982).

2. Ed Wilks, "'Birds Will Bust Their Tails' New Manager Herzog Says," *St. Louis Post-Dispatch*, 9 June 1980, 1.

3. Rick Hummel, "Players Take Blame for Boyer's Firing," *St. Louis Post-Dispatch*, 9 June 1980, 33.

4. *Ibid.*

5. Mike Littwin, "Expos Extend Dodgers' Nightmare 4–3," *Los Angeles Times*, 14 June 1980, 73.

6. "Let's Make the Streets Safer for Spaceman," *Ottawa (ONT) Journal*, 10 June 1980, 17.

7. Lewis Freedman, "Phils Erupt for 7 in First, Hold on to Beat Padres, 9–6," *Philadelphia Inquirer*, 14 June 1980, 21.

8. "Cromartie Crosses Up Phils; Hail Cesar! He is 5–5," *St. Louis Post-Dispatch*, 25 June 1980, 26.

9. Tom Cushman, "Expos Are No Joke," *Philadelphia Daily News*, 25 June 1980, 71.

10. "Royals' George Brett Sidelined with Ankle Injury," *Santa Fe New Mexican*, 11 May 1980, 16.

11. "Royals Foil Sparky's Strategy," *Battle Creek (MI) Enquirer*, 14 April 1980, 13.

12. Charles Champlin, "'Blues': A $30-Million Wreck, Minus Laughs," *Los Angeles Times*, 20 June 1980, 123.

13. Ibid.

14. Kristi Oleson, *The Blues Brothers*, directed by John Landis (Los Angeles: Universal Pictures, 1980).

15. Gary McLarty, *The Blues Brothers*, directed by John Landis (Los Angeles: Universal Pictures, 1980).

16. Mike Littwin, "Patek Puts 'Em in State of Shock," *Los Angeles Times*, 21 June 1980, 63.

17. *Ibid.*

18. "Farmer's 'Wild' Streak Has Royal Flushed with Anger," *Detroit Free Press*, 10 May 1979, 12.

19. Brian Bragg, "Cowens Suspended 7 Games, Faces Arrest," *Detroit Free Press*, 22 June 1980, 63.

20. *Ibid.*

21. Bob Logan, "Cowens Attacks Sox's Farmer, Suspended 7 Games," *Chicago Tribune*, 21 June 1980, 21.

22. "Sox Want Cowens Arrested for Slugging Reliever Farmer," *Carbondale Southern Illinoisan*, 21 June 1980, 16.

23. *Ibid.*

24. Michael Faber, "Most Expos Favor Leonard," *Montreal Gazette*, 20 June 1980, 11.

25. "Ryan, Sambito Stop Cards," *Salina (KS) Journal*, 20 June 1980, 15.

26. Rick Hummel, "Cards Scuffle After Another Defeat," *St. Louis Post-Dispatch*, 20 June 1980, 31.

27. *Ibid.*

28. "Bristol Decks Montefusco in Locker Room Brawl," *Santa Cruz (CA) Sentinel*, 19 June 1980, 37.

29. "Battered Montefusco Wants Out," *Daytona Beach (FL) Morning Journal*, 20 June 1980, 5B.

30. "Bristol Decks Montefusco," 37.

31. Rick Hummel, "Astros Turn Dome into Big Bird Cage," *St. Louis Post-Dispatch*, 19 June 1980, 21.

32. Richard Dozer, "Astros Keep Cubs Boiling, Losing," *Chicago Tribune*, 18 June 1980, 55.

33. Gordon Verrell, "Dodgers Land Vet Reuss to Aid Shaky Lefty Crew," *Sporting News*, 21 April 1979, 20.

34. *Ibid.*

35. "Not Perfect, but Reuss Happy with No-Hitter," *Anniston (AL) Star*, 29 June 1980, 35.

36. "But for Error, Jerry Reuss Was Perfect," *White Plains (NY) Journal News*, 29 June 1980, 33.

37. *Ibid.*

38. "A New Feeling for Jerry Reuss," *Appleton (WI) Post-Crescent*, 29 June 1980, 45.

39. David Knight, "Reds Loose in Practice, Troubled with 3d Place," *Indianapolis Star*, 27 June 1980, 37.

40. *Ibid.*

41. *Ibid.*

Chapter 5

1. Janet Maslin, "Screen: 'Airplane!,' Disaster-Film Spoof," *New York Times*, 2 July 1980, C17.

2. Charles Champlin, "'Airplane!' Sends Up a Comic Boom," *Los Angeles Times*, 2 July 1980, 97.

3. *Late Night with David Letterman*, (15 March 1982; New York:) YouTube https://www.youtube.com/watch?v=TPwNVG14OIM.

4. David Nightengale, "Piersall Attacks Suburban Sportswriter," *Chicago Tribune*, 3 July 1980, 41.

5. Jimmy Piersall and Richard Whittingham, *The Truth Hurts* (Chicago: Contemporary, 1984), 148.

6. David Nightengale, "Piersall Attacks Suburban Sportswriter," *Chicago Tribune*, 3 July 1980, 41.

7. *Ibid.*

8. *Ibid.*

9. "Expos Bitter Over 'Stars Selection," *Montreal Gazette*, 4 July 1980, 13.

10. *Ibid.*

11. "Another Baseball Brawl; Cubs Sweep Bucs," *Columbus (IN) Republic*, 5 July 1980, 8.

12. *Ibid.*

13. "Swan Promises He'll Get Even," *Reading (PA) Eagle*, 7 July 1980, 19.

14. *Ibid.*

15. *Ibid.*

16. "Ryan Reaches Milestone but Reds Crush Astros," *Marion (OH) Star*, 5 July 1980, 7.

17. *Ibid.*

18. Peter King, "Uncle Ned Has a Tip for Bruce," *Cincinnati Enquirer*, 5 July 1980, 11.

19. Dave Anderson, "Arm Ailment Imperils Tom Seaver's Career," *New York Times*, 2 July 1980, A23.

20. "Seaver's Problems Mount as Giants Rock Cincinnati," *Albany (GA) Herald*, 1 July 1980, 10.

21. "Rookie Rips Phils for Giants, 7–2," *New York Herald Tribune*, 31 July 1959, B1.

22. Dave Winfield and Tom Parker, *Winfield: A Player's Life* (New York: W.W. Norton, 1988), 107.

23. "Homer Not Enough to Sooth McCovey," *Montreal Gazette*, 5 May 1980, 53.

24. "Willie Mac Gives Fans Something to Remember," *Santa Cruz (CA) Sentinel*, 7 July 1980, 8.

25. Robert Markus, "Pirates Give Cub Bullpen a Lesson in Futility," *Chicago Tribune*, 7 July 1980, 29.

26. *Ibid.*

27. Ron Cook, "The Longest Day," *Beaver County (PA) Times*, 7 July 1980, 8.

28. "Cellar-bound Padres Fire GM Bob Fontaine," *Montreal Gazette*, 7 July 1980, 82.

29. *Ibid.*

30. "Coleman May Move Upstairs," *Huntingdon (PA) Daily News*, 7 July 1980, P5.

31. "Carpenter Says Phils Not Talking," *Reading (PA) Eagle*, 10 July 1980, 26.

32. *Ibid.*

33. "Three Cleared in Phillie Case," *Pittsburgh Post-Gazette*, 5 February 1981, 12.

34. *Ibid.*

35. Mike Schmidt and Glen Waggoner, *Clearing the Bases* (New York: HarperCollins, 2006), 90.

36. Murray Chass, "American Leaguers Predict Win," *Anniston (AL) Star*, 8 July 1980, 8.

37. "Stone Lauds Koufax and Veeck for Helping Career," *Baltimore Sun*, 8 July 1980, C5.

38. Howard Cosell, 1980 All-Star Game, ABC, (8 July 1980) YouTube, https://www.youtube.com/watch?v=ZpxH_cvMKI

39. *Ibid.*

40. *Ibid.*

41. *Ibid.*

42. Ross Newhan, "The American Way Continues to Be a No-Win Policy," *Los Angeles Times*, 9 July 1980, 70.

43. *Ibid.*

44. *Ibid.*

45. Richard Hoffer, "Where Were All the Instant Replays?" *Los Angeles Times*, 9 July 1980, 69.

46. "Richard's Stomach Pain a Pang to Astros," *Wilmington (DE) Morning News*, 18 July 1980, 31.

47. *Ibid.*

48. "Richard's Health Remains Mystery," *Reno (NV) Gazette-Journal*, 15 July 1980, 34.

49. *Ibid.*

50. Harry Shattuck, "Houston Has Own 'J.R.' Mystery," *Sporting News*, 2 August 1980, 11.

51. *Ibid.*

52. Peter King, "Bench Sets Homer Mark as Reds End Slump," *Cincinnati Enquirer*, 16 July 1980, 15.

53. Ray Buck, "Reds Won't Renegotiate Bench's Contract," *Cincinnati Enquirer*, 15 July 1980, 25.

54. *Ibid.*

55. "Brett's 'Incredible' Return Lifts Royals," *St. Louis Post-Dispatch*, 17 July 1980, 17.

56. *Ibid.*

57. Gary Mihoces, "Stargell Gets Star, Surprise at Tribute," *Pittsburgh Post-Gazette*, 21 July 1980, 11.

58. John Clayton, "Parker Feeling Mighty Low After Assault with Battery," *Pittsburgh Press*, 21 July 1980, 17.

59. Dan Donovan, "Parker Still Shaken, Wants to Be Traded," *Pittsburgh Press*, 22 July 1980, 22.

60. Tom Cushman, "Lefty Strikes It Rich," *Philadelphia Daily News*, 7 July 1980, 66.

61. Bill Conlin, "Hands Full Minus Bull," *Philadelphia Daily News*, 29 July 1980, 54.

62. David Condon, "Cubs No Kind of Organization: Gomez," *Chicago Tribune*, 27 July 1980, 43.

63. *Ibid.*

64. Dave Nightengale, "Cubs Fire Preston Gomez," *Chicago Tribune*, 26 July 1980, 141.

65. "Gomez Fired," *Sioux Falls (SD) Argus Leader*, 26 July 1980, 9.

66. Mickey Herskowitz, "Perhaps Our Biggest Fault Was Misunderstanding J.R.," *Houston Post*, 3 August 1980, 1C.

67. *Ibid.*

Chapter 6

1. Duke Snider Hall of Fame Induction Speech, YouTube https://www.youtube.com/watch?v=QaeMdQl3XF4.\

2. Hy Zimmerman, "Pitching Rated M's Strongest Suit," *Sporting News*, 9 February 1980, 35.

3. Ross Newhan, "Mariners Hire Maury Wills to Bail Them Out," *Los Angeles Times*, 5 August 1980, 36.

4. "Wills, Johnson ponder future of Mariners," *St. Joseph (MO) Gazette*, 6 August 1980, 33.

5. "Richard possibly out for season," *Bloomington (IL) Pantagraph*, 5 August 1980, 15.

6. *Ibid.*

7. William Nack, "Now Everyone Believes Him," *Sports Illustrated*, 18 August 1980, 22.

8. Jim Murray, "It Was All in His Head," *Los Angeles Times*, 8 August 1980, 248.

9. "Reds Clip Padres in 4-Game Sweep," *Marion (OH) Star*, 7 August 1980, 13.

10. "Braves' Cox Spitting Mad After Juicy Field Battle," *St. Louis Post-Dispatch*, 7 August 1980, 18.

11. *Ibid.*

12. *Ibid.*

13. Nolan Ryan and Harvey Frommer,

Throwing Heat: The Autobiography of Nolan Ryan (New York: Avon, 1990), 170.

14. "Astros Retain Lead on Ceden's 4 RBIs; Expos Gain a Split," *Louisville Courier-Journal*, 10 August 1980, 40.

15. Michael Hurd, "Winfield Didn't Take Pitch Lightly," *Houston Post*, 10 August 1980, C10.

16. Ken Nigro, "Birds Do It to Yanks Again, Trail by 3½," *Baltimore Sun*, 10 August 1980, 23.

17. *Ibid.*

18. Murray Chass, "Yanks Lose, 4–2, to Orioles' Stone," *New York Times*, 10 August 1980, A1.

19. Murray Chass, "Yanks Bow, 6–5; Lead Cut to 2½," *New York Times*, 11 August 1980, C1.

20. *Ibid.*

21. Al Mari, "Reggie Basks in Own Starlight After 399th," *White Plains (NY) Journal News*, 5 August 1980, 14.

22. *Ibid.*

23. "Jackson Scares Off Gunman," *Baltimore Sun*, 13 August 1980, C5.

24. *Ibid.*

25. Ray Didinger, "Green Blows His Top," *Philadelphia Daily News*, 11 August 1980, 76.

26. *Ibid.*

27. *Ibid.*

28. Rusty Pray, "Green Lashes Phillies for Lack of Hustle," *Camden (NJ) Courier-Post*, 11 August 1980, 19.

29. *Ibid.*

30. "Anxious Garcia Looks Forward to Spring Camp," *Akron (OH) Beacon Journal*, 11 February 1980, 31.

31. "Cleveland Indians' Rookie Stabbed," *Lafayette (IN) Journal and Courier*, 10 March 1980, 18.

32. Joe Charboneau, Burt Graeff and Terry Pluto, *Super Joe: The Life and Legend of Joe Charboneau* (New York: Stein and Day, 1981), 184.

33. Peter King, "The Man Who Saved Cleveland," *Cincinnati Enquirer*, 10 August 1980, 26.

34. *Ibid.*

35. "'Bird' Does Well, Blasts Anderson," *West Palm Beach (FL) Post*, 5 April 1980, 51.

36. "Anderson Answers: Fidrych Out of Line," *Boston Globe*, 6 April 1980, 42.

37. "Fidrych Loss Doesn't Dim Sparky's Excitement," *Columbus (IN) Republic*, 13 August 1980, 16.

38. Mick McCabe, "Bird Looks Good in 5–4 Loss," *Detroit Free Press*, 13 August 1980, 55.

39. "Tide Has Turned for Fidrych, and So Has Fans' Reaction," *Los Angeles Times*, 30 August 1980, 64.

40. Thomas Boswell, "Brett's Bat Is Red Hot; Brett Puts Mass into Production; Opponents Watch in Awe When He Steps to Plate," *Washington Post*, 23 July 1980, D1.

41. "Brett Raises Average to .401 in Royals' Win," *Chicago Tribune*, 18 August 1980, 37.

42. Kent Baker, "McGregor, O's Beat Yanks to Tie Series," *Baltimore Sun*, 18 August 1980, 25.

43. Murray Chass, "Orioles Beat Yanks; Trail by 2½," *New York Times*, 19 August 1980, C11.

44. Kent Baker Murray, "51,528 See Birds Bounce Yankees, 6–5," *Baltimore Sun*, 19 August 1980, C5.

45. *Ibid.*

46. "Ex-Journeyman Stone Credits Birds for Success," *Great Falls (MT) Tribune*, 21 August 1980, 15.

47. *Ibid.*

48. Murray Chass, "Distress Call Issues to Yanks," *New York Times*, 20 August 1980, D19.

49. *Ibid.*

50. *Ibid.*

51. Tom Callahan, "Baseball Had Left Behind Finley, Veeck," *San Bernardino County (CA) Sun*, 26 August 1980, 28.

52. David Israel, "Just Don't Try Any Fast Moves on Us, Mr. Debartolo," *Chicago Tribune*, 23 August 1980, 19.

53. "New Orleans Says: Finley to Chicago," *Chicago Tribune*, 23 August 1980, 19.

54. Cooper Rollow, "Kuhn 'Village Idiot,' Says Finley," *Chicago Tribune*, 19 June 1976, 169.

55. "Finley Finally Sells A's," *Boston Globe*, 24 August 1980, 48.

56. David Condon, "Fat Cats Won't Miss

Veeck, Charlie O.," *Chicago Tribune*, 24 August 1980, 57.

57. *Ibid.*

58. *Ibid.*

59. "Mauch Calls It Quits," *Reading (PA) Eagle*, 25 August 1980, 17.

60. *Ibid.*

61. Dan Stoneking, "Another Loss—And Then Came Shocker," *Minneapolis Star*, 25 August 1980, 34.

62. Doug Grow, "Twins Bowing Heads as Mauch Bows Out," *Minneapolis Star*, 25 August 1980, 34.

63. "Jenkins Arrested, Charged with Narcotics Possession," *Houston Post*, 26 August 1980, 2D.

64. "Jail Term Said Unlikely if Jenkins Found Guilty," *Montreal Gazette*, 28 August 1980, 19.

65. *Ibid.*

66. "L.A. Beats Phillies as Both Benches Empty," *Reading (PA) Eagle*, 26 August 1980, 33; "McGraw Receives Warning from Lopes," *Los Angeles Times*, 26 August 1980, Sec. III, 1, 7.

67. *Ibid.*

68. Tom Cushman, "A Pitch Thrown in Anger," *Philadelphia Daily News*, 26 August 1980, 63.

69. Bill Conlin, "Phils Lose Tug O'war," *Philadelphia Daily News*, 26 August 1980, 62.

70. *Ibid.*

71. Jayson Stark, "Carlton Holds Off Dodgers for No. 20," *Philadelphia Inquirer*, 28 August 1980, 49.

72. *Ibid.*, 52.

73. Jayson Stark, "Round 2 Goes to Fired-Up McGraw," *Philadelphia Inquirer*, 28 August 1980, 52.

Chapter 7

1. Jim Hawkins, "Peace, at Last," *Detroit Free Press*, 2 September 1980, 35.

2. "Cowens, Farmer Make Peace," *Crystal Lake (IL) Herald*, 2 September 1980, 5.

3. Jayson Stark, "Phillies Defeat Giants, Move into 1st," *Philadelphia Inquirer*, 2 September 1980, 15.

4. Hal Bodley, "Owens Erupts; Phillies on Top," *Camden (NJ) Courier-Post*, 2 September 1980, 21.

5. Ray Buck, "Foster Bats Reds to Fifth Straight," *Cincinnati Enquirer*, 2 September 1980, 37.

6. Mike Littwin, "Here's Howe Dodgers' Bullpen Has Held Up," *Los Angeles Times*, 1 August 1980, 53.

7. *Ibid.*

8. Gordon Verrell, "Dodgers Finding Their Road Full of Potholes and Hazards," *Sporting News*, 9 August 1980, 22.

9. *Ibid.*

10. Bill McGraw, "Off-And-On Fidrych Had an 'On' Day," *Detroit Free Press*, 3 September 1980, 45.

11. *Ibid.*

12. "Bamberger Will Quit Sunday," *Green Bay (WI) Press Gazette*, 6 September 1980, 17.

13. Steve O'Brien, "Brewers, Rodgers See Smooth Transition," *Stevens Point (WI) Daily Journal*, 6 September 1980, 11.

14. David Condon, "Debartolo Still May Lose Sox to Local Group," *Chicago Tribune*, 4 September 1980, 54.

15. "AL Vote Anti-Veeck: Steinbrenner," *Chicago Tribune*, 17 December 1980, 64.

16. David Israel, "Big Sox Deal Touches Off a Most Significant Trivia Duel," 18 December 1980, 75.

17. Mike Littwin, "Dodgers Beat Phils, Lead by 2 Games," *Los Angeles Times*, 8 September 1980, 57.

18. *Ibid.*

19. Mike Littwin, "Dodgers Boot Away Half Their Lead," *Los Angeles Times*, 10 September 1980, 72.

20. "Dodger Notes," *Los Angeles Times*, 10 September 1980, 78.

21. Kenny Hand, "Astros Tie L.A. for Lead on Cruz's Homer," *Houston Post*, 11 September 1980, C1.

22. "Astros Get Even with Dodgers 6–5," *San Bernardino County (CA) Sun*, 11 September 1980, 65.

23. Peter King, "No Time to Look Back with L.A. in Town," *Cincinnati Enquirer*, 12 September 1980, 37.

24. Mike Littwin, "Dodgers Win One and

Lose One," *Los Angeles Times*, 13 September 1980, 73.

25. Bill Conlin, "Phils Kid Wins 1st Against Mets," *Philadelphia Daily News*, 11 September 1980, 64.

26. Jayson Stark, "Bystrom Blanks Mets on 5 Hits," *Philadelphia Inquirer*, 11 September 1980, 21.

27. Ian McDonald, "Gullickson Fires Masterpiece as Expos Maintain NL Lead," *Montreal Gazette*, 11 September 1980, 21.

28. "Expo Rookie's 18 Strikeouts Stifle Cubs," *Chicago Tribune*, 11 September 1980, 42.

29. *Ibid.*

30. "Ron Leflore Alleges Expos, Fans Racist," *Wilmington (DE) Morning News*, 29 August 1980, 25.

31. "Les Racists?" *Akron (OH) Beacon Journal*, 29 August 1980, 33.

32. Thomas Boswell, "Expos: Divided but Still Conquering," *Washington Post*, 18 September 1980, F1.

33. "Dawson Is Not in Accord with LeFlore Racial Views," *Toronto Globe and Mail*, 30 September 1980, S2.

34. "Blue Jays Ruffle Feathers over George's Charge," *White Plains (NY) Journal News*, 13 September 1980, 11.

35. *Ibid.*

36. *Ibid.*

37. Ken Nigro, "Stewart Wins in Relief; Weaver Ejected," *Baltimore Sun*, 18 September 1980, C9.

38. "Earl Weaver Umpire Fight," https://www.youtube.com/watch?v=rpS-XFXxJvE.

39. *Ibid.*

40. "Was Weaver Set Up to Argue?" *Baltimore Sun*, 24 September 1980, B2.

41. Chuck Woodling, "Royals Clinch Division Title," *Lawrence (KS) Journal World*, 18 September 1980, 8.

42. "Half-Champion Royals Targeting Yanks, Series," *St. Louis Post-Dispatch*, 18 September 1980, 47.

43. *Ibid.*

44. "Brett, Templeton May Be Exceptions to Rule 10.23," *Marshall (TX) News Messenger*, 17 September 1980, 10.

45. Ross Newhan, "Even Hitting .356, Cecil Cooper Remains in Shadows," *Los Angeles Times*, 31 August 1980, 99.

46. *Ibid.*

47. Tom Wheatley, "Hot Cooper Frets as Media Follow Even Hotter Brett," *Green Bay (WI) Press Gazette*, 31 August 1980, 22.

48. Newhan, "Even Hitting .356, Cecil Cooper Remains in Shadows," 99.

49. Mick McCabe, "Oakland Hurler Makes It 5 in a Row," *Detroit Free Press*, 26 July 1980, 27.

50. Ken Nigro, "A's Langford Stops Birds, 3 to 2," *Baltimore Sun*, 7 September 1980, 36.

51. "A's Set Complete Game Record, May Cost Orioles Division Title," *Hattiesburg (MS) American*, 8 September 1980, 17.

52. "Henderson Steals Record," *Santa Cruz (CA) Sentinel*, 18 September 1980, 36.

53. *Ibid.*

54. "Brett Reaches .400," *Reno (NV) Gazette Journal*, 20 September 1980, 22.

55. *Ibid.*

Chapter 8

1. Peter Gammons, "Zimmer Gets That Fatal Call," *Boston Globe*, 2 October 1980, 1.

2. Larry Whiteside, "Zimmer's Gone, but the Players Won't Forget," *Boston Globe*, 2 October 1980, 1.

3. *Ibid.*

4. "Tamargo Helps Expos in Pinch," *Philadelphia Daily News*, 30 September 1980, 62.

5. Frank Dolson, "Fun Is a Tight Race in Stretch, but Someone Forgot to Tell Phils," *Philadelphia Inquirer*, 30 September 1980, 33.

6. Ray Didinger, "Bitter Taste to Phils Win," *Philadelphia Daily News*, 30 September 1980, 64.

7. *Ibid.*, 63, 64.

8. *Ibid.*

9. *Ibid.*

10. David Leon Moore, "Dodgers Fend Off S.D., Stay Close," *San Bernardino County (CA) Sun*, 28 September 1980, 48.

11. John Hall, "So Help Me," *Los Angeles Times*, 3 October 1980, 65.

12. Mike Littwin, "Dodgers Lose, Now

Must Sweep Astros Just to Tie," *Los Angeles Times*, 3 October 1980, 63.

13. Kenny Hand, "Astros One Win Away from NL West Title," *Houston Post*, 3 October 1980, 1C.

14. *Ibid.*

15. "Expos, Phils Keep Pace; Yankees Maul Indians," *Huntingdon (PA) Daily News*, 2 October 1980, 13.

16. Rick Hummel, "Cards Effort, in a Word: Embarrassing," *St. Louis Post-Dispatch*, 2 October 1980, 39.

17. Murray Chass, "Indians Rally to Beat Yankees, 12–9; Lead Shrinks to 2½ Games," *New York Times*, 1 October 1980, B9.

18. Frank Dolson, "Cool Hand Tug Saves the Cheers," *Philadelphia Inquirer*, 4 October 1980, 23.

19. David Tucker, "Phils Win Crucial Opener with Expos," *Huntingdon (PA) Daily News*, 4 October 1980, 10.

20. "Astrolog," *Houston Post*, 4 October 1980, 4C.

21. David Leon Moore, "There's Still a Race in the NL West," *San Bernardino County (CA) Sun*, 4 October 1980, 40.

22. Mike Littwin, "Garvey and Reuss Leave Astros in a Haze, 2–1," *Los Angeles Times* 5 October 1980, 127.

23. *Ibid.*

24. Kenny Hand, "Astros Lose to Dodgers; Lead Cut to One," *Houston Post*, 5 October 1980, 1C.

25. Murray Chass, "Jackson Clout Breaks 2–2 Tie," *New York Times*, 5 October 1980, S1.

26. "Jackson Hits 3rd Homer in Three Days," *Palm Beach (FL) Post*, 5 October 1980, 302.

27. *Ibid.*

28. Rick Carpiniello, "Yankees, Royals Meet Again," *Port Huron (MI) Times Herald*, 5 October 1980, 24.

29. *Ibid.*

30. Phillies at Expos, 10/4/80, https://www.youtube.com/watch?v=Q94uOGRZf0o

31. *Ibid.*

32. *Ibid.*

33. Kenny Hand, "Scratched Finger Casts Doubt on Ruhle's Status," *Houston Post*, 5 October 1980, 14C.

34. Kenny Hand, "Dodgers Force Astros into Playoff," *Houston Post*, 6 October 1980, 6D.

35. Tommy Bonk, "Right Down to the Wire," *Houston Post*, 6 October 1980, 1A.

36. Mike Littwin, "As Astros Hit the Wall, the Dodgers Clear It—Again," *Los Angeles Times*, 6 October 1980, 53.

37. "Missing Astro Ingredient to Return, Morgan Vows," *Houston Post*, 6 October 1980, 2D.

38. Kenny Hand, "Dodgers Force Playoff for Division Crown," *Houston Post*, 6 October 1980, 1D.

39. Littwin, "As Astros Hit the Wall, the Dodgers Clear It—Again," 63.

40. David Israel, "Dodgers Goltz Seeks Redemption," *Chicago Tribune*, 6 October 1980, 50.

41. *Ibid.*

42. Littwin, "As Astros Hit the Wall, the Dodgers Clear It—Again," 52.

43. "Astrolog," *Houston Post*, 6 October 1980, 2D.

44. Kenny Hand, "Niekro, Howe Team Up," *Houston Post*, 7 October 1980, 1E.

45. Kenny Hand, "Astros Make Up for Lost Time," *Houston Post*, 7 October 1980, 4E.

46. *Ibid.*

47. Kenny Hand, "Niekro, Howe Team Up," *Houston Post*, 7 October 1980, 1E.

48. Mike Littwin, "Astros Win First Prize: Two Days in Philadelphia," *Los Angeles Times*, 7 October 1980, 47.

49. *Ibid.*

50. Kenny Hand, "Astros Make Up for Lost Time," *Houston Post*, 7 October 1980, 4E.

Chapter 9

1. "Phils Feel Chances Better Against Astros than L.A." *Houston Post*, 7 October 1980, 3E.

2. Howard Cosell, 1980 NLCS Game 1, https://www.youtube.com/watch?v=ox5myljqMY4.

3. Jayson Stark, "Phillies Top Astros in Opener 3–1," *Philadelphia Inquirer*, 8 October 1980, 26.

4. Kenny Hand, "Phils Take Opener on Luzinski's HR," *Houston Post*, 8 October 1980, 1D.

5. Thom Greer, "Gura's Great, by the Book," *Philadelphia Daily News*, 9 October 1980, 66.

6. Warren Mayes, "Yankee Killer Gura Upholds Reputation," *Springfield (MO) News Leader*, 9 October 1980, 25.

7. Dan George, "Win Bolsters Royals' Morale," *Springfield (MO) News Leader*, 9 October 1980, 27.

8. *Ibid.*

9. Don Drysdale, 1980 NLCS Game 2, https://www.youtube.com/watch?v=NhXxkB2xq2w&t=8854s

10. *Ibid.*

11. Kenny Hand, "Pressure on Phils in Spacious Dome," *Houston Post*, 9 October 1980, 1D.

12. Bill Conlin, "Phils' Elia Has Troubles as a Traffic Cop," *Philadelphia Daily News*, 9 October 1980, 10/9/80, 74.

13. Mike Littwin, "Astros Get the Split They Needed," *Los Angeles Times*, 9 October 1980, 79.

14. Phil Rizzuto, 1980 ALCS Game 2, https://www.youtube.com/watch?v=56nTHghGra8.

15. Leigh Montville, "Steinbrenner Keeps a Stiff Upper Lip," *Boston Globe*, 10 October 1980, 42.

16. Brian Bragg, "Steinbrenner Blasts Coach," *Detroit Free Press*, 11 October 1980, 33.

17. Dave Anderson, "Steinbrenner Criticizes His 3rd Base Coach," *New York Times*, 10 October 1980, A28.

18. *Ibid.*

19. Leigh Montville, "Steinbrenner Keeps a Stiff Upper Lip," *Boston Globe*, 10 October 1980, 42.

20. Kenny Hand, "Astros Trip Phils, Need One More Victory," *Houston Post*, 11 October 1980, 1B.

21. Tommy Bonk, "Morgan's Triple Was Just in Time," *Houston Post*, 11 October 1980, 1B.

22. Keith Jackson, 1980 NLCS Game 3, https://www.youtube.com/watch?v=ucBPiK8bM3E

23. Howard Cosell, 1980 NLCS Game 3, https://www.youtube.com/watch?v=ucBPiK8bM3E

24. Kenny Hand, "Astros Trip Phils, Need One More Victory," *Houston Post*, 11 October 1980, 6B.

25. Ray Didinger, "A Tale of Two Cities," *Philadelphia Daily News*, 11 October 1980, 38.

26. Bill Conlin, "Phillies Are Down," *Philadelphia Daily News*, 11 October 1980, 39.

27. Phil Rizzuto, 1980 ALCS Game 3, https://www.youtube.com/watch?v=w_6jpcyJEUk&t=7279s.

28. 1980 ALCS Game 3, https://www.youtube.com/watch?v=w_6jpcyJEUk&t=7279s.

29. "Royals Win, by George!" *Decatur (IL) Herald and Review*, 11 October 1980, 66.

30. Murray Chass, "Royals Win the Pennant with 4–2 Victory Over Yanks," *New York Times*, 11 October 1980, 15.

31. "Kaycee Stops Yanks with a Royal Flush," *Matoon (IL) Journal Gazette*, 11 October 1980, 13.

32. Rick Hummel, "Brett's 3-Run Homer Wipes Out Yanks," *St. Louis Post-Dispatch*, 11 October 1980, 5.

33. Russ Franke, "Brett's Blast Cooks Yankees' Goose," *Pittsburgh Press*, 11 October 1980, 7.

34. Joe Morgan and David Falkner, *Joe Morgan: A Life in Baseball* (New York: W.W. Norton, 1993), 248–249.

35. Howard Cosell, NLCS Game 5, https://www.youtube.com/watch?v=9mKKuvxRqP0

36. *Ibid.*

37. Scott Heimer, "Phils' Fate Is Crystal Clear," *Philadelphia Daily News*, 15 October 1980, 3.

38. "GI Maneuvers Trip to World Series," *Philadelphia Daily News*, 15 October 1980, 26.

39. Bill Conlin, "The Spirit of 7–6," *Philadelphia Daily News*, 15 October 1980, 88.

40. Danny Robbins, "In Pain, Brett Heads for Kansas City Hospital," *Philadelphia Inquirer*, 16 October 1980, 26.

41. Rick Hummel, "Royals Homesick

After Loss to Phillies," *St. Louis Post-Dispatch*, 16 October 1980, 39, 42.

42. Bill Conlin, "Phils Just Two Tough," *Philadelphia Daily News*, 16 October 1980, 78.

43. Hummel, "Royals Homesick After Loss to Phillies," *St. Louis Post-Dispatch*, 16 October 1980, 42.

44. *Ibid.*

45. Danny Robbins, "In Pain, Brett Heads for Kansas City Hospital," *Philadelphia Inquirer*, 16 October 1980, 21.

46. Rick Hummel, "Revived Royals Finally Have Some Fun," *St. Louis Post-Dispatch*, 18 October 1980, 5.

47. *Ibid.*

48. Ray Didinger, "Willie May Aikens Earns Respect," *Philadelphia Daily News*, 18 October 1980, 40.

49. Joe Garagiola, 1980 World Series Game 4, https://www.youtube.com/watch?v=UquJHv1SwLE.

50. 1980 World Series Film, https://www.youtube.com/watch?v=j1cEeIkoAjU.

51. Rick Hummel, "Beanball Riles All but Target—Brett," *St. Louis Post-Dispatch*, 19 October 1980, 83.

52. *Ibid.*

53. Rick Hummel, "Royals Heroes Trip as Phillies Rally, 4–3," *St. Louis Post-Dispatch*, 20 October 1980, 21.

54. *Ibid.*

55. Bill Conlin, "Phils One Win Away," *Philadelphia Daily News*, 20 October 1980, 82.

56. *Ibid.*

57. *Ibid.*

58. Bill Conlin, "Tired Carlton Ready to Try for Clincher," *Philadelphia Daily News*, 21 October 1980, 76.

59. Larry Eichel, "Second Guessing, Gloom Pervade Royals After Game 5," *Philadelphia Inquirer*, 21 October 1980, 15.

60. *Ibid.*

61. 1980 World Series Film, https://www.youtube.com/watch?v=j1cEeIkoAjU.

62. *Ibid.*

63. Tony Kubek, 1980 World Series Game 6, https://www.youtube.com/watch?v=vLDRIk9SgQM.

64. Robert Gordon, *Then Bowa Said to Schmidt...* (Chicago: Triumph, 2013), 167.

65. Tug McGraw and Don Yaeger, *Ya Gotta Believe* (New York: New American Library, 2004), 149.

Epilogue

1. Kalas, Harry, https://www.youtube.com/watch?v=usT6uHdLOYM.

2. *Ibid.*

3. *Ibid.*

Bibliography

Newspapers and Periodicals

Akron Beacon Journal
Albany Herald
Anniston (AL) Star
Appleton (WI) Post-Crescent
Arizona Republic
Asbury Park (NJ) Press
Baltimore Sun
Battle Creek (MI) Enquirer
Beaver County (PA) Times
Binghamton (NY) Press and Sun-Bulletin
Bloomington (IL) Pantagraph
Bridgewater (NJ) Courier-Times
Carbondale Southern Illinoisan
Chicago Tribune
Cincinnati Enquirer
Columbus (IN) Republic
Daytona Beach (FL) Morning Journal
Decatur (IL) Herald and Review
Detroit Free Press
Fort Myers (FL) News-Press
Great Falls (MT) Tribune
Green Bay (WI) Press Gazette
Hartford Courant
Hattiesburg (MS) American
Honolulu Star-Bulletin
Houston Post
Huntingdon (PA) Daily News
Indianapolis Star
Lafayette (IN) Journal and Courier
Lawrence (KS) Journal World
Longview (TX) News Journal
Los Angeles Times
Louisville Courier-Journal
Marion (OH) Star
Marshall (TX) News Messenger
Mattoon (IL) Journal Gazette
Miami News
Minneapolis Star-Tribune
Minneapolis Star
Montreal Gazette
New York Herald Tribune
New York Times
Odessa (TX) American
Ottawa (ONT) Journal
Palm Beach (FL) Post
Philadelphia Daily News
Philadelphia Inquirer
Pittsburgh Post-Gazette
Pittsburgh Press
Port Huron (MI) Times Herald
Poughkeepsie (NY) Journal
Reading (PA) Eagle
Reno (NV) Gazette-Journal
St. Joseph (MO) Gazette
St. Louis Post Dispatch
Salina (KS) Journal
San Bernardino (CA) County Sun
Santa Cruz (CA) Sentinel
Santa Fe New Mexican
Sayre (PA) Evening Times
Sporting News
Sports Illustrated
Springfield News (MO) Leader
Stevens Point (WI) Daily Journal
Tampa Times
Tampa Tribune
Toronto Globe and Mail
Washington Post
West Palm Beach (FL) Post
White Plains (NY) Journal News
Wilmington (OH) News Journal

Books

Baylor, Don, and Claire Smith. *Don Baylor—Nothing but the Truth: A Baseball Life*. New York: St. Martin's, 1989.

Charboneau, Joe, Burt Graeff and Terry Pluto. *Super Joe: The Life and Legend of Joe Charboneau*. New York: Stein and Day, 1981.

Dawson, Andre, and Tim Bird. *Hawk: An Inspiring Story of Success at the Game of Life and Baseball*. Grand Rapids, MI: Zondervan, 1994.

Giles, Bill, and Doug Myers. *Pouring Six Beers at a Time and Other Stories from a Lifetime in Baseball*. Chicago: Triumph, 2007.

Gordon, Robert. *Then Bowa Said to Schmidt....* Chicago: Triumph, 2013.

Hagman, Larry, and Tom Gold. *Hello, Darlin': Tall (and Absolutely True) Tales About My Life*. New York: Simon & Schuster, 2001.

Howe, Steve, and Jim Greenfield. *Between the Lines: One Athlete's Struggle to Escape the Nightmare of Addiction*. Grand Rapids, MI: Masters Press, 1989.

McGraw, Tug, and Don Yaeger. *Ya Gotta Believe*. New York: New American Library, 2004.

Morgan, Joe, and David Falkner. *Joe Morgan: A Life in Baseball*. New York: W.W. Norton, 1993.

Porter, Darrell, and William Deerfield. *Snap Me Perfect: The Darrell Porter Story*. Nashville: Thomas Nelson, 1984.

Ryan, Nolan, and Harvey Frommer. *Throwing Heat: The Autobiography of Nolan Ryan*. New York: Avon, 1990.

Schmidt, Mike, and Glen Waggoner. *Clearing the Bases*. New York: HarperCollins, 2006.

Winfield, Dave, and Tom Parker. *Winfield: A Player's Life*. New York: W.W. Norton, 1988.

Websites

BaseballProspectus.com
Baseball-Reference.com
ESPN.com
Retrosheet.org
SABR.org
YouTube.com

Index

Index

Index

Index